A CAMBRIDGE MOVEMENT

By the Same Author

CANDIDATE FOR TRUTH.   (Church Book Room Press.)
PIONEERS.   (Tyndale Press.)

HOLY TRINITY CHURCH AND THE HENRY MARTYN HALL
IN THE EIGHTEEN-NINETIES

A CAMBRIDGE MOVEMENT

by

J. C. POLLOCK

With a Foreword by

THE LORD BISHOP OF LIVERPOOL

LONDON

JOHN MURRAY, ALBEMARLE STREET, W.

First Edition . . 1953

Printed in Great Britain by
Wyman & Sons, Ltd. London, Fakenham and Reading
and published by John Murray (Publishers) Ltd.

CONTENTS

LIST OF ILLUSTRATIONS

Facing Page

FOREWORD

By the LORD BISHOP OF LIVERPOOL
(The Right Rev. C. A. Martin, D.D.)

I HAVE been asked to write a foreword to this book and I
do so with pleasure. It is the story of a particular religious movement in Cambridge and while it is full of
interest to those who have been associated with the Inter-
Collegiate Union, the value of the book is by no means
limited to them. It should be read by all who are interested in the spread of the Christian Gospel, for what has
happened at Cambridge during the past eighty years is
important to an understanding of the religious movements
of our time.

The story is told in a clear, scholarly and imaginative
style, and reveals a keen appreciation of the crucial issues
which are raised. There has been no attempt to hide the
independent and critical attitude which has characterized
the C.I.C.C.U. in its relations with other religious bodies,
but while this factor is mentioned and cannot be ignored
it is by no means the most important one.

On the contrary, the reader cannot fail to realize that
here is the story of a religious movement in Cambridge
which has influenced the whole University. The Inter-
Collegiate Union has not always succeeded in gaining
unqualified approval from the religious leaders in the
University but it is true to say that its members have always
been respected for their deep sincerity and undoubted
integrity. Moreover, the whole life of the Church, both at
home and overseas, has benefited by the contribution which
has been made by men brought to faith in Christ or quick-
ened or strengthened in their Christian life through their
association with the Union during their days at Cambridge.

The record unfolded in these pages goes on to show that a movement which started in Cambridge has now spread into Universities the world over, and is undeniably the strongest religious influence within them. What is its secret?

Those who want to understand the contemporary situation will find much food for thought in this book. They may not agree at every point with the author's interpretation of the facts but the facts themselves they should not ignore.

To one who in years gone by has profited greatly by association with this movement this story is of profound interest. Many of the names mentioned recall memories of men with strong faith, undoubted courage, and unswerving loyalty to our Lord Jesus Christ. Such men I have known in the fellowship of the C.I.C.C.U. and for them I give thanks.

CLIFFORD LIVERPOOL

PREFACE

I owe much to the work and generosity of others. I wish especially to thank the Bishop of Liverpool for so kindly writing the Foreword; the Bishop of Barking (the Rt. Rev. H. R. Gough, O.B.E., M.A.), who has given me help at every stage; and the Rev. J. T. C. B. Collins, M.A., who read the book in manuscript and made many valuable suggestions. A further list of Acknowledgements will be found as an Appendix.

I am very grateful to successive Presidents of the Cambridge Inter-Collegiate Christian Union from 1949 to 1953, for honouring me with the invitation to write this book, for leaving me completely free in my treatment of the theme, and for giving me all assistance in their power.

Finally I should like to thank Sir John Murray for his close personal interest and help.

J. C. P.

PROLOGUE

THE HOOP INN

EARLY on Saturday, 18th November 1876, two young men might have been seen leaving the Sidney Street gate of Master's Court, Trinity College, Cambridge. They turned left, crossed the road and entered the Hoop Inn opposite.

It was a fine late-autumn morning, warm for the time of year, and the curious carved heads of the once-famous coaching inn gleamed in the sun. Shortly afterwards, more undergraduates walked up to the Hoop, and before the clocks of Cambridge, Trinity's double-strike outlasting the rest, had chimed eight, some sixty men had converged from all directions, from Jesus Lane and Bridge Street, from Green Lane and narrow, dark All Saints' Passage, and had entered the Inn. Upstairs, places were laid for breakfast. In the seat of honour, as the meal began, sat the Reverend Sholto Douglas, a tall, massive-chested clergyman, not yet forty and tanned from a recent tour in the East. On his left and right sat the two Trinity men, W. F. T. Hamilton and William Mitchell-Carruthers, his hosts. The large party they had invited, now chatting merrily on either side of the long table, were all undergraduates save a few Bachelors and one Master of Arts, and were representative of every walk of University life.

The breakfast was ample, though not exceptional. Fish, followed by cutlets or cold ham with poached eggs or an omelette, and toast, rolls and marmalade. When all had done, and Mr. Palmer the landlord had seen the tables cleared, the sixty men rose and sang a hymn. The sound, so unusual for the hour, drifted across to wake lazy men in Trinity or Sidney Sussex, and echoed in the quiet street below, catching the ears of carters as they lumbered in from the country to Cambridge market. The hymn over, Sholto Douglas began to speak. It was midday before the party broke up, after eleven speeches and much discussion.

This meeting passed unnoticed. Senior members of the University had plenty to talk about, for the previous week's elections had given the Council of the Senate its first liberal majority for years; undergraduates were preparing for the last day of College Sports and the Trial Eights on the river. The great world outside was discussing the Eastern Question, the Americans were in the throes of the strangest presidential election in their history, the Queen was still at Balmoral, and Lord Beaconsfield's Cabinet was debating the danger of war with Russia. The Hoop Inn, Cambridge, on that November morning of 1876, seemed insignificant and the men who met there were unknown. Yet from their deliberations sprang a movement which has influenced universities all over the world—the Cambridge Inter-Collegiate Christian Union.

The activities of young men in the somewhat sheltered atmosphere of a University might seem a trivial subject, and seventy-five years of youthful effort limited in interest. But the significance of the story is not only found at Cambridge, nor even in the student movements which drew thence so much of their inspiration. It is found in the faith, love and self-sacrifice which immured cultured men in the slums for the sake of their fellows; which sent them into the Congo or up the Yangtze when they could have lived comfortably at home; or in parliament and industry made them risk reputation for the sake of truth. Lives which otherwise might have passed in honourable but self-centred devotion to things temporal have been reorientated through experiences at Cambridge; characters refashioned, ideals renewed and ambitions transformed.

It is a tale of human relationships and human endeavour, spiced not only with courage and adventure but with frailty. Yet it is more than a human tale, and thus pertinent to the present. The mass of facts, figures and names which a full history would demand has been discarded therefore in favour of a straightforward approach, related to the national scene, but devoid of wearisome detail in which, for all but a limited circle, the inspiration of the story so easily could be lost. The focus is on the ideas and actions of undergraduates, the thought and work of their seniors being seen only as it affects or is affected by them, and where possible the players in the drama speak for themselves. The story by no means ends with the book.

The Hoop Inn Conference of November 1876, gave birth to the C.I.C.C.U.[1] It was not an isolated, unpredictable episode, but a development from the past. To understand it and the long series of events to which it led, nearly a hundred years must first be retraced.

[1] From the start the Cambridge Inter-Collegiate Christian Union was known by its initials, C.I.C.C.U.—pronounced as a word.

CHAPTER I

STUBBORN SOIL

IN February 1779, a nineteen-year-old freshman, Charles Simeon, attended a service of Holy Communion in King's College Chapel which changed the course of history.

Two hundred years had passed since Hugh Latimer, fellow of Clare Hall, had startled town and University by asserting openly that heart and life counted more than outward forms. The old White Horse Inn, where Latimer, little Bilney, Coverdale and their friends had met in secret 'to smell the Word of God,' still stood a short way down the street from King's, but the ideals of the White Horse set were forgotten.

Cambridge men had led the Reformation in England. Seventeenth-century Cambridge, for all its wranglings, had known its saints. The eighteenth century saw the University in decay.

Academically its learning was thin. Morals were lax; religious life barren. Graduates had to subscribe their loyalty to the established church, all fellowships obliged their holders to take Holy Orders or resign, and Chapel was compulsory in the colleges, but, as a contemporary, a fellow of Jesus wrote, it was 'attended by the generality of the undergraduates with no seriousness of devotion, and seldom by the fellows at all.' Holy Communion was administered at the three great festivals and otherwise only once a term. The moral decadence was relieved, as elsewhere in England, by some who lived up to their lights; such was the poet Gray. But the University remained almost untouched by the vigorous Christianity of the Wesleys and Whitefield. John Berridge of Clare, Vicar of Everton on the road to Bedford, who scandalized his less zealous brethren by open-air preaching in their parishes, occasionally came to Cambridge, while the eloquence of Robert Robinson, Minister of the Particular Baptist Chapel in Saint Andrew's Street, attracted a number of gownsmen, of whom one, Rowland Hill, had come up from Eton in 1764 already a follower of Whitefield. With a few undergraduate friends Hill used to study the New Testament in Greek, visit the sick and prisoners, and do good works in the surrounding villages where they were bold enough even to preach. Such activities won scant favour from their seniors and Hill was threatened with expulsion. He said later that the only man in his College to give him a smile was the shoe-black.

By 1771 Hill had gone down; after several rebuffs from bishops afraid of his enthusiasm he received deacon's orders, and spent most of his life in a ministry highly successful if ecclesiastically irregular at Surrey Street Chapel in London. His friends had left also, the mild disturbance they had created was forgotten and Cambridge religion continued in its customary torpor.

Neither Provost Cooke of King's nor his dean presumably saw anything unusual in the terminal Sacrament of Lent, 1779. Nor was there anything about Charles Simeon, fresh from Eton, to suggest that the Provost's note informing him of his obligation to attend should have had the effect which it did. Except for one brief and somewhat self-conscious phase of fasting and prayer at school, he had shown no predisposition to differ from his fellows. Yet when he understood that the Provost 'absolutely required' his attendance at the Communion, 'conscience told me that Satan was as fit to go there as I; and that if I *must* go I *must* repent, and turn to God, unless I chose to eat and drink to my own damnation.'

He had three weeks to prepare. He bought William Law's *The Whole Duty of Man*, the religious best-seller of the day, and 'made myself quite ill with reading, fasting and prayer.' February came and the terminal Sacrament duly attended, but in his rooms in King's Old Court beside the gate of Trinity Hall, Simeon remained depressed and perplexed, until during Passion week, while reading a book by Thomas Wilson, sometime Bishop of Sodor and Man, he came to a passage on the meaning of the Old Testament sacrifices. 'What!' thought Simeon; 'may I transfer my guilt to another? Has God provided an offering for me, that I may lay my sins on another? Then I will not bear them on my own soul a moment longer.' And then and there, as he wrote, 'I sought to lay my sins on the sacred head of Jesus.' Peace of mind did not follow immediately, but on Easter Day he awoke with an over-whelming sense that Christ was risen. 'From that hour peace flowed in rich abundance into my soul; and at the Lord's Table in our chapel I had the sweetest access to God through my blessed Saviour.'

Simeon was determined, so he related thirty years later, to share his discovery with others. His courage was not equal at first to accosting fellow-gownsmen; early efforts were directed towards his bedmaker. He further related that three years passed before he met anyone else with his outlook. The few in Cambridge who shared it were so isolated that it was not until Simeon's ordination in 1782 that they discovered him to be as sincere as themselves.

He was not only sincere but effective. 'In less than seventeen Sundays,' wrote Henry Venn, whose son was at Sidney, 'by preaching in a church at Cambridge, he filled it with hearers—a thing unknown there for near a century.' The church was St. Edward's, where Latimer had preached. A few weeks later, after some dispute, Charles Simeon was appointed incumbent of Holy Trinity, at the age of twenty-three, the new Bishop of Ely being a family friend.

Simeon's ministry of fifty-four years at Holy Trinity has often been described; how he had to contend with the active opposition of his churchwardens, who tried to stifle his preaching by locking the doors of the old high pews. How at first he found almost every man of influence in town and gown against him for preaching what they ranked fanatical methodism; how not least among his troubles was his own quick temper and impatience. In process of time Simeon acquired allies among the dons, but even they were slow to appreciate his worth. 'For some years,' remarked Isaac Milner, President of Queens', with sublime self-righteousness, 'I rigorously scrutinized the character and conduct of Mr. Simeon, and for a time entertained some doubts of his sincerity. But now,' he was pleased to add, 'I am perfectly convinced of his truly Christian spirit and usefulness.'

Isaac Milner, however, President of Queens' from 1788 until his death in 1820, became a staunch friend to Simeon. Milner, a large, bluff Yorkshireman, with an enormous voice and a hearty laugh, was a brilliant mathematician and for a while combined in his ample person the Jacksonian and Lucasian Professorships, together with his presidency and the deanery of Carlisle. His brother was a noted evangelical in Hull but as an undergraduate Milner showed no such inclinations. For some years afterwards the direction of his life was undecided, and he lived in two worlds; Wilberforce, then a gay young Member of Parliament, took him abroad for good company, yet they ended by reading the New Testament together. When he became President he wrote to Wilberforce, by then more staunch a Christian than himself, 'I dare say I deceive myself but I have it strongly in mind to lead *something of a new life.*'

He had not deceived himself, and his presidency of Queens' made his decision an asset to Christianity in Cambridge. He ruled Queens' with a strong hand, gave the tutorships to fellows who would care for the well-being of their men and although making little effort to proselytize was a guide and a guardian to 'young men of a religious disposition.' His methods were not always popular, for to carry out his professed determination 'to have nothing to do with Jacobins or infidels' he would forcibly remove unsuitable fellows to college livings.

One of Milner's friends was Joseph Jowett who became Professor of Civil Laws in 1782. 'He loved his Bible,' Milner said of him after his death in 1813. He was held in great respect by the University and was thus of considerable help to Simeon. 'Who dared ridicule the preacher to whose discourses Dr. Jowett was frequently known to listen?' Henry Jowett, his brother, was another of the set, as also William Farish, tutor of Magdalene and Vicar of St. Giles.

4

Although these men played their part, Simeon's influence was paramount. In the course of his long life as fellow of King's and incumbent of Holy Trinity his fame spread far from the Cam; he preached, he wrote letters and gave advice, he supported missionary work, encouraging Cambridge men such as Henry Martyn to devote their lives to the heathen, and he purchased livings, 'fixing the gospel there in perpetuity.' Simeon thus became a name honoured, loved and abused thoughout the three kingdoms and beyond. But his chief work was at Cambridge. He was primarily a clergyman and only secondarily a don.[1] He had therefore both more time and more opportunity to mould the young men who gathered around him. He would invite them to conversation parties, when they would crowd to his rooms in Gibbs' Building, to be greeted with smiles and gawky courtesy, while Simeon noted down new names in his pocket-book and set all at ease. Then, with windows tight shut for fear of fresh air, while a servant handed round tea ('a part of the entertainment which most of us could have well dispensed with' was one smug comment) they would ask Simeon questions and listen to his teaching. These parties, somewhat severely formal though they were, proved a training ground for future clergy and taught both pastoral skill and the grounds of faith.

He led his men firmly. He had no truck with conduct contrary 'to the modesty that becomes a young man, and a religious professor in particular.' He was quite prepared to report to their tutors any who neglected studies to visit the sick. He held that there was a time for both, and that the indolence and indiscipline of the average undergraduate gave no 'Simeonite' any excuse to be idle because he was religious.

It became inevitable that most undergraduates should hear Simeon's preaching in their time. Some sought him out. The majority came from curiosity or even less worthy motives. Thus two King's men, Richard Godley and John Sargent, once entered his church during service 'in a most disorderly way.' 'As usual, I fixed my eyes

[1] Though for a while he was Dean and later Vice-Provost of King's.

upon them with sternness, indicative of my displeasure.' One looked suitably ashamed. But the other ('the only one that ever was daring enough to withstand my eye') stared back. Simeon sent for him next day, and told him never to go to that church again unless 'in a very different spirit.' He did come again, and both of them, as Simeon triumphantly could claim, eventually became 'blessed servants of the Most High God.'

Simeon left an impression on Cambridge which lasted long after the wane of similar influence at Oxford. And he was peculiarly fitted for the work he undertook. Being no one's convert, and having for three years built his faith in a spiritual isolation reminiscent of St. Paul's Arabia, he remained independent in thought and outlook. He saw that 'truth is not in the middle, and not in one extreme, but in both extremes. . . . Sometimes I am a high Calvinist and sometimes a low Arminian.' He detested controversy and his attitude to those who preached his gospel but differed in detail is well expressed by his remark as a young man to the veteran Wesley. 'We will cordially unite in those things wherein we agree.' He based his whole life on the revelation of God in Scripture—on 'the grand whole, the vast scheme of redemption as from eternity to eternity,' and his great desire in preaching was 'never to speak more or less than I believe to be the mind of the Spirit in the passage I am expounding.' He was loyal to the Church of England, loved its liturgy and disliked irregularity; on the few occasions he was provoked into ecclesiastical indiscipline he suffered twinges of conscience. Unlike Berridge of Everton, he did not despise learning although not a scholar of weight. His spirit of moderation, regularity, loyalty to the Bible and dislike of controversy imperceptibly became part of the Cambridge tradition.

His influence sprang chiefly from his character. His close friends knew, and Simeon knew, that his warm humanity had its quota of imperfections. This little man with his beak nose, his awkward gait and often grotesque gestures could be irritable, hasty and vain. His attention to detail could make him as fussy as any other bachelor don of his day. Being rather emotional and introspective, he was easily depressed. It says much for his religion that not only were these faults overcome but that in a society quick to criticize and eager to condemn he became honoured as a saint—and a cheerful saint. He was kind and courteous, warm-hearted and full of humour, though deadly serious in what he held were vital matters of life; he cared for the bodily needs as well as for the souls of his people and was generous almost to a fault. By such qualities, wrote a friend towards the end of Simeon's life, 'he was gradually won a popularity at Cambridge which now seems to triumph over all prejudice and persecution.'

Behind lay a devotional life of rare power. He rose early each morning to study the Scriptures, and often could be seen pacing the roof above his rooms as he prayed for friends and enemies. If ever a man walked with God, it was he. And he knew that no merit of his own had made him what he was. The expression he used of himself as he lay dying in 1836, 'the chief of sinners and the greatest monument of God's mercy,' was no shallow death-bed platitude but lifelong conviction. Milner, Jowett and the rest played their part, together with the changing outlook of the nation, in transforming Cambridge religion and setting the scene for the future, but Simeon bears the palm.

A young gentleman of the early days of the Regency, making the six-hour run on the *Telegraph* or *Star* coaches from London to Cambridge for his first term would have found a very different University from that of his father or grandfather, although except for the half-finished buildings of Downing's long-deferred college little had changed outwardly. Had he been so minded he would have had no difficulty in finding dons whose Christianity meant something, and even if he risked being cheerfully dubbed a 'Sim' he would not, like Rowland Hill, have been obliged to rely for sympathy on the college shoe-black. Whoever he was, he was sure at some time to visit Holy Trinity. 'As for the gownsmen,' wrote Simeon at about this time, 'I am forced to let them go up into the galleries, which I never suffered before, and notwithstanding that, multitudes of them are forced to stand in the aisles for want of space.'

7

But however changed the religious life of Cambridge, there was no question yet of any organized initiative on the part of junior members of the University. This was shown by the affair of the British and Foreign Bible Society in 1811.

Early in November a number of undergraduates thought they would start an auxiliary branch of the Bible Society in Cambridge. The Society was seven years old and to such rigidly orthodox Anglicans as Dr. Marsh, the Regius Professor of Divinity, smacked strongly of Dissent. The undergraduates chose an informal committee to discuss their scheme with Milner, Farish, Simeon and Dr. Jowett whom, to their disgust and dismay, they found most un-enthusiastic. Farish 'sat with his head on his hand and said very little'; Jowett looked kind, but 'was suspected by us of lukewarmness.' Milner, ever on the watch for Jacobins—for Buonaparte was still very much alive—thought of 'the danger of encouraging insubordination by appearing as a leader in any plan which originated with undergraduates.' The dons advised the committee that its one hope of success was to leave the whole matter in the hands of their seniors.

This they did. But as soon as the project was rumoured abroad 'every person without exception,' as Simeon wrote, 'threw cold water upon it, on this principle that if they were suffered to proceed in this way about the Bible they would soon do the same about politics.' The undergraduates began to get restless. Their seniors seemed to be doing nothing. They themselves had called without success on the Vice-Chancellor at Christ's and on the Master of Trinity, who happened to be Bishop of Bristol. Finally they decided to act 'by ourselves, neglecting the seniors, without delay,' and fell to discussing ways and means. At the last moment, when plans for a great meeting were all but settled, one of them prevailed upon the others to go with him again to Simeon, who by this time was writing that he 'would have given a large sum that we had not stirred at all.' Simeon persuaded them once more to be patient.

Wilberforce in London then secured the support of the

Duke of Gloucester, the King's nephew and Chancellor-elect of the University, who for all his odd ways and his nickname 'Silly Billy' was a cut above the average Hanoverian, and at last the Bible Society auxiliary was launched at a somewhat rowdy public meeting on December 12th, at which the original undergraduate sponsors of the scheme were scarcely mentioned.

Sixteen years later, in 1827, times had changed sufficiently for undergraduate initiative to meet more favour. It was a period of growth and inspiration in the University. Numbers had doubled since 1811. Many names afterwards great were on college lists or about to enter: F.D. Maurice was in his third year, Tennyson, Hallam and Darwin came up in '28 and Thackeray shortly afterwards. The Union, once suppressed as subversive was flourishing; regular racing on the river, the Varsity cricket match, and the highly intellectual and almost secret society of the Apostles date from this time. That something of the same pioneering spirit should inspire those whose predominant interest was the extension of Christ's Kingdom is not surprising.

In the early spring of 1827 five men walked back in the sunshine from Holy Trinity Church one Sunday morning and sat discussing the sermon in a summer-house behind Tennis Court Road. All but one were first year men, and all but one from Queens. Simeon must have stressed the need to prove faith by works, or had spoken of the pagan ignorance prevailing around Cambridge, for as they talked one of them, James Wright, remarked: 'It seems a pity that we could not spend some part of our time in Sunday School teaching.'

They wondered if any parish would like their help. One said he had already asked all the town parsons and been turned down. Another suggested Barnwell, 'a sadly neglected place and near enough; why not try to do something there?' Barnwell was a straggling village on the Newmarket Road, still separated from the town by fields through which ran Jesus Lane. It was growing fast, had an unsavoury reputation ('heathenish and dissolute') and

9

a very small church dating back to the old priory which had stood between the road and the river.

The originators of the idea felt no need this time to submit their plans to the seniors. They do not seem even to have consulted the Vicar of Barnwell before dividing his parish into sections for house-to-house visiting. The Vicar was probably an absentee, for shortly afterwards a don favourable to the scheme managed to obtain the living in order to help them. They did, however, call on Professor Farish, Vicar of St. Michael's in Trinity Street, and on young Professor Scholefield, Vicar of St. Peter's, to ask if they might send the children to their churches. Both received them very courteously and agreed to help, but did not think the scheme would last.

The next need was a suitable building. The Friends' Meeting House in Jesus Lane, apparently only used once or twice a year, was suggested, the trustee written to, and when no reply was received two of them hired a gig, drove over to the village near Ely where the Quaker lived and called on him. Their dilatory correspondent proved only too willing to help now that letter-writing was unnecessary, and they returned to Cambridge in triumph.

By this time the scheme had some enthusiastic adherents in other colleges, and together they spent a week visiting the homes, some in pairs, some singly, in order to recruit the children. 'I was most kindly received everywhere,' wrote one of them, 'and found the inhabitants of Barnwell a very different set of people from what I had supposed.' Some parents, however, asked how much they would be paid for each child sent. Others would listen to the solemn pleas and warnings of the undergraduates, and then politely agree to send the children merely 'to oblige the gentlemen.'

The scholars' list lengthened and on a Sunday morning about three weeks after the summer-house meeting, the Jesus Lane Sunday School was opened. Some two hundred and twenty boys and girls had arrived. 'I shall not readily forget the shouting and uproar which saluted our ears on entering the building,' said one of the founders. He and his friends succeeded in quietening their 'unruly, boisterous, dirty and ragged' pupils and lessons began. The children were illiterate and the first task each Sunday morning was to teach a few letters; the teachers would then dictate a text of Scripture which the children wrote as best they could on their slates. Its meaning would be explained and the children repeat the text and be questioned on it. The first selected was from the third chapter of St. John, and the sixteenth verse: 'God so loved the world that He gave His only begotten Son, that whosoever believeth on Him should not perish but have everlasting life.' In course of time all the great doctrines of the faith were taught in this simple way.

The founders of the Jesus Lane Sunday School lived to see it become an honoured and loved institution. After six years in Jesus Lane it moved round the corner to King Street, and in 1867 to new quarters specially built in Paradise Lane nearer Barnwell, though keeping its original name. Prompt results were evident in the lives of some at least of the children. Two of the dirtiest were sons of a drunken glazier in Abbey Street, 'a bad husband and a worse father.' Within a few weeks one of the brothers was missing. The other, when questioned, burst into tears and said 'He's in Heaven, Sir.' One of the staff went round to the home, and found the father lying on his filthy bed, also dying, but in a most unexpectedly 'humble and penitent state of mind.' 'Oh, Sir," he said, 'there was no resisting the prayers and entreaties of that dying boy. He made me ashamed of myself.'

Whatever the effect on the children, the Sunday School influenced the lives of the teachers. It became a joint enterprise in which dons, bachelors and undergraduates worked together, thus forging a valuable link between them for generation after generation. It was a training ground where men learned to prove their faith, to enjoy fellowship which could not become an end in itself, and to understand something of the lives of those less fortunate than themselves. In course of time many who were to play important parts at Cambridge or elsewhere passed through Jesus Lane Sunday School; Conybeare, Howson, Vaughan, Westcott and Montagu Butler taught there, and it was 'always a place where the Lord Jesus Christ as the only hope of the sinner or of the believer, was the sum and substance of what was taught.'

In 1836 Simeon died, seen to his grave in King's Chapel by vast crowds of mourners, while every shop in the town was closed. At Oxford the next ten years were filled with quarrels and disputes, but Cambridge was scarcely touched. *Tracts for the Times* met with little response and there was no Professor Hampden to raise further controversial issues.

Simeon's movement thrived and during the 'thirties and 'forties had firm hold on the churches of Cambridge and considerable power in the colleges. Not every evangelical don was as high principled as Simeon. Benson, afterwards Archbishop, had a fine story of his mathematical coach, 'a pronounced evangelical' who was always in bed when his pupils arrived and would conduct his supervision through a chink in the bedroom door while dressing, 'singing hymns all the time with immense unction'; but Simeonites earned their share of academic distinction. C. J. Vaughan, who was bracketed Senior Classic in 1838 and F. J. A. Hort, also from Arnold's Rugby, are names enough, while Joseph Barber Lightfoot, though not a Jesus Lane teacher, was as an undergraduate a follower of Carus, Simeon's successor at Holy Trinity. 'Sims' were found in profusion on the river. The original crew of what became Second Trinity were said to have been 'Sims' to a man and the club dubbed 'the Hallelujah.'

By 1847, the year when to Queen Victoria's disgust Prince Albert's election as Chancellor was contested, the religious life of Cambridge undergraduates seemed set fair. The Simeonites were secure. Continued opposition was inevitable but seldom strong. There was patronage and protection from above and continually renewed vigour from below. Then came 1848.

CHAPTER II

CONVERGENT STREAMS

ON 20th March 1848, in the rooms of A. A. Isaacs of Corpus, took shape the first of the three immediate forerunners of the Cambridge Inter-Collegiate Christian Union.

The times were out of joint. Louis Philippe had landed in exile a few weeks before and in London the Chartist affair was less than a month away. Such events could not ruffle Cambridge, although within two hours and eight minutes of London by the new railway. But in the University the disputes which ended with the Reforms of the 'fifties had broken out in February, though scarcely of interest either to the earnest-minded Isaacs or to more frivolous contemporaries.

Albert Augustus Isaacs had come up to Corpus in January 1847. He was already a determined Christian and looking forward to ordination. He had no cause to feel lonely; Corpus already had as much reputation as Queens' for evangelical ardour among both fellows and undergraduates. His first contact with Christians in the University came the morning after his arrival. It was not, however, a Corpus man who knocked on his door but Frederick Gough of St. John's. It was particularly kind of him to come round so soon, for University etiquette frowned on third year men who paid attention to freshmen. Yet Isaacs at once found himself introduced to 'the various works which Christian young men were carrying on in the town and University, and,' he continues, 'the first Sunday I spent in Cambridge I was inducted into the office of a teacher in the Jesus Lane Sunday School.'

One factor in Frederick Gough's life gave him a marked

position among his friends; he was to be a foreign missionary. Henry Martyn, Thomason, Buchanan and others of Simeon's day were not much imitated in the 'forties, but honour was paid to those preparing for what was held 'the highest calling.' Affection, therefore, was blended with profound respect in Isaacs' feelings towards Gough. Gough's intention, when he had been ordained and served a short curacy, was to sail for China. The journey alone took six months and, except for the Treaty Ports opened six years before, the country was closed to Europeans. The life of an English missionary in China was restricted, arduous and, thanks to the constant civil wars of the period, often dangerous. Gough had been provisionally accepted for the small pioneer party of the Church Missionary Society at Ningpo.

'About the beginning of May 1847,' said Isaacs many years later, 'Gough was taking tea with me in the rooms which I occupied above the Combination Room.' As they sat talking in the gathering dusk (no one had afternoon tea in 1847) Isaacs' thoughts ran to the uncertain future. He reminded Gough that before long they and other friends would be separated, and suggested that 'we might agree among ourselves to meet in the spirit of prayer in whatever part of the world our lot might be cast.' His idea was that before they went down they should select a particular hour and day in the month on which they could pray for one another. Gough thought this an excellent suggestion. Before he left Corpus that evening he had agreed to get others together to discuss it, Isaacs being too junior to vent his ideas on his betters. They were all teaching each week at Jesus Lane and Gough would have no difficulty in reaching them.

Days passed and crept into weeks, and nothing happened. Isaacs at last sent Gough a note of reminder and when lessons were done at Jesus Lane on the following Sunday, had the satisfaction of hearing Gough call him and their friends together to discuss the idea.

A few days later six of them met in Free School Lane, at the rooms of Edmund Carr of St. John's, and prayed and talked into the night. If, they felt, the project was to survive the years they should throw it into a definite form and Gough and Isaacs agreed to draw up a few simple rules. Frederick Gough, his mind already in China, seems to have had poor memory, for the Long Vacation and the Michaelmas term of 1847 were past before further steps were taken. Gough, in fact, was far from Cambridge, preparing for ordination and his Birmingham curacy when Isaacs' project finally materialized at the meeting in Corpus of March 1848.

By this time the idea had grown. Originally to be limited to the few immediately concerned, it was now, at a first committee meeting, formally launched, minute book and all, as *The Cambridge Union for Private Prayer, for Members of the University preparing for the Ministry*. The rules were straightforward, but rigorous. The members were to pray for each other on the second Monday of each month, from six to seven o'clock in the morning, 'or the first convenient hour' later. They were to pray for the Church at home and abroad, and for 'the raising up of a devoted ministry.' Members were to write to the secretary each year, extracts being published in a report, and the annual subscription was a shilling.

Of the committee of 1848, one was in his first year as fellow of Trinity, four of the seven were scholars, three members came from Corpus, one each were from Caius, Christ's and St. John's, and all were undergraduates except the Trinity man. Some, like Edmund Carr, were rich men's sons, some were poor. One at least, Robert Walker, was a most solemn and severe character, Edmund Carr quite the reverse. George Moule became a missionary bishop but the rest spent lives of solid but unmarked service. Something of the beliefs which moulded them may be gathered from a letter which Carr wrote shortly afterwards. They should always teach, he told his friends in brief but succinct phrases, 'the doctrines of man's fall, the ruin and bankruptcy of his nature, his restoration in Christ, the blessings of redemption made over to him by faith, the operation of the Spirit in conversion and His subsequent co-operation in daily renewal; the necessity of personal holiness, consistency, and separation from the world, and the sovereignty of God in the disposition of His gifts both in providence and grace.'

The seven men of 1848 could not have foreseen the further developments of their scheme, both in Cambridge and beyond. Their original union was limited. New members had to be preparing for orders but still unordained. Yet they had a hundred members by 1849. In 1850 they removed this restriction on the ordained and numbers mounted. In 1854 they admitted Anglicans who were neither in orders nor reading for them, and shortened the title to the *Cambridge University Prayer Union*. By their Silver Jubilee, in 1873, they had just short of a thousand members. Except for local branches of missionary societies, this Cambridge Prayer Union was the first organized religious union at Cambridge, though it had no corporate meetings and was a handmaid to the regular life in the churches and college chapels. In its expanded form it provided a link between Cambridge Christians, undergraduate and graduate, in residence and gone down. Though it became very much a preserve of the seniors, and in the latter years before its final demise in 1934 of little significance, it plays a clear part in the expansion of Christian life in the colleges.

Beyond Cambridge its effect was no less pronounced. A letter which Isaacs wrote almost at once to Valpy French of Oxford, afterwards the great bishop of Lahore, met with little response. 'Matters are not ripe' for such a scheme, French replied. But at the end of 1850 Oxford men were brave enough to follow the Cambridge example and started their Prayer Union. The following year, 1851, the scheme was taken up both by officers of the Army and of the Navy, their Prayer Unions eventually joining together as the Officers' Christian Union, and in 1852 a further Prayer Union was formed by lawyers.

Thus Cambridge undergraduates led the way; and it is significant that their first effort to have had more than a local effect was connected with prayer.

Ten years later came the founding of the Cambridge University Church Missionary Union.

The Simeonites, still so called, continued to flourish in the 'fifties, years of change in the University, as the Royal Commission of 1849 led to one reform after another and Cambridge was catching up with the nineteenth century. Samuel Butler, at St. John's, includes Simeonites in his bitter jibes at the religion of the day. His description in *The Way of All Flesh* of the sizars of St. John's most of whom were 'Sims,' may have a grain of truth: 'they were rarely seen except in hall or chapel or at lecture, where their manners of feeding, praying and studying were considered alike objectionable.' He cleverly, if unfairly, generalizes from the poor sizars to all Simeonites, 'unprepossessing in features, gait and manners, unkempt and ill-dressed beyond what can be easily described, these poor fellows formed a class apart. . . .' 'The Simeonites,' he writes, 'held themselves to have received a very loud call to the ministry. To most of them the fact of becoming clergymen would be an *entrée* into a social position from which they were at present kept out.' Thus he disposes of their manners and their motives. As for their methods, they certainly, as he records, dropped tracts in letter-boxes by night. As late as 1889 B. K. Cunningham met such a tract in his post: 'very startling, very forcible.' In *The Way of All Flesh* Ernest Pontifex writes a parody of a tract and drops it on the leading Sims. The subject was Personal Cleanliness and it 'concluded by exhorting Simeonites to a freer use of the tub.' A tract in Butler's own handwriting survives, dating from his second term, in 1855. 'What can ten fools do among three hundred sinners?' he asks bitterly. 'They can do much harm and had far better let the sinners seek peace their own way in the wilderness than ram it down their throats during the night.' Pathetic advice, if Butler's own history be recalled.

At the end of the 'fifties, in the last days of 1857, David Livingstone addressed the University.

Livingstone, then forty-four, had been sixteen years in Africa and had discovered the Victoria Falls the year before. Since his return he had been fêted and lionized rather to his distaste, and already had spoken at Oxford. He came to Cambridge in the first week of December to stay with W. H. Monk, curate of Barnwell, without any intention of what he called 'public spouting.' Monk, 'an energetic but somewhat eccentric personage,' as an undergraduate of the time described him, was determined not to let his lion lie. On 4th December therefore, Livingstone found himself in the Senate House, with the veteran Professor Sedgwick in the chair, the platform crowded with Heads of Houses, the floor with graduates and undergraduates and in the galleries a crush of crinolines.

The acclamations over, Livingstone began to speak. 'He stood before us,' wrote Sedgwick, 'a plain, single-minded, cheerful man—somewhat attenuated by years of toil and with a face tinged by the sun of Africa. And he addressed us in unadorned and simple words.' He described his travels and discoveries, the horror of slavery, and the commercial possibilities of the continent. But Livingstone had not come to Cambridge as an entertainer. He went on to speak of matters nearest his heart and to call for followers. 'The sort of men who are wanted for missionaries are such as I see before me—men of education, standing, enterprise, zeal and piety.' It was not sacrifice they would make if they came to Africa: 'I never made a sacrifice. Of this we ought never to talk, when we remember the great sacrifice which He made Who left His Father's throne on high to give Himself for us.' Other motives were brought in, not without humour: 'the missionary can earn his living by his gun—a course not open to a country curate. I would rather be a poor missionary than a poor curate!'

He spoke for over an hour and held his audience spellbound. 'I beg to direct your attention to Africa,' he concluded quietly, 'I know that in a few years I shall be cut off in that country, which is now open; do not let it be shut again! I go back to Africa to try to make an open path for commerce and Christianity: do you carry out the work which I have begun. I leave it with you.'

Livingstone, who also lectured to the town the following day, was delighted with his reception. 'It beat Oxford hollow,' he wrote to a friend. And when he had returned to Africa, with his library restocked by Cambridge gifts and two dozen of Trinity audit ale in his baggage, his words still echoed round the University: 'I leave it with you.' The senior men moved slowly. By summertime Livingstone's lectures had been printed, with a long and stirring preface from Sedgwick. Negotiations with Oxford proceeded, but it was not until 1st November 1859, at a Senate House meeting, Gladstone and Bishop Wilberforce representing Oxford, that the Universities Mission to Central Africa was founded.

W. H. Monk of Barnwell, determined also to follow up his guest's visit, forthwith founded a missionary association for Cambridge. For many years the two great missionary organizations, the Society for the Propagation of the Gospel and the Church Missionary Society, had kept somewhat loose ties with the University, but Monk's association was to include men of all schools of thought. He soon found that such alliances prove lukewarm. He therefore linked his project to the society the most represented in the University and announced it, in the early weeks of 1858, as the Cambridge University Church Missionary Union 'to encourage a more extended missionary spirit by frequent meetings for prayer and the reading of papers, and for bringing forward an increased number of candidates for missionary employment.' Quite a number of senior men and undergraduates joined, but other enthusiasms soon replaced the Church Missionary Union in the heart of its eccentric founder, and for some months it was little but a name, until in the following Long Vacation a fellow of Emmanuel took it over, formed a new committee and picked for secretary an undergraduate who was just the man for the task.

John Barton, who thus took the secretaryship of the Missionary Union in the summer of 1858, was starting his third year at Christ's, at the age of twenty-one. He came from Quaker stock, though his parents were Anglican. As a boy he had made friends with the Wright family in Derbyshire, whose vast Victorian mansion, its battlements quaintly formed into a Scripture text visible for miles, testified to their industrial wealth and uncompromising Christianity. Through one of the Wrights, then at Cambridge, John Barton came to what he recalled as 'a crisis in my inner life' during a walking tour in Wales, whilst still a schoolboy. During his second year at Christ's his convictions were sharpened by decision to be a missionary.

Strengthened by the Mutiny tragedies which were filling the newspapers, Barton's missionary call was for India. He saw no reason why anything less than utmost determination and loyalty should follow such a call. Livingstone's visit thrilled him, and he pressed the missionary cause on his friends while the opportunity lasted. He had persuaded the Prayer Union to have its hour of prayer once a week instead of once a month; when he was appointed Secretary of the Missionary Union he saw it as a God-given responsibility.

Until Livingstone's visit, overseas service had not been popular among Cambridge men. Less than a dozen of the eight thousand in Orders were known to be missionaries. John Barton's leadership of the Church Missionary Union broke down this indifference. He saw to it that members did not take their responsibilities lightly. On 6th April 1859, as a faded manuscript in Barton's handwriting testifies, thirteen of them signed a series of resolutions which turned Monk's original project into a union deep and lasting: 'We the undersigned members of the University of Cambridge, who have felt that the call to missionary work abroad has been especially addressed to ourselves; and have resolved in God's strength to give ourselves to that work if He makes our way plain before us; being desirous of strengthening one another's hands in this work by mutual sympathy and intercessory prayer for and with each other, have agreed to the following propositions. . . .' They shall meet once a month for prayer in the rooms of the President, a senior member. They shall pray for each other and for 'the missionary cause in the University' every Friday evening. 'Every member shall do his utmost to increase the missionary spirit . . . and by his life and consistent Christian walk and conversation to glorify that cause on which he has embarked.' Any member of the University may join, and by signing the roll signifies his 'willingness and intention to go out as a missionary if God should enable him.' In that spirit the Church Missionary Union went forward, and laid a solid foundation for the future.

The third and most important of the three foundations was that of the Daily Prayer Meeting four years later in 1862.

Christian activity at Cambridge had been shaping over the years in a way that seemed more than a matter of chance. After Simeon's pioneering, the Jesus Lane School, the Prayer Union and the Missionary Union had formed a pattern; service, prayer and then, on a wider field, service again. But there were limiting factors. All three movements were strictly Anglican, yet the effective entrance to the University of Nonconformists for whom no provision was made, could not long be delayed. The strength of Christian work, controlled for better or for worse by senior members, still depended on the succession of men coming up with lives moulded already by love and loyalty to Christ. Should such a succession decline or evangelical sympathies among the senior men weaken, the ideals which Simeon and his friends held dear might no longer find expression at Cambridge. In the England of 1859–60 anything might happen. The religious world had been shaken by the production of *Essays and Reviews* which, mild and sincere as they were, seemed an assault on the Bible as supreme and trustworthy guide, and an open door to the strong scepticism of Germany. At Oxford in the summer of 1860 Bishop Wilberforce's ill-conceived ridicule of Darwin's theories in his *Origin of Species* had precipitated a hammer-and-tongs battle between science and religion. On the other hand, though some older evangelicals were tending to suspect innovations and to endanger the sincerity of their faith by a dead-weight of tradition a new spirit was breathing across the land: 1859 was the year of the Great Revival, which filled churches and congregations with a fresh sense of Divine power and love and in many parts of the country seemed a return to the days of Wesley and Whitefield.

By 1862 Cambridge had shown no sympathy to either

of these opposing movements. Neither Darwin nor the Revival of '59 had met with response. But in that year a number of young men forced their seniors' hands, and in the right direction.

J. F. B. Tinling and Alfred Maynard had been boys at Liverpool College. Both came from Christian homes and both, like their contemporary Thomas Barnardo in Dublin had been influenced by the Revival. At school they used to meet together to pray for their friends, using for the purpose a quiet corner at the back of the school hall. On one such occasion, so Tinling records, the headmaster, Dr. Howson, 'sharply questioned us as to our business in that part of the building.' Howson, with his Cambridge friend Conybeare already famous for the *Life and Letters of St. Paul* had as an undergraduate taught at Jesus Lane. The boys told him what they were doing, and Howson 'said warmly "go there as often as you will for that purpose."' Their prayers were not unavailing, for Maynard recalls 'the awakening of *many* of our school-fellows.'

In 1860 Tinling went up to St. John's, followed in '62 by Maynard who had won a minor scholarship to Clare. Some weeks later they called together on Perowne, Dean of Corpus, and on Clayton, tutor of Caius and Vicar of Holy Trinity, the two evangelical leaders in Cambridge, offering a startling suggestion. With a few like-minded friends they wished to start 'a daily meeting for prayer, to ask for the outpouring of the Holy Spirit on our University.' This daily prayer meeting should be held throughout each full term, should be short, and open to any member of the University who cared to come. They said that it was only after 'earnest and long-continued prayer for divine guidance' that they had resolved on this course. They saw the University as one of 'the headquarters of the Ministry of Great Britain' and their praying should have 'special reference to those who shall hereafter constitute part of the clergy of this country.' Many future clergy were around them, often ignorant, easy-going and without the essential experience of the invigorating and re-newing power of the Holy Spirit; the Cambridge Prayer

Union and Missionary Union were admirable but made little effort to reach any not like-minded, though this might be done by individual members. Surely, said the two undergraduates, there could be no doubt of 'the effect which an answer to our prayers, in the increased holiness and earnestness of the ministry, must have upon our own country and upon the world.'

Perowne and Clayton bristled with objections. They were not in any way opposed to extempore prayer, but that a prayer meeting should be public was not to their liking. Then there was fear of that 'excitement' which often seemed to accompany such meetings among 'the lower orders of the people.' Did they not also already have 'sufficient means of Grace and perfect Liturgies?' Another objection was that 'the use of such open and un-precedented means would be detrimental to the cause of religion by lessening the individual influence of religious men.' This objection, obscure in meaning, seemed to Maynard and Tinling scarcely serious. But these were not all. They were roundly told that 'such efforts are inconsistent with your present position as undergraduates' and, secondly, that 'assuming the propriety of the move-ment, *you* are not called upon to undertake it.'

Thus rebuffed, Maynard and Tinling returned to the other undergraduates who were with them in the project and continued to think and pray, by no means certain what was right. Maynard, however, was a near neighbour in Yorkshire of the great Dr. Vaughan, just resigned from the headmastership of Harrow and now Vicar of Don-caster, a few miles from the village where Maynard's father was parson. It was decided that Maynard should write to Vaughan, while their old headmaster, Howson, should also be consulted.

Charles John Vaughan, fellow of Trinity, who appointed headmaster of Harrow at the age of twenty-eight in 1844, had raised it from a broken-down, ill-disciplined rabble of sixty-nine boys to be one of the leading public schools of the day in fact as well as in name, was a brilliant classical scholar, a great teacher and preacher, and the most humble of men. He had already refused the bishopric of

Rochester and with it, as was generally believed, the certainty of Lambeth. For the rest of his life, first as Vicar of Doncaster and later as Master of the Temple and Dean of Llandaff he devoted himself primarily to training men for the ministry. And to have been one of Vaughan's 'doves' was perhaps the best training a man could have. He loathed controversy, and stood aside from ecclesiastical parties. His great love was for the Bible, and it was said of him that in his teaching and commentaries he imparted to his pupils the conviction that 'every word which the sacred writers have written down at the mouth of God is worth all the labour of mastering its meaning and making it their own for ever.'

This was the man, gentle in voice and manner but with penetrating insight and resolute will, who read his young friend Maynard's letter in the vicarage at Doncaster in the autumn of 1862. And though Vaughan in his reply 'urged carefulness and moderation' he 'certainly did not oppose our movement.' Nor did Howson. Having thus tested the advice of dons against that of headmasters, Maynard and Tinling came to believe that Perowne's and Clayton's objection, whatever they had said, was primarily against the very idea of undergraduate initiative and leadership.

Tinling and Maynard decided to go ahead, believing 'that we were therein guided by God.' By this time they had formed a committee of some dozen men. Together they drew up a leaflet explaining their purpose and inviting undergraduates to join them and placed it in nearly every college room. Tinling, Maynard and two others, George Wilson of Caius and George Edwards of St. John's, signed the invitation as conveners. The day selected for the opening meeting approached, and the four conveners, conscious of the disapproval of their seniors and the scoffing and gossip with which most of their invitations had been received, solemnly drew lots for the leadership of the first Daily Prayer Meeting. The lot fell on Maynard.

On Monday 24th November 1862, Alfred Martin Maynard stood 'in fear and trembling' before some twenty undergraduates crowded into a minute room behind

Hutt's Bookshop in Trinity Street, opposite the Blue Boar.[1] Outside in the University, the senior men were discussing the *Alabama* crisis or arguing the proposed removal of Religious Tests, while many of the juniors were hurrying down to the river or making their way to the few rugger fields In the great world beyond, the opposing American armies were skirmishing before Fredericksburg. But in the quiet of the little room above Trinity Street these twenty undergraduates sang a hymn, listened to the reading of Scripture and prayed, one after another, short extempore prayers. All was over within twenty minutes. Though they did not know it as they clattered downstairs again, they had begun a tradition which except for a few short months during the First World War when the University was all but closed down, was to continue unbroken day after day in Full Term.

They had taken the plunge. But opposition did not cease. 'Our prayer-meeting,' they wrote in April 1863, 'has met with the disapproval of many of the most esteemed men in our University.' Leslie Stephen, his father one of Simeon's close friends but himself turning agnostic and throwing up his Orders and Trinity Hall fellowship for conscience' sake, might well be expected to write, in his anonymous *Sketches from Cambridge*, 'I should be sorry to speak of these well-meant efforts because I could not describe them in the simplest terms without making them ridiculous.' Nor was he probably far wrong in his estimation that 'ordinary undergraduates' were classing such things under the head of 'awful bosh.' But Clayton, Perowne and their friends were also slow to approve, though none of their dire predictions were being fulfilled. Opposition never took an active form, and the Daily Prayer Meeting prospered. It was divided for convenience into two sessions of fifteen minutes; a hymn, Scripture reading and time of prayer in each. Once a term a general meeting was held, addressed by an outside speaker or, when their prejudice had been overcome, by a senior

[1] Hutt's Bookshop was at 29 Trinity Street, later a post office and subsequently the shop of Arthur Roper, Ltd., tailors.

man. At this meeting tea and cakes went the rounds and to it they 'invited any whom we thought might be influenced for good.' Numbers at D.P.M., as it was soon known after the Cambridge habit, began to creep up, though not in the first year above thirty at best.

Names afterwards famous in the religious world begin to cross the records, such as Boyd Carpenter, the 'silver-tongued' Bishop of Ripon, together with others, like Tinling and Maynard themselves, whose lives were dedicated and valiant, but obscure. Of the many names in these early years one in particular may provide a fitting epilogue to the founding of the Daily Prayer Meeting.

James Gordon, who entered Trinity in 1865, was son of the fifth Lord Aberdeen and grandson of the Crimean Prime Minister. He combined a deep and utterly uncompromising loyalty to Christ with a dare-devil love of adventure. His father, though shy and sensitive, had always made plain his faith by word and action, and had died in 1864 after a life of self-sacrifice, liberality and courage. His brother George had gone to sea under an assumed name in the American merchant marine, first before the mast and later as captain. But instead of developing characteristics common to those who run away to sea he became known as an outstanding Christian as well as a first class sailor. Jim Gordon himself, while an undergraduate, paddled a canoe alone across the Channel, and up and down several rivers in Europe. He rowed for the University in the great race of 1867. He was a crack shot, though so reckless as to frighten his friends. With a character full of 'merriment and boyish light-heartedness' he was intensely popular, and known far and wide as a Christian. He taught at Jesus Lane and regularly attended D.P.M. 'Though his piety,' said a contemporary, 'was unobtrusive, he was not ashamed of it,' and both by the example of a remarkably consistent life and by straight talk when occasion offered 'he encouraged others to seek the peace which he himself had found.' 'You must give your whole heart to Jesus,' he once wrote to a friend, 'keep nothing back. Remember He gave up all for us.' Or again: 'I used to think that Christians were cowards because they were afraid of displeasing God; but now I see that I was the coward and they were the brave warriors, fighting the fight of faith. I was a coward because I was afraid of joining their ranks, I was afraid of being laughed at. I was afraid of having to give up many pleasures.' Jim Gordon, with his courage and faith, his ability and the enthusiasm which made him plan to finance and take out a pioneering missionary colony to Kaffirland, might have become one of the leaders of his generation. But on 12th February 1868, while dressing for dinner in his rooms, he somehow set off his gun and was shot dead. Such was the power of his life that the flags of every boathouse on the river were flown half-mast the next day.

Some words of Jim Gordon's might well have been addressed by men of the early D.P.M. to the University, hovering as it was at the end of the 'sixties between Christian loyalty and a devastating inrush of scepticism: 'Oh why will you halt between two opinions? What could the Lord do for you that He has not done? Has He not watched over you every moment? Has He not been knocking at the door of your heart continuously? And will you keep the King of Glory outside? . . .'

CHAPTER III

FULFILMENT

FOR Cambridge men in the early eighteen-seventies the Jesus Lane Sunday School, the Church Missionary Union and the Daily Prayer Meeting together formed a powerful spiritual stimulus and a smooth-flowing channel of Christian service; in the background the Cambridge Prayer Union continued to link past and present members of the University. It might have seemed that no further initiative was needed. But step by step during the decade matters worked up to the climax of 1877, when the Inter-Collegiate Christian Union was founded.

The Jesus Lane School was normally superintended by an undergraduate or bachelor but control was in the hands of the dons. From Jesus Lane other Sunday Schools had sprung, catering both for college choirs and for the rapidly growing districts of St. Paul's and St. Barnabas' near the railway, in which the lead came principally from fellows of Trinity.

The Church Missionary Union met for prayer every Monday night, while once or twice a term papers on missionary matters were read by undergraduates, dons or visitors, with a senior man in the chair. By Lent term 1875, as the Treasurer's book testifies, there were two hundred and twenty-six undergraduate members out of a University total of about two thousand.[1] Comparatively few C.M.U. members were intending to go overseas nor were all to be ordained; it was enough to be interested in the mission field. Some twenty, however, joined the

[1] Corpus had the highest proportion with thirty-seven, the larger colleges Trinity and St. John's had forty each; Queens' had forgotten past glories and dropped to eight, and King's and Trinity Hall each had only one member.

Church Missionary Society abroad in the ten years before 1882, while others went elsewhere. C.M.U. men would also valiantly dun their college neighbours for five-shilling payments to the parent society. 'It is terrible work,' wrote G. A. Lefroy of Trinity, afterwards Bishop of Calcutta, 'about the most unpleasant that I was ever employed on.' Even H. H. Montgomery (the Field-Marshal's father) a few years earlier, who was courageous enough to have jumped, as very few have done, the twenty-three steps of Trinity in one leap, confessed the same: 'Nothing I have ever had to do since has seemed so formidable . . . to knock at a man's door, to find him at breakfast with others, to explain in halting terms what I wanted to a man who may have had the dimmest idea of the C.M.S. and to be asked in return how much I wanted in order to get rid of me as soon as possible, and to feel that five shillings was a cheap riddance!' On the other hand someone 'whose after-life has been a warning' suggested to the youthful Edward Lyttelton a better way to deal with such a caller; 'Offer him a brandy and soda and he won't stop long!'

The Missionary Union and the Daily Prayer Meeting shared much of their membership, and their place of meeting. Both had used the room behind Hutt's Trinity Street Bookshop until 1870, when they moved to All Saints' Passage, leasing a large, dark and ugly room from George Carpenter, a tailor. From a quarter to two until a quarter past on week days some twenty or thirty men would be present in Carpenter's Rooms for D.P.M., still run in two self-contained sections of equal length, each led by a different man. On Sundays a graduate, generally a fellow, would take the meeting, to which a hundred men or more would come, and after the hymn he would not only read the chosen passage of Scripture but comment on it. In October 1873, a *Special Requests Book*, for prayer and praise, open to all, was laid on the table. 'It is hoped that gentlemen who lead in prayer will consult this book; but it is left entirely to their own discretion as to whether or not they should bring forward any petition found in it.' The petitions were not only concerned with Cambridge. A request from some Trinity dons 'engaged in a Mission in Liverpool'; prayer for the repression of intemperance; for famine relief in India, and for missions in villages around Cambridge are all found in the first few pages, together with prayer for an undergraduate dangerously ill and for two sick Sunday School scholars, as well as for evangelistic efforts in the University. 'The Daily Prayer Meeting,' wrote a Johnian of this period, 'was the barometer of spiritual life at the Varsity. If the meetings were well attended one could be sure there was real work for God going on, if badly attended then the reverse, and all the more need for prayer.'

The movement had spread beyond Cambridge, although it was 1867 before Oxford had followed suit in spite of a long letter written by the original committee in April '63 and backed by visits from Maynard and Tinling; but in Cambridge itself, as the C.M.S. collectors knew, the heart of the average undergraduate was not only a spiritual wilderness but scarcely reached by any compelling Christian influence. Much thought was being given to what Westcott called 'the religious office of the University,' but chapel, which was still compulsory, was to most men stultifying. The town churches, though evangelical, had comparatively little effect on the unbeliever, and the meetings which the Daily Prayer Meeting men had arranged from time to time in small public halls or in the drawing-rooms of friendly dons had never proved very effectual. The full force of scientific agnosticism had raised intellectual barriers to belief where previously there had only been moral. Here and there a man would find faith through friendship with don or college friend; Henry Parker, who afterwards succeeded the murdered Hannington as bishop in Uganda was converted by Jani Ali, himself a convert from Islam. Most of those who prayed in Carpenter's Rooms and gathered round the great theologians of the Cambridge School were already believing and practising Christians when they came up. Victorian England still ensured an ample supply, but times were changing. The future could not depend only on them, while the present, if thoughtless or antagonistic, was also perplexed.

This was the challenge of the times. And there were men to take it up.

'Six of us knelt in prayer. As we rose from our knees, someone quoted the words, "Launch out into the deep." We felt that it was a message from God.' Thus, thirty years later, Sir Algernon Coote described a meeting in October 1873 which had world-wide effect.

Algernon Coote was then nearly twenty-six. He had taken his degree the year before, was just married and had returned to live in Cambridge. His father was a vicar in Kent and premier baronet of Ireland. On leaving Eton Coote had started as a railway engineer at Victoria Station. Less than a year later, with startling suddenness, as he relates, 'I was led to decision for Christ through the instrumentality of that honoured servant of God, Mr. Stevenson Blackwood.' Blackwood, who thus helped Coote as many other young men, was a picturesque and unusual mid-Victorian figure. An old Etonian and Trinity man, his handsome looks and gay nature had won him the nickname 'Beauty.' On returning from the Crimean War, where he served as a commissary, the whole direction of his life was changed by a few short months in 1856. A Bible Reading at an Admiral's, thoughts at the Queen's Ball ('world in my heart. God in my conscience'), the friendship and determination of a Guards officer, a meeting in a cottage in Kent, all played their part. The final push was given by a visit to Christ Church, Barnet, to hear the noted William Pennefather. 'I came into this church darkness,' Blackwood burst out to a stranger as the church was emptying after service, 'I am going out of it light in the Lord.'

Shortly afterwards he married a young widowed duchess and together (she incorrectly keeping her title) they devoted themselves to the spread of the gospel they loved. Blackwood was a Civil Servant, ending up at the head of the Post Office.[1] In his spare time he travelled the country preaching, conducting Bible Readings and seizing every

[1] Stevenson Blackwood was knighted in 1887 but preferred to use his second name and thenceforth was known as Sir Arthur Blackwood.

opportunity to tell his good news to rich and poor. He turned his back completely on the gay world, but such was his charm and good nature that though often misunderstood he was always loved. His religion, wrote Algernon Blackwood his son, was 'genuine, unfaltering, consistent and sincere. He knew a vivid joy, a wondrous peace, his pain being for others only.'

This was the man who met and won the young Coote in 1866. Two years later Coote threw up engineering and went to Cambridge, planning to take Orders though in fact he never did. After his degree he married and returned to Cambridge as honorary representative for the Bible Society, and it was he who had convened that small meeting in October 1873 which heard the call to 'launch out into the deep.'

'There were,' writes Coote, 'a large number of out and out Christian men—leaders, too, in boating and athletics—whose one aim and prayer was the desire to lead other men to Christ.' As usual, an influx of freshmen in the October term presented an opportunity and Coote had called together a few of the more senior undergraduates to discuss ways and means and pray. They were not long in deciding what the call to launch out must mean: they would take the largest hall in Cambridge, and send for 'Beauty' Blackwood.

The Guildhall in the Market Place, capable of seating thirteen hundred, was taken for Sunday evening, 17th November. There was about a month to run. Invitations were printed and it was determined that every undergraduate should be asked personally. 'I do not mean,' continues Coote, 'that a card was put into the man's door and left there, but the one who had undertaken to ask him went until he found him; whatever the consequences might be, whatever the language used might be, he went until he found him.' Meanwhile constant prayer was made. It was said that upwards of forty meetings for prayer were held. In the *Special Requests Book* a somewhat blotted and much underlined scrawl requests prayer 'for a blessing on Mr. Blackwood's visit that many may attend the meeting but especially that *souls may be awakened.*'

When the Sunday evening came Coote sat by the door of the Guildhall and with a mixture of delight and awe watched the men 'literally pouring in.' It was estimated that well over half the undergraduates of the University were there. The room was packed with them, while away in a corner, secure from manly eyes, were four valiant women determined to watch and hear. 'There were brought to the Guildhall,' wrote one of these ladies, Mrs. Professor Babington, 'some of the wildest and most un-likely—some who, as they acknowledged, came solely to please the friends who brought them, and deliberately determined that no gospel address should touch them.' As Stevenson Blackwood stood up, without introduction or formality, an intense quiet spread over the hall. This, for an undergraduate meeting, was unusual and en-couraging. Furthermore, scarcely a soul left before the end. 'I am going to speak to you men,' began Black-wood, 'on the secret of true happiness.' When, at the end of the meeting, all stood and Blackwood prayed, an immense impression had been made. His striking figure and straightforward language, his strong con-victions and his own sense of what he had missed at Cam-bridge by not being a Christian, all made his talk memor-able. He himself knew that behind everything was the power of prayer.

In the *Special Requests Book* next day 'For an abundant answer' was written on the page for Praise opposite the original request. Below was a further request, 'that the impression made by Mr. Blackwood's visit may not pass but deepen in all our hearts.' Several had stayed behind to talk with the speaker. Others had long conversations with friends back in their rooms. It was the start of a new life for many, and it heralded a new vigour on the part of the Christian men.

The year 1874 continued and strengthened what 1873 had begun. In February Blackwood was up again, but the chief advance in 1874 was not led by an Englishman but by an American Quaker business man, Robert Pearsall Smith.

Pearsall Smith and his wife Hannah, her beauty such that she was called the Angel of the Churches, came to England from Philadelphia late in 1873. By 1875 Smith was out of the picture with a mental breakdown, but in that short time the two had contributed something fresh and lasting to English religion.

They had rediscovered the spiritual secret, curiously forgotten in nineteenth-century England and America, that the Christian life need not be an unsteady struggle without any real attainment, but a constant and happy sense of God's presence through His Holy Spirit in the heart. When a sin was known and recognized it could be overcome. Joy rather than conflict should be the keynote of Christianity, though all depended on complete consecration to the will of God. They called this 'The Higher Life.' Their enemies, who were many, called it Pearsall Smithism, and claimed it unscriptural, dangerous, and smacking of sinless perfection. 'Heresy! Damnable heresy!' was the public verdict of one leading evangelical: 'I hold that it is for the glory of God that we should fall into sin, that He may get honour to Himself by drawing us out of it.' When the Pearsall Smiths had landed in England they were soon addressing small meetings in London. Blackwood and several clergy and laymen supported them, having either discovered the same experience for themselves or having 'come into the blessing,' as the phrase went, as a result of what the Pearsall Smiths said. On the other hand J. C. Ryle, the most prominent evangelical and soon to be first bishop of Liverpool, gave a decided voice against them and was joined by the *Record* newspaper.

In spite of this atmosphere of controversy, Algernon Coote and his wife once again took the initiative and asked Pearsall Smith to stay with them in Cambridge. They held a breakfast in their house, for any senior men who wanted to meet the American. Many came and Handley Moule, the young Dean of Trinity, stayed on long after the others had left. Moule, already showing the gifts which made him a few years later one of the most influential men at Cambridge, had come back for a short period at Trinity between two curacies with his father in Dorset. At the time of

Coote's breakfast, as he wrote afterwards, 'I was specially interested in the problem of the fuller life through a remarkable work of grace among the boys of the Choir School,' of which Coote's brother-in-law was the undergraduate superintendent. The happiness of these boys seemed to Moule in sharp contrast with his own rather melancholy faith. He dreaded, however, what he had heard of one side of the 'Holiness' teaching, which had undoubtedly encouraged crack-pot emotions. Pearsall Smith had a long talk with him after breakfast, closing with prayer which, said Moule, 'he offered in beautiful and childlike terms.' But Moule came away unconvinced, and though never joining the outcry and heresy-hunt it was ten years before he found for himself what the Pearsall Smiths had found.

Later, in May, Pearsall Smith came again for several days of meetings. 'When life's great sorrow, sin, is over,' was his message, 'Heaven truly begins. I do not believe the command "Rejoice evermore" can be obeyed save along the narrow line of a holy life. Obey at once; obey simply, unhesitatingly and therefore easily—the first moment is the right moment—obey at once.' This, expanded and explained from Scripture and centering on the power of the Holy Spirit to reproduce Christlike life in the Christian, brought a new vision and experience to men, and to women from the new college at Girton. Despite the extremes which were so much feared, nothing ugly was seen as yet at Cambridge; merely a deeper determination to serve God.

As the term closed several of the men were discussing the hope of getting away during the vacation for a few days of quiet and prayer, to think more of these things and to prepare for the following term. Pearsall Smith had told them how in America they used 'to go out into the woods for a week or ten days, and seek together in long breaths to draw in the influx of the Spirit. The result has been wonderful.' The Cambridge men wished they could do the same.

Shortly afterwards Pearsall Smith was talking with a prominent landowning Member of Parliament and his wife, and mentioned the Cambridge men and how he would like to help them. 'Tell them' replied the M.P. ('on impulse' said his wife) 'that my place is at your service if you will accept it.' He did accept it. The M.P. was William Cowper-Temple and the place Broadlands.

Broadlands, a pleasant Georgian house set in spacious lawns on the banks of the River Test in Hampshire, was famous in the nineteenth century as the home of the great Lord Palmerston, as in the twentieth as that of the Mount-battens. William Cowper-Temple, Palmerston's stepson and heir and author of the religious clause in the Education Act of 1870 had been bred in much the same paganism as that in which Palmerston lived and died. But about 1832, possibly through the influence of Lord Shaftesbury, his brother-in-law, he became a decided and happy Christian. He and his wife, Georgina Tollemache, a great beauty in her day, did not turn their backs on the world as the Blackwoods did, and Georgina said of her William that 'after a party or ball he was as ready for prayer as if he had been at a religious meeting.' But they set themselves to let Christ show His love in their lives and actions, as well as by their words. They were utterly unpretentious, and far less Victorian than many of their more unchristian contemporaries. Georgina especially, as G. W. E. Russell said of her, became a 'champion of people whom the world casts out of its synagogues.'

When they first issued their invitation the Cowper-Temples told Pearsall Smith to arrange and conduct the conference. But their own touch was soon in evidence. Some hundred guests assembled on 17th July 1874, filling the house to the attics and overflowing into the inns of Romsey outside the gates; not only the enthusiastic and delighted undergraduates from Cambridge had arrived, with some from Oxford, but a party which cut right across Victorian life and religion. Stevenson Blackwood jostled with Father Stanton; Andrew Jukes of the strange 'Apostolic Church' with George Macdonald, Basil Wilberforce with the Nonconformist millionaire Morley; Charlotte Yonge and Mrs. Sumner of the Mothers' Union, with the stalwart evangelist Miss Marsh. 'High Church, Low Church, Broad Church, Tories and Whigs, actors and writers and all social ranks,' wrote Georgina, 'and,' adds G. W. E. Russell writing of the whole series of conferences of which this was the first, 'preaching negresses and ritualistic curates and vegetarians and clairvoyants, all these have met in that beautiful house amid an unequalled environment of Italian pictures, and gardens.'

The complexion may have been mixed, but the purpose for which they were invited was plain. They were to study 'The Scriptural possibilities of faith in the life of the Christian in the daily walk, as to maintained communion with God and as to victory over all known sin.' Which meant, in the plainer language of one of the guests, 'Never mind the world, nor the devil, so long as you have the sunshine of Jesus' smile in your heart.'

The day began at seven with Holy Communion in Romsey Abbey or with private prayer. The main meetings were held 'in a glorious grove of beeches on the lawn,'— readings, addresses, hymn-singing and corporate prayer. Much time was given for guests to think and pray alone or in groups, and it must have seemed strange to the people of Romsey to see men and women kneeling in Palmerston's park. After tea and a reading from George Macdonald, dinner and family prayers, they would separate for the night, 'each with our candle presented to us by the solemn-looking butler.' The day would end, says Mrs. Pearsall Smith, with 'a visitation in wrappers from room to room, when confidences were poured out.'

In this atmosphere the Cambridge men prepared for the coming term. They could be happy in the thought that their own request to Pearsall Smith had led to Broadlands. And they had set forward a movement that did not stop there. For Broadlands was followed by a public convention at Oxford the following month. The next year, 1875, this public convention was at Brighton, and the whole movement nearly made shipwreck on Pearsall Smith's mental collapse. But another convention, for the north, was held at Keswick the next month, and under Harford-Battersby, Vicar of Keswick, the lake district eventually became the annual home of the convention. Cowper-Temple made the Broadlands conference annual as well, and each year a party from Cambridge were included among his guests. The next moves at the University, therefore, were all discussed and prayed over in the peace of a Hampshire park in those summers of the later 'seventies.

The academic year which began in October 1874 made plain the value of the first Broadlands conference. 'There has been indeed an unmistakable outpouring of the Holy Spirit,' wrote Lang, Dean of Corpus, in the Prayer Union annual report of February '75. New blood strengthened the ranks. Ion Keith-Falconer, fresh to Trinity from Harrow, was the most colourful of the new personalities. Son of a Scots earl of ancient lineage, who was not ashamed to be known as an evangelist, he had fighting blood in his veins and was a giant of a man. He had a brilliant mind which won him University prizes, a double-first in the tripos lists, and a Cambridge professorship at the age of twenty-nine. His fame as an athlete kept pace with his fame as a scholar, and he was an international bicycling champion in days of boneshakers and penny-farthings. His most notable feat, of the many, was to bicycle the thousand miles from Land's End to John o' Groat's in thirteen days on a 'fifty-eight incher' of nearly half a hundredweight.

Both at Harrow and Cambridge Keith-Falconer was deeply respected for fearless faith and intense singleness of mind, coupled with a strong sense of humour. G. W. E. Russell, his school friend and contemporary who himself became an Anglo-Catholic, said of him that 'he had the intuitive peace of an unclouded faith.' This was no easy acceptance of a father's creed, for he 'had faced difficulties and thought out problems and weighed and compared differing and sometimes conflicting views of religious truth.' All this was as a boy at Harrow. At Cambridge he seemed so free from intellectual difficulties that they thought he had never known them. His faith was reflected in every corner of his life. Russell described him as 'an *accomplished* Christian,' a powerful influence in his school house and 'at all times and in all things a loyal and loving soldier of the Lord Jesus.'

With men such as he coming up and with the infectious spirit of Broadlands about, it is not surprising that the undergraduates of 1874–75 went ahead. Tyndall's assertions at the Belfast British Association could not affect them, nor *Supernatural Religion*, the best seller of the year, demolishing faith with much show of learning only to be so utterly demolished itself by Lightfoot that it glutted the second-hand market. Blackwood came once more in November ('Great Hall nearly filled. About six hundred' he wrote to his wife. 'Deep attention for one hour . . . daily prayer meeting attended by seventy downright men— a marvellous sight. Then down the river to see Boat Race. Great fun. Saw one man who wished me to be hanged . . .') and in the following year there was a combined mission to town and gown but it was not until 1876 that the climax came, with the visit of Sholto Douglas.

Like Keith-Falconer, Sholto Douglas was a Scot of old family, and a handsome giant. As an undergraduate he had been one of the founders of the Daily Prayer Meeting, and in 1876 was thirty-seven, Vicar of All Saints, Derby (the future cathedral) and just home from a missionary tour in the East. An evangelistic address every Michaelmas term had by then become a habit and the usual preparations were made. But when Douglas arrived, on Saturday 11th November, it was soon sensed that events would prove less usual. In preparation for the morrow, two hundred men came to the small Guildhall. Sholto Douglas was no orator. But he had such mastery of Scripture and such sense of urgency that his address burned its way into the consciousness of everyone present. He took an Old Testament text, 'On whom dost thou trust . . .?' from 2 Kings 18, 20. Douglas, who believed that unceasing study of God's word and unceasing concern for the spiritual welfare of others was vital, seemed to unearth hidden truths and fling them at his audience. Small wonder that one of his hearers wrote in his diary that night that the power of God was felt.

On the Sunday evening in the large Guildhall Douglas'
main address was given. He spoke on 'Man's Wrong
Idea of God's Dealings towards Man.' Here also the sense
of power was present. Douglas believed nothing to be
more urgent than immediate decision for Christ. He used
what a contemporary called 'a new, blazing method of
evangelistic proclamation,' which had somewhat shocked
the more solemn of older leaders and during the Bishop of
London's Mission in '74 had troubled the highly evangelical,
select and august congregation of Portman Square 'well-
nigh to hysteria.' Cambridge undergraduates thrived
on it.

Yet it was not the Sunday evening which made 1876
different from previous years. During the following week
Douglas stayed on, though no programme had been
arranged. Each day he went to two or three informal
meetings in the colleges, speaking of his experiences in the
East, and encouraging the undergraduates to work and
pray as never before. When his last day came Hamilton
and Mitchell-Carruthers of Trinity gave the Hoop Inn
breakfast in his honour at which the sixty guests discussed
'how best to carry on God's work amongst undergraduates
by undergraduates.'

It was Saturday, 18th November 1876—an auspicious
day: forty years earlier, on Saturday, 19th November 1836,
Charles Simeon had been buried in King's College Chapel.
Before the sixty undergraduates had separated and Douglas
had caught his train back to Derby, he had convinced them
that such conferences should be held more often, to co-
ordinate and buttress the work of the informal unions of
Christians which he had visited in the colleges. More
planning and co-ordination was needed. Though the
Daily Prayer Meeting was indispensable its committee
made little attempt at organization. A regular inter-
collegiate conference could harness the scattered strength
of the college meetings, and ensure continuity, and arrange
evangelistic efforts beyond the scope of the college unions.

'We all fell in with the idea,' wrote Mitchell-Carruthers,
and that very evening a further meeting was held in
Carpenter's Rooms. The invaluable Coote, with the

wisdom of a Master of Arts (of a year's standing) and the buoyancy of an undergraduate was in the chair, and Mitchell-Carruthers was chosen secretary. On the following Friday, to quote Mitchell-Carruthers' diary, 'we had our first "representatives" meeting,' twelve undergraduates and two graduates in the secretary's rooms. When all were present, the secretary rose. 'We are met together,' he said, 'a few of us, to consider how we may best bring about closer union and sympathy between men of different colleges, and even between members of the same, who are engaged in working for Christ. I am sure if our operations are founded on the Word of God, and begin in the spirit of earnest, believing prayer, having God's glory as our sole object, that they will be blessed and acknowledged by Him. . . .' As the oil lamps burned low in the room on D staircase of Master's Court, Trinity, overlooking the grass plot, the 'Garden of Eden,' they talked until there was only time to get back to their colleges before leave expired at twelve. Many doubts and perplexities were discussed. Though centred firmly, as the secretary said, on prayer and Holy Scripture, and though one in their object to work for Christ, the college Christian unions were an unwieldly assortment. There were problems of varying years and backgrounds in an age stiff with etiquette and convention. There was the attitude of senior men to be considered, the extra time office-holders would have to give, the question whether men of Trinity or St. John's would submit to direction from Downing or St. Catharine's.

One thing was clear; the movement, once started, must go on. Term was nearly over, and it was decided to meet again early the following term and arrange the next step.

On Friday, 9th March 1877, four months after Sholto Douglas' great address, 'On Whom dost thou trust?' the smaller room at the Guildhall was once more filled with some two hundred and fifty men. Douglas was present, this time in the background, and Coote was in the chair.

A few weeks earlier the representatives of the college unions had met once more. 'The term "representatives" was advisedly chosen,' explains Mitchell-Carruthers, 'the design being that such men should consult others of their respective colleges before attending our meetings, and thus "represent" their views as a whole.' Eventually they drew up and printed a letter, dated 3rd March and signed in each college by the college representative, which was sent to any thought to be interested, inviting them to a 'social conference' on March 9th. Its threefold object, they wrote, was 'to promote prayerful sympathy between those who are seeking the advance of Christ's Kingdom in the University, and a more entire self-consecration to God's service; to give information generally concerning God's work in the various colleges; and to make suggestions as to the best means of carrying on the work.'

The conference met at half-past seven, and after three-quarters of an hour of tea and coffee and conversation the proceedings began. The informal committee had sent to Oxford, and seven men had come over to help them. Oxford, home of the ancient Pusey, the hunting-ground of Tractarians, Broad Churchmen and agnostic philosophers, had echoed only feebly as yet to the Cambridge initiative. Canon Christopher (a Cambridge man) was working hard to make St. Aldate's another Holy Trinity but the Oxford seven were, as they said, 'representatives of a rather meagre body of evangelicals.' Twenty years later one of the Oxford men, R. F. Horton of New College, by then distinguished as a Free Church theologian, wrote down his memories. 'There comes back to me a sense of rushing life and assured enthusiasm, young men buoyant and even rollicking, overflowing with animal spirits, but still more with the Spirit Divine. I seem to remember some speeches which had the ring of boyish eloquence in them, and the shout of a King in the midst.' It was very different from the chill formalities and proprieties of Oxford. There was a spirit of freedom in the air. Horton and his friends were astonished that such large-hearted religion could flourish among undergraduates. One speech in particular made a deep impression. H. C. Wright of Trinity Hall spoke 'like a Hotspur of Evangelical zeal flinging himself on a dead and stupid world.' Those who knew him best were the most moved, for they remembered how only a short while before he was a foul-mouthed boy turning his parson father's hair grey. Now he stood, 'a very lovable spirit,' on the Guildhall platform, a first-year man urging on his elders. And like Hotspur he was robbed of his youth for he died suddenly a few years later, after being ordained to a London curacy.

The conference made certain that Douglas' suggestion for the better running of the work in Cambridge would not be still-born. Six days later the committee met again to put itself on a firm basis, rules of procedure being drawn up and a brief constitution framed. There was no question of wide membership; in itself the new organization was to be nothing more than a committee of men elected by the colleges. Each college had, or could have, its own informal union. These should henceforth send representatives to the inter-collegiate union, who would meet under a president chosen by themselves. As each man went down, he would nominate his own successor who would be approved by his college if he was to be their representative, or by the inter-collegiate committee if he was to be president or secretary. A minute book was opened,[1] and a title was assumed which had suggested itself naturally; The Cambridge Inter-Collegiate Christian Union. 'We determined,' writes Coote, 'that every college in Cambridge where an out-and-out Christian man could be found should be represented on the Union, one such man from each College to be on the executive committee—and we found such men in sixteen out of the seventeen colleges in Cambridge.' On somewhat insecure circumstantial evidence King's may be indicted as the defaulter. 'Before many terms had passed,' concludes Coote, 'the seventeenth College had also its representative.'

Thus forty years after Simeon's death and ninety-eight after his conversion, a lasting form was given to the work which he had begun among Cambridge undergraduates.

---

[1] This minute book was lost within a few years. Further losses occurred in 1914 and 1939, and the extant minutes of the Executive Committee date back no further than 1926; those of the General Committee, to 1919.

This new Cambridge Inter-Collegiate Christian Union was the product of a Biblical theology. The original members, and their successors, were united by loyalty to certain basic beliefs. The first was that God has spoken to man. They accepted humbly the authority and inspiration of the Bible, and held that its truth is wholly independent of changes in human thought and philosophy. Secondly they believed firmly that God has acted in Christ to save man. The Cross of Christ was at the very centre of their theology, and they gloried in the Cross, acknowledging Christ's death as nothing less than substitutionary, and accepting it as the only ground of man's forgiveness and of his reconciliation with God. Thirdly, the Union was founded with an uncompromising belief in the necessity of the new birth, the gift of God to the sinner who is justified by faith in Christ. They were convinced that without such new birth no true life was possible; and it was this conviction, and their sense of responsibility, as justified sinners, towards those as yet without personal faith in Christ, that had led the men of 1877 to found the new Union.

On the truth of these basic doctrines the C.I.C.C.U. was built. As a movement of youth it might at times express and act upon them crudely; but without them, neither its activity nor its continuance is explicable.

That God, our Father, may give an abundant and lasting blessing on the gathering of Christian men to take place on Friday next (March 9th) → tonight.

The Daily Prayer Meeting *Special Requests Book*,
March, 1877.

CHAPTER IV

VICTORIAN UNIVERSITY

ARRIVING by railway from London in 1880 or 1881 the first sight of Cambridge would be the unfinished buildings of Cavendish, the working-men's college which failed after fifteen years and was later bought for Homerton. Nothing else of town or university could be seen save a possible glimpse of King's College Chapel, before the train drew up at the long wooden platform of the station. Horse-trams, infrequent and slow, would then take you the mile and a half to the centre of the town, clanging their rhythmic way beside cabs, carriages and country carts.

In Station Road a few new villas (and a tombstone factory) were built among the trees, and at the junction with the main road stood the Albert Benevolent Asylum 'for decayed tradesmen,' with the Botanical Gardens behind. As the tram turned towards the town centre you passed a farm, then the red brick of St. Paul's Church and a glimpse of mean streets opposite, and a little further Pugin's small Roman Catholic chapel, set back a hundred and fifty yards from the road at Hyde Park Corner. Hills Road became Regent Street and the houses began, but the leisured atmosphere of ancient country town remained unbroken as the tram rattled past the University Arms to Christ's, for the slums of Cambridge were hidden away to east and south-east. Around Christ's, Petty Cury and the Market Place, town and university jostled one another, but King's Parade to the west and Trinity Street seemed to mark the boundary. For between the open country beyond and their line of colleges, with the Senate House and Library, were only the Backs and the college gardens. Newnham, with its little suburb on the way to the Grantchester meadows, was as isolated a village as Girton or

45

Chesterton, although Barnwell on the east was already joined to the town by the houses along Jesus Lane and Maid's Causeway.

The Backs, where the river flows past six colleges from Queens' to St. John's was still the scene of the ceremonial Procession of Boats, though the racing had always been down-river. It was the great period of Jesus College's supremacy—ten years Head of the River from 1875 to 1885. Other games, rugby and association football, hockey, lawn tennis, were becoming popular, although Blues were granted only for rowing and cricket until 1885, when the rugger men won the right to them.

In government and atmosphere the University in the early 'eighties hovered uncertainly between the past and the future. Classics and Mathematics no longer monopolized examinations, and the modern Tripos system was taking shape. The reforms of the Statutory Commission, set up in 1877, were about to become law, and thenceforth the University would be ruled on less ancient lines. From 1882, also, dons could marry (twenty brides or more were brought to Cambridge in 1882-3) and were no longer obliged to take Holy Orders. The two women's colleges, Girton and Newnham, were working their way into the confidence of a suspicious University. Science had begun to take its proper place, with the opening of the Cavendish Laboratory in 1874 and the appointment of Lord Rayleigh as the second Cavendish professor in 1879.

On the other hand, many of the colleges remained small and hedged about with entrenched customs and privileges. King's though no longer confined to Etonians, had only seventy undergraduates in 1882. St. Catharine's had fifty, Downing was even smaller. At Corpus, conservative in every way, the porters still levied a tax (to benefit their own pockets) on every letter they delivered to undergraduates.

Cambridge had its quota of characters and oddities—Dr. Corrie, Master of Jesus, who died aged ninety-two in 1885, his death hastened, it was said, by a fall from an apple tree; Dr. Worsley who had become Master of Downing the year Simeon died, and Robinson of St.

Catherine's, who had won the mastership by his own vote and was ostracized for the rest of his life. Among younger men, Lumby of St. Catharine's—'omniscient and omnipotent but (thank heaven) not omnipresent'—or the famous Oscar Browning of King's, brilliant and popular, yet spoiled by absurd vanity, snobbishness and querulousness—'a genius flawed by abysmal fatuity.'

It was still possible for an undergraduate to pass his time in utter idleness. The 'Jesus Lane Lot,' men of various colleges who lived in that locality were famous for spending the whole of their time in roystering. 'Some of them rode,' writes one critic, 'some played games; but the majority were addicted to Bacchanalian orgies and gambling in different degrees of excess, and not one of them made any attempt whatever to do any honest reading for his degree.' Drunkenness was found often enough among dons, who too frequently turned blind eyes to the evils around and even encouraged them. There was much cribbing—at any rate in Little-go, the 'rather absurd and very exasperating' freshman's examination. Extravagance was not discouraged—it was not unknown for a man to buy two or more pairs of boots a week. Such excess was confined to a fairly small circle; most men sported gay waistcoats and no one would have dreamed of going out without a hat or a walking-stick, but flamboyant clothes were frowned on by undergraduate opinion. There might be some excuse for the boots, for as games were not universal the majority of men went out walking every day on 'grinds' through neighbouring villages, or further afield for as much as five or six hours. Even the fifty miles to London were sometimes walked.

Edward Lyttelton, who captained the cricket eleven in 1878 and was afterwards headmaster of Eton said that for the freshman 'there was no inducement to do more than float with the stream . . . nobody seemed to care whether the raw youth wasted his time or not.' He laments 'the lack of bracing moral teaching and the haziness which prevailed as to fundamental principles.' His picture is sweeping; nor can generalization be accurate, for even in a

University of less than three thousand undergraduates it was possible to remain in one set for the whole period of residence and know nothing of others. Intellectually, the Darwinian movement was strong, the new scientific determinism at its crudest and most assured, and the air heavy with the dust of exploded beliefs. Many of the younger dons were openly agnostic although, as the future proved, their convictions were as unstable as they were clamorous. It was an upsetting atmosphere for boys fresh from school, eager to be up to date and easily convinced of the inerrancy of those a few years older than themselves. Yet there was, in the words of a contemporary article, 'no active propagandism of unbelief, no regular sceptical teaching, at Cambridge. There may be observed even, not seldom, a kind of chivalrous caution on the part of teachers themselves sceptical not to influence the younger members of the University in a sceptical direction.' Furthermore there was the striking influence of the Christianity of many leading scientists of the day—Clerk-Maxwell, first Cavendish professor, and to a lesser extent his successor Lord Rayleigh; Babington the botanist, Paget, professor of physics, Macalister the anatomist, all were openly and decidedly Christian. Sir George Stokes, known as the second Newton not only for his learning but because, like Newton, he was Lucasius professor of mathematics, burgess of the University in Parliament and a theologian in his spare time, though some of his theological ideas were not popular, had an outstanding beauty and gentleness of character and a fearless Christianity which gave him an influence far beyond his own college of Pembroke. Yet most of these Christian scientists were of the older generation. The younger men were easily swayed by the steadily increasing intellectual assault on the Christian position, not only in Cambridge but throughout the country.

Over against the moral laxity and the scepticism, which to some seemed the chief feature of the Cambridge atmosphere, there was a Christianity singularly united and active. Differences were more of emphasis than of doctrine. A very small group of Puseyite graduates, ardent

48

tractarians, gathered in the chapters of the Confraternity of the Holy Trinity (the S.T.C., founded in 1857), but they were isolated and ineffective; their ideas made little headway among their juniors and the undergraduate would not normally meet doctrinal strife. Wherever he went, whether he listened to Westcott, reverently unfolding the wonders of the Incarnation, perhaps spending a whole hour on one word of Scripture; or talked with the more active deans and tutors such as Appleton and Blenkin of Trinity, Parry of Caius, Lang of Corpus or Charles Prior of Pembroke for whom, so C. F. Andrews felt a few years later, 'the love of Christ constrained every word and thought during the day'; or whether he attended any of the principal churches of Cambridge or the meetings convened from time to time in the Guildhall, the undergraduate of 1880 heard and felt the strength of a Christianity squarely based on the inspiration of the Scriptures and the reality of Christ, and on the necessity of individual faith in His incarnation, atonement and resurrection.

This Christianity, strong and united though it was did not by any means influence all who came up to Cambridge. They might pack Great St. Mary's to the doors on a great occasion such as Lightfoot's farewell in '79. Lightfoot himself might say when he returned for the opening of Selwyn in 1881, that having spent thirty years in the University it was 'his deliberate conviction that in the later years of that period there existed among undergraduates a greater desire to work for Christ and to do good service for Christianity.' Westcott as far back as 1872 might contrast the spiritual advantages a young man had then with those of twenty-five years before. Yet most men saw no further than the dreariness of compulsory chapel, and the dead-weight of Paley's *Evidences*, 'swotted' for Little-go. An anonymous writer in the *Church Quarterly Review* for October 1881 assured his readers that 'the evidence of religious zeal among the undergraduates seem to us to be very remarkable, and to have been on the increase in recent years.' Yet when he concluded by expressing his belief that there was real ground for hope that any young man coming up to Cambridge 'with desire for what is right' would find his way into a set 'the prevailing tone of which will not hinder but will help forward his own Christian character,' he unconsciously revealed the limitations of Cambridge Christianity. There was the Church Missionary Union, the Daily Prayer Meeting, and the Prayer Union. There was the Church Society, founded in 1872 'to foster a deep and earnest resolve to devote time and energy in after-life to Christian study and Christian work' by discussion and mutual help. For its limited aims this Church Society drew the loyalties of all shades of Anglican opinion; the abolition of religious tests had at last enabled the University to draw effectively on Nonconformist strength. But in any age, and especially in the early 'eighties, to admit that real hope of benefit was limited to those who came up 'with desire for what is right' was a condemnation and a challenge.

The Cambridge Inter-Collegiate Christian Union had been founded to overcome this limitation. Its early members saw no reason why only those few who came up with desire for what is right should receive the blessings of the Gospel. In this they had the tacit approval of Westcott and most of his fellow-theologians. But more support was needed. It was found in the return to Cambridge of two outstanding personalities—John Barton, who became Vicar of Holy Trinity in 1877, and Handley Moule, who arrived as Principal-elect of the new theological college, Ridley Hall, in October 1880.

John Barton had spent nearly twenty years in India. Tall, bearded, a man of few words but of deep feeling, he had lost none of that love and spiritual skill which had made him such an effective leader for the Cambridge Church Missionary Union back in '58. He had no selfish ambition, and three times refused an overseas bishopric. He and his (second) wife made their new Vicarage in Brookside a centre of hospitality for undergraduates. It was 'a large roomy house; fourteen bedrooms and six sitting-rooms, with a drawing-room specially planned to suit large gatherings of undergraduates.' Mrs. Barton also mentions in passing that there were eight children and two other

relatives, and a household of twenty (including the gover-
ness), and all was evidently maintained on about £600 a
year. They had, over and above their own parish, 'a
large and steadily increasing family of "sons in the University"—never less than two hundred on our books,
introduced by parents, guardians and clergy, and all were
invited to the Vicarage two or more times every term. . . .
We used to ask men into breakfast, lunch and dinner,
three or four at a time, and seldom had a meal alone, or
half an hour we could call our own.' The men appreciated
this Victorian largesse—'We meet all our friends in your
house'—but it was not the hospitality, nor the Bible readings nor the hymn singings on Sunday nights which were
most welcomed, nor the friendships which shy and lonely
freshmen would form in the Brookside Vicarage, but John
Barton's wise and understanding leadership. They could
trust him when they might have resented the intrusion of
another. 'A long talk in the study ending with prayer
decided many an important question, and though we did
not always like, or always follow the advice we then
received, we did sincerely respect the one who gave it,
and generally found that he was right.'

It was John Barton who brought Moule back to Cambridge. Handley Carr Glyn Moule, afterwards Bishop of
Durham, was not quite forty when he was made first
Principal of Ridley. He came from a remarkable home.
His father, Moule of Fordington, was one of a group of
Dorset country parsons famous for their courage and
faithfulness in days when so many were idle and un-
concerned. Handley was youngest in a large family.
His brother George was a founder of the Prayer Union in
'48, and with another brother had become a China missionary. He himself went up to Trinity in 1860. He was
popular, rather soberly gay, and fond of practical jokes.
He soon showed that he had his share of the family's
intellectual ability, being bracketed (with F. W. H. Myers)
second Classic of his year, and later winning a Trinity
fellowship. But in spite of some desultory first-year
attendance at the Church Missionary Union, as became
Moule of Fordington's son, he showed little of the family

spiritual zeal; his interests were soon absorbed by the classics. He confessed afterwards that not only had his religion at this time been second-hand, but that 'a painful invasion of intellectual perplexity and doubt' had assailed him. It was not until 1866, during a brief assistant-mastership at Marlborough that he was able, as he described it, 'to realize the presence, pardon and personal love of the Lord, not reasoned, just received.' 'My trust is,' he wrote to his father in February 1867, 'that this very Christmas vacation, after a time of much mental wretchedness, I was able to find and to accept pardon and peace through the satisfaction of the Redeemer, as I had never done before; and to feel a truth and solid reality in the doctrine of the Cross as I have ever been taught it at home.'

For the next fifteen years he acted as curate to his aged father, except for a brief though influential period as Dean of Trinity. In 1880 his father died. John Barton asked him to Cambridge to take the Evening Lectureship at Holy Trinity, a post which was separate from the incumbency, and shortly afterwards he was appointed to Ridley Hall.

He was the man for the post. As a former fellow of Trinity, a Carus Prizeman and double Browne's medallist, and well up to the mark of contemporary scholarship, he held the respect of the University. He was an able teacher, whether in lecture-room or pulpit. He had passed through intellectual doubts and had found a settled faith to which he could point others. In particular he had come to a happy and satisfying belief in the Bible which no theories of criticism or scholarship could shake: 'When my Lord Christ became a living and unutterably necessary reality to me, I remember that one of my first sensations of profound relief was: "He absolutely trusted the Bible, and though there are in it things inexplicable and intricate that have puzzled me so much, I am going, not in a blind sense, but reverently, to trust the Book because of HIM."' Thus his Bible expositions went deep into the consciousness of his students, as morning by morning, 'the Principal, book in hand, holds up each word . . . and examines it with the critical eye of the scholar and the loving insight of the saint.'

Moule was shy and sensitive. He seemed to radiate an infectious goodness. His saintliness tended to isolate him from mundane affairs—however deeply aware theologically of the corruption of human nature he was only too easily caught by its guiles—yet his counsel was much sought after, and freely given. He was a minor poet of distinction and a prolific prose writer, though his classical and analytical mind, his desire to avoid giving unnecessary pain, his anxiety that every possible qualifying factor should be mentioned, together with a deep reverence which excluded humour, combined to stretch Victorian style to its limits. He wrote a number of theological and pastoral works, but his fame was built on his Bible expositions and commentaries, and on his devotional books. Some of his disciples later regretted that he never produced a *magnum opus*; its influence would probably have been less than that of the numerous little books which he did write, and which made him the friend and adviser of Christians all over the world.

Whatever his defects, Moule came to Cambridge just when he was needed, as the next years were to prove; a great teacher, a humble-minded and sympathetic pastor, a man of prayer and a sane saint.

Thus, in the first years of the C.I.C.C.U.'s existence, Cambridge stood at the cross-roads. Both scepticism and Christianity seemed on the increase, with the issue in doubt. It might remain so for years, or else a sudden impact from either direction might set a clear course for a decade or more. This was the question. It was answered from an unexpected quarter.

CHAPTER V

THE MAN FROM THE MIDDLE WEST

EARLY in 1882 J. E. K. Studd, undergraduate of Trinity, Captain of University cricket, President of the C.I.C.C.U., proposed that the American evangelists Moody and Sankey be invited to Cambridge the following Michaelmas term.

Dwight Lyman Moody, whose name had become prominent in Great Britain during the previous decade, was born in 1837 of old, though insignificant New England stock. After working as a boy in Boston, he 'went west to grow up with the country' at the age of nineteen, seeking his fortune in the small though rapidly expanding prairie city of Chicago. He was already a confessed Christian; the great religious revival of 1857 led him to throw up business and devote himself entirely to evangelistic work. He began with marked success among the wildest, most dissipated of Chicago youth. During the Civil War he was an unofficial chaplain with the Union forces, doing notable work for the wounded and for the Confederate prisoners. It was not, however, until he came to England in the early 'seventies, following a further spiritual experience, that his power as an evangelist became widely known.

For two years he and his companion, the singer Ira D. Sankey, travelled throughout Great Britain, drawing immense crowds wherever Moody preached and Sankey sang. The more conservative in the religious world were doubtful at first of these unconventional Americans, with their strong accents, their easy, familiar use of Scripture, and their straightforward, simple services in theatres and music-halls. Lord Shaftesbury was uneasy because Moody told stories 'oftentimes bordering on the humourous, almost to the extent of provoking a laugh!' The *Record* religious newspaper felt that it was 'impossible not to feel the need of caution.' Most of the national papers were scathing—'a ranter of the most vulgar type. His mission appears to be to degrade religion to the level of the "penny gaff"' was the comment of the *Saturday Review*. But when the evidence multiplied of lives transformed among the roughest and hardest in city underworlds, and of good effect on churches and chapels throughout the country, honest criticism began to wear thin.

The climax came with their great London campaign from March to July 1875. In London Moody showed his startling ability to reach both the highest and lowest in the land. He preached in the East End in the early evening to the poor of the docks and the slums, and would then drive across London to speak at Her Majesty's opera house at nine. 'The scene in the Haymarket,' wrote an eyewitness, 'baffled description. It was literally flocked with the carriages of the aristocratic and plutocratic of the land; the struggle for admission was perhaps even more severe in the West than the East.' Moody and Sankey were undoubtedly one of the sights of London in the summer of '75, a spectacle for the curious and a butt for the witty. Their hymns were sung by errand boys and ground out by barrel-organs; cheap photographs and copies of sermons, bogus and true, were hawked in the streets. But of the two and a half million people who heard him in London, thousands of all classes were deeply and lastingly touched. The Princess of Wales told an evangelical peer what a help Moody had been to her, Lord Chancellor Cairns and Shaftesbury, and even Gladstone and Matthew Arnold sat at the feet of this unlettered man.

Moody was of middle-size, rather stout, with a short neck and a massive chest, his face bright rather than handsome, and frequently lit up with a delightful smile. He was a most genial man, and none could doubt either his sincerity or his love. Many who went to hear him expected flights of tub-thumping oratory. But there was no rhetoric. 'Perhaps his most distinguishing characteristic,' wrote Canon

Hay Aitken, who worked with him at this time, 'was a singular simplicity and directness of speech. His sermons never assumed the character of orations. They were straight, homely talks.' 'They are calm,' adds Lord Shaftesbury, 'without an approach to the fanatical or even the enthusiastic. They seem neither to terrify nor to puff up.' Instead there was this direct speaking lit with anecdotes, often more comic than Shaftesbury cared to admit, but always to the point and backed by Moody's great skill in dealing with the personal problems of individuals. And if Moody's words brought the crowds to the feet of Christ, it was Sankey's singing which first stirred them. 'I am no musician,' Sankey used to say, and this was true in that he had no professional training, but the natural beauty of his baritone, with its warmth and reality, racked mid-Victorian hearts wherever he sang.[1] The two evangelists thus worked together, a well-balanced and highly effective team.

R. A. Torrey, to some extent Moody's successor, once gave seven reasons 'Why God used D. L. Moody.' First, 'every ounce of that two-hundred-and-eighty-pound body of his belonged to God.' He had as a young man heard someone say that 'It remains to be seen what God will do with a man who gives himself wholly to Him,' and had resolved to be that man. Secondly, he was a man of prayer. 'Everything he undertook was backed by prayer and in everything his ultimate dependence was upon God.' Then he was 'a deep and practical student of the Bible.' He rose at about four every morning to study the Bible—a further secret must have been ability to do without sleep—and Torrey believed that it was largely by the thorough knowledge he thus gained that this man of little formal education (though he read widely and systematically and never despised learning) drew such crowds. A fourth reason why God used D. L. Moody was his humility; another, his freedom from all love of money. And not only was he 'definitely endued with power from

[1] Fifty million copies of Sankey's collection, *Sacred Songs and Solos*, are said to have been sold in Britain and America.

on high' but he had 'a consuming passion for the salvation of the lost—a man on fire for God.'

This then was the man whom young Kynaston Studd proposed as missioner to the University in 1882. Handley Moule, asked to add his signature to the invitation, was disturbed. Though Moody had preached, unofficially, at Eton, and though the West End had flocked to the mission seven years before, Moule feared that the University would not be reached. To launch the simple Americans on one of the most difficult and intolerant audiences in the world seemed to court disaster. Studd thought differently. He knew that in 1875 the undergraduates (three hundred of them, so he believed) had tried to get Moody to Cambridge. If they had done so, why should not their successors? Nor could he forget how his own father, a wealthy retired planter, had at Moody's touch left a life of selfish extravagance to devote himself to Christ almost to excess. If Moody could win Edward Studd at the age of fifty-five, he would not fail at Cambridge.

Moule signed the invitation ('but reluctantly') and so did John Barton and other senior men. It was agreed that the mission be planned to reach both town and gown. The evangelists, whose energy was inexhaustible, should hold services for the town each morning, afternoon and early evening and then address the University.

Preparations were pressed ahead. As early as April the Cambridge Prayer Union committee was considering special meetings 'to ask of Almighty God that it would please Him to grant to our University a measure of the religious revival which has lately been vouchsafed to other parts of His church.' Nearly all the clergy in Cambridge were co-operating and during the Long Vacation prayer meetings were held in the Alexandra Hall of the Y.M.C.A. In the first week of October John Barton went down to Plymouth to see Moody and Sankey. As term began, Cambridge was plastered with posters and every undergraduate received a personal invitation ('advertised and forced on men's attention, *ad nauseam*' grumbled one critic), and in the week preceding the mission special preparatory meetings were held. Moule wrote in his diary, 'Lord, be

Thou really with me in this coming anxious, responsible time.'

And when the first day came, it looked as if his forebodings were right.

The 5th November at Cambridge, as T. R. Glover has said, 'was a night consecrated to disorder, to bonfires and fireworks and to fights between town and gown.' In 1882 it fell on a Sunday, the day the mission opened. Though the Guy Fawkes celebrations were supposed to be held over to the Monday, 5th November remained an unfortunate choice of date. There were other disturbing factors. The new, vast, ugly Corn Exchange, where the Sunday meetings were to be held had poor acoustics, and a hustings-like platform which created the atmosphere of a political meeting.

The first services for the town had gone smoothly. The weather was fine, and the hall, which had been adapted to hold nearly twenty-five hundred, was nearly full.

Then came the University meeting. Seventeen hundred men in cap and gown were counted entering the building, everyone being provided with a hymn-book. 'In they came, laughing and talking and rushing for seats near their friends.' While the hall was filling the choir—seventy undergraduates of courage ('I would not join that lot for £200' said one Jesus man to a Corpus friend as they entered) sang hymns. The audience responded with rowdy songs. Others began to build a pyramid of chairs. From outside, a fire cracker was thrown against a window. Then the platform party entered—Professor Babington, Moule, Barton, the Dean of Corpus and other clergy and dons, followed by Moody and Sankey. From parts of the hall they were greeted with derisive cheers and jokes. After the choir had sung 'Jesus, Lover of my soul,' Barton stood to lead in prayer. The 'ill-mannered youths' (as someone tartly described them) responded with 'Hear! Hear!' and Sankey's first solo, though he says they heard each verse in silence, produced shouts of 'encore.' Barton and several M.A.s, including proctors, went down the hall and quietly ejected the more noisy men and then sat at the back to keep watch. Moody himself, with courtesy and humour, asked them to remember 'that it is a religious meeting and not a political one, where perhaps you might resort to such means. The service is God's and such proceedings are irreverent.' Even so, disturbances continued throughout the evening—bursts of laughter, loud talking, shouts of 'Well done!' and pert questions. 'We went meaning to have some fun,' said one man next day 'and, by Jove, we had it!'

Tyndale-Biscoe of Kashmir, who was present as an undergraduate from Jesus, makes in his *Autobiography* the rest of this first meeting a riot. 'First the Moody and Sankey hymn books were used as ammunition, then the hassocks, and lastly the chairs were flying all over the hall and on to the platform.' Ladies faint, proctors and bulldogs enter and are thrust out and finally the police arrive and clear the hall by baton charges 'with the exception of about forty undergraduates.' Tyndale-Biscoe, who wrote many years after the event, was presumably confused by memories of a Salvation Army meeting two years later, which did end in this way. At the Corn Exchange in 1882 there were no ladies and no hassocks, and the contemporary accounts, which do not ignore the cheers and encores, know nothing of a free fight.

In plain fact, the meeting was carried through to the end. Moody, with his broad American accent, unfortunately had chosen to speak on Daniel, and 'his favourite one-syllabled pronunciation of *Dan'l* was the signal for repeated outbursts.' There was also some excuse in that many at the back could not hear, and started to shuffle and stamp their feet—a time-honoured Varsity reaction to boredom, not then unknown at University sermons. The majority, however, according to the *Cambridge Review*, paid 'every attention to the service and marked their deprecation of the conduct of the minority in no uncertain manner,' though even this must have added to the confusion.

When the meeting closed, with another solo from Sankey, John Barton suggested that those who wished should remain for a brief while and pray. Some four hundred stayed, including in fact some of the rowdiest—by now 'quiet, impressed and apparently ashamed of their recent behaviour.' Moody spoke briefly again, sweating with nervous exhaustion but still in good humour and still on Daniel. And then slowly the Corn Exchange emptied.

When they had returned to their hotel, Moody said as he took off his dripping collar, or so the story went, 'Well, Sankey, I guess I've no hankering after that crowd again.' The two then knelt and prayed, fervently and unhurriedly, for the coming days.

As for the C.I.C.C.U. men, 'with heavy hearts we took our way to our respective colleges.' The next day Studd sat down and began a letter to the *Cambridge Review*, and then pencilled into the *D.P.M. Special Requests* book: 'Special prayer is requested that God would over-rule any disturbance that may take place tonight.'

They had arranged that the week-day meetings should be held in the Gymnasium, a building in Market Passage which could be made to seat five hundred. The town meetings were increasing in numbers and attention, but when on the Monday, writes W. H. Stone, one of the C.I.C.C.U. committee, 'we assembled in the Gymnasium, the sight was enough to depress the spirits of the most sanguine.' Not much more than a hundred were present. But if numbers were small the Gunpowder spirit did not interfere and though one observer thought he detected 'some signs of latent irreverence,' these wore off as the vigorous address on the New Birth proceeded. Studd's prayer was answered.

Nor were numbers a true indication of affairs. That very day Gerald Lander, a Trinity man of a fast set, one of the rowdiest of the Sunday night, who had excused his behaviour with the conceited comment, 'if uneducated men will come to teach the Varsity they deserve to be snubbed,' had been to see Moody with an apology from himself and his friends, had stayed for a long talk, and was in the Gymnasium that evening. Furthermore, the sparse attendance enabled Moody after the meeting to move round the hall speaking to every man in turn. When Stone saw him ask one man, later in the Varsity boat, if he were a Christian and heard the reply 'No, but I wish to be one,' he felt that their effort had not been in vain. 'Last night,' recorded Moule in his diary next day, 'it is said five men were brought to Christ at the University meeting. Lord, make it *stand* and carry it on.'

On the Tuesday, so one of the local papers reported of the town meetings in the Corn Exchange, 'the eagerness of the public was greater than on previous occasions,' and by 6.30 the building was packed. At the Gymnasium, though numbers were up, and attention was better, it still seemed an uphill task and there was little to report.

The next day, as the choir leader, a Johnian wrote, 'exceeded our strongest faith and showed us how little we really had.' Wednesday, 8th November 1882, was the start of the most astonishing five days the University had seen.

In the morning Studd's letter appeared in the *Cambridge Review*, the University weekly. He pointed out that the Americans were guests. 'This being the case you may imagine the disgust which I and many others felt when . . . some fifty, or it might have been a hundred so far forgot themselves and their assumed character as gentlemen' as to create disturbance. He politely supposed that these members of the University could not have realized the evangelists' position 'or they would not have treated the guests of some of their fellow undergraduates, who are also visitors to our country, in such a very ungentlemanly way.' After expressing a hope that they would 'come and hear Mr. Moody speak and Mr. Sankey sing and that by their attention will show how much they regret having so misunderstood the facts of the case' he concluded with a neat suggestion that this would also forestall any criticism that Cambridge men could not behave as well as Oxford men, 'or even as well as those far below them in the social scale.'

Studd carried weight as Captain of Cricket. His letter was backed by another, anonymous ('One who was present') and less restrained. These two letters started a correspondence which wandered through a dozen letters and five issues until the end of term. Edward H. Dasent of Jesus, later a schoolmaster at Bedford and a prominent rugger coach, scoffed in the issue of 15th November at the 'strain of low comedy . . . the coarseness and levity of the meetings' and implied that the Americans got what they deserved. An editorial note of dissent from Dasent's views was printed and in the following week he was answered by several correspondents including Arthur Ropes (King's), afterwards famous as the librettist of the *Merry Widow*, and Owen Seaman (Clare), later the great editor of *Punch*, who claimed that 'Mr. Dasent defends the abuse of liberty.' In the issue of 29th November, a young High Church parson from Yorkshire attacked the clergy who 'so degrade their office and ignore their capabilities as to approve of such men as Moody and Sankey,' but he was promptly snubbed by Arthur Ropes again and others in the last issue of term.

Studd's letter was not the only hammer on the opposition that Wednesday. Moody himself was working along another line. The town meetings were now crammed, crowds pouring in from the surrounding villages and even from Huntingdon and beyond. When the afternoon meeting was over Moody collected, 'with infinite tact and wisdom' some hundred and fifty or two hundred mothers to pray for the young men he would address that night, 'some Mothers' sons.' The heart of an undergraduate in the 'eighties could be effectively touched by the plea to 'honour your mother's God'; and this appeal equally could be reversed. Moody afterwards described this mothers' meeting as unique in his experience: 'mother after mother, amidst her tears, pleaded for the young men of the University.'

The Gymnasium that night was still not full, but the atmosphere was far removed from that of the Sunday. As Moody spoke he could sense that those mothers' prayers would be answered, and at the end of the address he determined to prove it: 'I have not yet held an inquiry meeting for you, gentlemen,' he said, 'but I feel sure many of you are ready and yearning to know Christ. When you are in difficulties over mathematics or classics, you do not hesitate to consult your tutors. Would it be unreasonable for you to bring your soul-trouble to those who may be able to help you? Mr. Sankey and I will converse with any who will go up to the empty gallery yonder. . . . Let us have silent prayer.'

There was a pause. The gallery, normally used as a fencing room, was reached by a steep iron staircase from the centre of the Gymnasium. To reach it a man would have to face his friends and acquaintances; and even if they were supposed to be praying the clatter of the iron steps would open scores of inquisitive eyes. Moody did not want shallow decisions; as he said another night that week, 'No one can have really received Christ in his heart if he does not confess Him to his friends, if only by some small action.'

No one moved. Then 'amidst an awful stillness' a young Trinity man got up, and 'half hiding his face in his gown, bounded up the stairs two at a time.' Soon the stillness was quite gone, as one man followed another up the iron staircase, while the choir sang a further hymn. Mr. Moody remarked, 'I never saw the gowns look so well before,' and with Sankey and other helpers went up the stairs himself. He found fifty-two men in the gallery. Among them was Gerald Lander, the rowdy of Sunday night.

It was clear by now that this was to be a highly unusual week. One of the local papers wrote, 'Never within the recollection of the oldest inhabitant have there been such immense gatherings in Cambridge for religion.' The Corn Exchange was filled to overflowing twice a day, with extension meetings in Holy Trinity Church. The Gymnasium, on the Thursday night, was fuller than ever. Moody was drawing every rank and age in town and University. Mrs. Barton noticed Welldon and Ryle of King's, both afterwards bishops, and even Oscar Browning among the dons daily at the Corn Exchange. At the Gymnasium the most unlikely people would greet each other with the mutual question 'What on earth are *you* doing here?'

Moody's address at the Thursday University meeting was on 'sowing and reaping.' One of the senior members present described it a few days later as 'the most solid contribution to moral influence that has ever been made, by way of public appeal, for many a day.' The service began, as usual, with a hymn led by the choir, and then Sankey took the platform. 'An immense bilious man,' recalled Arthur Benson of King's, the Archbishop's son and afterwards Master of Magdalene, 'with black hair, and eyes surrounded by flaccid, pendent baggy wrinkles,' he came forward 'with an unctuous gesture, and took his place at a small harmonium, placed so near the front of the platform that it looked as if both player and instrument must inevitably topple over; it was inexpressibly ludicrous to behold. Rolling his eyes in an affected manner he touched a few simple chords, and a marvellous transformation came over the room. In a sweet powerful voice, with an exquisite simplicity combined with irresistible emotion, he sang *There were ninety and nine*. The man was transfigured. A deathly hush came over the room, and I felt my eyes fill with tears; his physical repulsiveness slipped from him and left a sincere, impulsive Christian, whose simple music spoke straight to the soul.'

When Sankey had done, Moody began to speak. The men had got used to his American accent. Their suspicions of tub-thumping had been cleared away. And although, as Benson said, 'he had no grace of look and gesture,' there was a plain sturdiness in his manner of preaching that attracted and held their attention, lightened with his rich vein of humour and graphic illustrations. Moody's address held nothing back. 'The scathing denunciations of sin at times were terrific,' recalled a gay young Trinity Hall man, an M.P.'s son, who became an overseas missionary as a result of this week, 'but were always balanced by the wonderful love of God to the sinner.' 'He had not spoken half a dozen words,' said Arthur Benson, 'before I felt as though he and I were alone in the world. . . . After a scathing and indignant invective on sin,' continues Benson, 'he turned to draw a picture of the hollow, drifting life with feeble, mundane ambitions—

utterly selfish, giving no service, making no sacrifice, tasting the moment, gliding feebly down the stream of time to the roaring cataract of death. Every word he said burnt into my soul. He seemed to me to probe the secrets of my innermost heart; to be analysing, as it were, before the Judge of the world, the arid and pitiful constituents of my most secret thought. I did not think I could have heard him out . . . his words fell on me like the stabs of a knife. Then he made a sudden pause, and in a peroration of incredible dignity and pathos he drew us to the feet of a crucified Saviour, showed us the bleeding hand and the dimmed eye, and the infinite heart behind. "Just *accept* Him," he cried; "in a moment, in the twinkling of an eye you may be His—nestling in His arms—with the burden of sin and selfishness resting at His feet."'

The following night the gallery up the iron staircase was packed. Over a hundred were counted. Moody had spoken on the text, 'Come, for all things are now ready,' enlarging on the excuses men offered when rejecting the divine invitation—'I'll wait . . . I don't feel like it. . . . The Bible so hard. . . . A Christian must be gloomy.' '*Gloomy?*' echoed Moody. 'Give a condemned criminal a pardon to make him gloomy? Give a starving man bread, a thirsty man water to make him gloomy?' After asserting that behind these excuses lay simply 'want of moral courage,' he had pretended to frame a letter: 'To the King of kings. On November 10th 1882 in the Gymnasium, Cambridge, one of your servants earnestly invited me to the marriage feast of your son. I pray Thee have me excused.' He asked who would sign it. Then he offered another reply, accepting not merely an invitation but Christ himself. Among those who heard him was Barclay Buxton, a Varsity tennis player, who was sitting beside his father, the great slave-liberator's son. 'There and then,' wrote Buxton in later years, 'the decision was made. Christ came and for fifty and more years has been my Saviour, Shepherd and King.'

As the choir sang 'Almost persuaded, Christ to receive . . .' the iron staircase rang once again as the men pressed up it. Moule was amongst the helpers in the fencing-room. He spoke first to a Japanese, Wadagaki, whom he later baptized, and then to a Trinity man and to Dover of Pembroke, 'the last full of sceptic trouble.' G. E. Morgan of St. John's wrote down his impressions of the scene: 'Here one man is in prayer with an undergraduate. A freshman is explaining the Way of Life to a third year man. . . . I saw two B.A.s who only found peace two nights ago busily leading others into the light. I watched the faces of a few who bid Mr. Moody good-night, and one rather stylish man, as Mr. Moody asked him if it was all right, explained with tears in his eyes, "Yes: thank God I ever came in here."' W. H. Stone overheard one man admit to Moody 'that his mind was made up for Christ but he really could not face one of his friends.' 'What is your name?' asked Moody. When he told him Moody said 'Is your friend So-and-so?' 'Yes' said the other, in great surprise. 'You two are afraid of each other,' said Moody, with a broad smile, remembering an identical talk the previous evening, 'go and tell your friend what has happened.'

Others preferred to get alone. Arthur Benson, the night before, 'went out into the night, like one dizzied with a sudden blow . . . my only idea was to escape and be alone.' For Benson followed long hours of agonized praying for light, 'until an intolerable weariness fell upon me and I slept,' never in the weeks of depression ahead to find the complete contentment of which Moody had spoken. Others, like Arthur Polhill-Turner of Trinity Hall went away to come again, until at the final Sunday service he was drawn by the text in Isaiah, 'God is my salvation; I will trust and not be afraid,' and 'decided for Christ that night.'

As midnight approached, the remaining undergraduates hurried home, and senior members and the missioners stayed a while for prayer, before the gas-lights were at last turned out.

For both town and university the climax came on Sunday 12th November. On that day, wrote a local newspaper, were held 'four such meetings as have never before been witnessed in this town.' Charles Simeon's spirit once more seemed to hover over the proceedings, for this second Sunday in November 1882 was the centenary of his first sermon in Holy Trinity Church and the forty-sixth anniversary of his death. In spite of the sharp frost and the murky weather, the Corn Exchange was packed at 8 a.m. for an address by Moody on 'The Holy Spirit's power in service.' The two town meetings were more crowded than ever. The Simeon celebration sermons in the churches added to the sense of expectancy.

The last University meeting was to be back in the Corn Exchange. In spite of Thursday and Friday nights (a meeting was not held on the Saturday) there was no guarantee that the much larger Corn Exchange would be full, or, if it was, that there would be no repetition of the previous Sunday's disturbances.

When the service began all doubts were at rest. The building was crowded. Some townsmen and graduates were present, but it was reckoned that well over half the undergraduates of Cambridge, eighteen hundred men or more, were in the Corn Exchange that night. From the start there was 'not the shadow of opposition, interruption or inattention.' One journalist judged it 'the most remarkable meeting we have ever seen at Cambridge, and our experience extends over a quarter of a century.'

After the singing was over, Moody announced his text from the second chapter of St. Luke: 'The Angel said unto them, Fear not: for behold I bring you good tidings of great joy, for unto you is born a Saviour, which is Christ the Lord.' 'The angels called it good news,' he began.[1] 'It was either such or it was not such. If it is good news you certainly ought to be glad to hear; if it is not good news, the quicker you find it out the better, and dismiss the whole subject.

'Now I firmly believe it is the best news that ever came from Heaven to earth. I think there is nothing compared with the glad tidings. God makes no mistakes. If man had not needed a Saviour, Jesus Christ would not have

---

[1] The substance of the address was reported by the *Cambridge Express*, but much of what he said must have been omitted.

come. God sent Him to save the world. What better news can man hear than that? Christ came to set men free from sin, that was His mission. Then He died. He died to make Atonement. If a man will but believe the Gospel and accept the finished work of Christ, he becomes a free man. Christ came to set men at liberty. And He commanded His disciples to go and preach the Gospel to every creature; to preach universal salvation by belief. And when Christ had ascended they went back to Jerusalem and preached to those men who had murdered the Son of God; and the work commenced right there. There is a class of men who tell you that they do not believe that Jesus Christ has risen. But that is one of our fundamental doctrines. I believe that the Son of God rose from Joseph's sepulchre as much as I believe He is here to-night.

'A young man was at my room last night talking about these things and he said he didn't believe in the resurrection. I said it was a good deal harder not to believe than it was to believe it. . . .'

After speaking of the evidence for the resurrection, Moody continued, 'Now, I want to tell you why I believe in the Gospel. The Gospel of the Son of God has removed out of my path my bitterest enemies. Before I possessed the power of the Gospel I feared *death*. In my native town it used to be the custom to toll out the ages of persons who died. I used to count the bell. If it tolled 80 or 90 I thought "Death is a long way off." but if it were for a boy in his 'teens it used to be very serious, and many times I have lain awake fearing death. That fear is now gone. I like to live, but to die is gain. The sting of death is gone. "The wages of sin is death, but the gift of God is eternal life." If I have got Christ's life, death cannot touch It.

'*Sin* is a terrible enemy; men may say their sins do not trouble them. I know better. There is a time when it troubles them; when sin haunts them and their conscience rebukes them. Christ came to break the power of sin and put it away by the Sacrifice of Himself. Out of love to our souls God has cast our sins behind His back. He has justified us and made us joint heirs with Christ.

'Then there is another enemy. I used to think it was a

terrible thing to go into the grave, and I have lain awake many a night and looked into the grave, and said, "Oh how dark." But it's gone now. I can shout "Oh grave, where is thy victory?" There was a time when I thought death took Christ and dragged Him into Joseph's sepulchre, but now I know that He went down after death, and bound death hand and foot and on the third day He burst His bonds asunder and came out. And if you believe you will live also.'

A further enemy was God's throne of Judgment. 'I used to fear that when I approached before it all my sins would be brought to light, but I found that the judgment was already passed. Christ was bruised for my iniquity and with His stripes I am healed. We shall all have to go into judgment for our works; but we are not going into judgment for our sins. No, we are free. He died for us. And no better news could you men present hear than that these enemies are swept away. Gone for time and eternity, and all by accepting His gospel as a gift.

'But the angels not only brought glad tidings, they brought peace. "Glory to God in the highest, and on earth, peace." When a man has faith in God it brings peace. Men seek after peace. They try to find it in companions, wealth, books, ambition, games. And they try to find rest for their souls, but they cannot. But here is eternal rest. "Come unto Me, and I will give you rest." You have not got to make any reconciliation on your part. It is made. You have only to enter into power by belief, and you can have peace.'

Then, 'in perfect stillness,' Moody said: 'I don't know if I shall ever have the privilege of speaking to you again. If you take my advice you will decide the question, and decide this night. If there is no reality in the Christian religion, it is time you knew it. . . . If the Bible can't be relied upon, burn it. If infidelity is right, and Christianity a myth and failure, the sooner you find it out the better. Deny Christianity, burn the Bible, turn the churches into theatres, and eat, drink and be merry—for the sooner you are gone the better!

'But if the God of the Bible is real, then take your stand,

and take it boldly. Don't be religious with religious people, and make sport when with scoffers. . . .'

After repeating the warning, 'Jesus Christ said, "if ye believe not, ye shall die in your sins: whither I go ye cannot come,"' Moody said: 'One last word. I've enjoyed preaching to you students as much as anything I have ever done in my life. I shall never forget this week, though you may forget me. I thank God I ever came to Cambridge, but I should like to give you one text before closing. "Seek ye *first* the kingdom of God."' He told them another story to illustrate the dangers of delay, reminded them that they were starting in life and their characters were forming, and ended with the words, 'Believe the Gospel and make room for God in your hearts.'

After the choir had sung 'Just as I am, without one plea,' Moody led in prayer, while all knelt or sat. Then he asked that those who had received blessing during the week should rise quietly in their places, silent prayer continuing and all eyes closed. And Moule, kneeling next to Moody on the platform heard him say under his breath as he looked up and saw some two hundred on their feet: 'My God, this is enough to live for.'

CHAPTER VI

THE CAMBRIDGE SEVEN

MOODY and Sankey went straight on to Oxford, to experience much the same initial opposition and final triumph.

At Cambridge, they had reached all sorts and conditions of men. Inevitably there were some to whom Moody's visit was a vivid but transient experience, but Handley Moule knew of 'scores of true deep, lasting conversions,' including 'not a few of men of well-known and of powerful influence.' Such were Gerald Lander,[1] Sidney Swann the rowing blue, and Douglas Hooper of Trinity Hall, 'a difficult selfish young man,' so his own sister described him, 'a heavy smoker and devoted to racing,' who kept his own horse and trap to take him to Newmarket. Hooper had been stirred by what he saw of the preparations for the Moody Mission. The sudden death of a friend on the way back from Newmarket, and the reluctant reading of a tract given him by one of his family in the summer vacation, brought him to his knees before the start of term and the mission completed the process. Some of the converts came from Christian homes, such as the future bishop who promised his mother to hear Moody, put off his visit until the last night, and found himself then and there deciding for Christ. Most of the men, in the eighteen-eighties, must have had some previous consciousness of Christian truth, although their new-found faith might not prove popular in their homes.

The moral effect of the mission was marked. The tone of more than one college was said afterwards to have been 'lastingly raised.' Moody's own attitude was straight-

[1] Afterwards Bishop of Hong-kong. J. E. K. Studd, the President who had invited Moody, became Lord Mayor of London in 1928–29.

forward. When someone asked him if a Christian should 'give up racing and shooting and hunting and balls,' he replied, 'Racing means betting and betting means gambling, and I don't see how a gambler is going to be a Christian. Do the other things as long as you like. . . . And as soon as ever you have won a soul you won't care about any of the other things.' At Cambridge the attitude of his converts was well expressed by the man whose friends, having heard of his conversion on the last Sunday night, came in on the Monday morning to rag him. 'I say, old man, we are all coming round this evening to have a card party in your room.' 'Oh no, you are not. Last night I decided for Christ. No more card parties for me.'

Moody imbued his converts with a sense of purpose. The mission 'permanently altered' the position of the infant Ridley Hall. It had only fourteen members in October 1882. But after November, 'it became my privilege,' said the Principal, 'to get inquiries about entrance more and yet more, and from men whom it was a joy to welcome.' In 1884 the Vice-Principal remarked to Eugene Stock of the C.M.S., as they sat at breakfast with the men, 'I think there is not one man here whose life was not influenced more or less by Moody's Cambridge Mission.'

But it was in the increase of missionary zeal that the impetus given by Moody was the most marked. The seeds of growth had been sown when John Barton first came to Holy Trinity and Moule to Ridley. Till then interest in foreign missions had been steady but slight. Barton reorganized the Church Missionary Union collecting system, thereby increasing returns. First Barton presided at the weekly meetings and then, in December 1882, Handley Moule succeeded him as president. The Moody Mission increased the sense of responsibility for the foreign field by emphasizing the cardinal doctrines of the faith, and its power and vital significance for every human soul. Many of Moody's converts were soon sensing a call to the foreign field, both Gerald Lander and Douglas Hooper, for instance, subscribing handsomely to the C.M.U. within a few weeks of their conversion. During 1883 and early in 1884 offers were being received by the Church Missionary Society, while other men went to Ridley with definite intention of going overseas when ordained.

In the autumn of that year came the formation of the Cambridge Seven, by which the significance of the spiritual revival in the University was brought suddenly and vividly home to the consciousness of the whole nation.

That seven young men should create such a stir—and no mere passing sensation—by setting out as missionaries to China can only be explained by reference to their background and past. Some years earlier the Seven would have been indistinguishable from any other boys of their class. William Cassels, the eldest, son of a Portugal merchant, was at Repton, devoted to games if not so very distinguished. Stanley Smith was also at Repton. Dixon Hoste, at Clifton, the only one of the Seven who was never at Cambridge, was son of a major-general and followed his father as a gunner. Montagu Beauchamp, another Reptonian, already tall and of strong physique, was son of a Norfolk baronet and landowner. The two brothers, Arthur and Cecil Polhill-Turner, their father a Member of Parliament, were at Eton, and in the holidays getting their fill of hunting or cricket in the leisured life of Howbury Hall, Bedfordshire. Charlie Studd, also at Eton, came from an even more wealthy home; on retirement from prosperous tea-planting in India his father had bought Tedworth Hall near Andover, where no one lacked for anything.

They thus had before them all that birth, wealth and education freely offered in aristocratic England. To this most of them had added a further passport to popularity and success—athletic distinction. Cecil Polhill-Turner was in the Eton XI of '78, but though in his short time at Cambridge he had no claim to fame, he could offset it by his commission in a crack cavalry regiment and a good reputation for polo. His brother Arthur played both cricket and football for Eton; Smith had rowed for Trinity and had stroked the Cambridge boat, while Beauchamp had rowed in the trial eight. Charlie Studd, the most prominent of the Seven, became a household name in cricket—'The most brilliant member of a well-known cricketing family,' was W. G. Grace's account of him, 'and from 1881 to 1884 had few superiors as an all-round player. His batting and bowling were very good . . . one of the finest of our young players.'

The world lay before them. But neither sport nor position proved decisive.

The first link in the chain was the impression made by Moody's Cambridge visit on William Hoste, Dixon's elder brother and a Trinity undergraduate, who was already a Christian. Dixon Hoste, a year younger than William, was then twenty-one and a gunner subaltern, leading, so he afterwards said, a life 'entirely indifferent to the claims of God.' There were occasional stirrings of conscience, and the influence of a religious if rather severe upbringing; but when in the following vacation William wanted to take his younger brother to Moody he met surly response. Persistence triumphed, and Dixon eventually found himself, like so many others, with eyes and ears glued to the American evangelist. 'A deep sense of my sinful and perilous state laid hold of my soul with great power. On the other hand, the realization of what it would cost to turn from the associations and habits of the life I was then living, and the knowledge that I should be exposed to the opposition, ridicule and dislike of my worldly companions, held me back from definite decision for Christ.' For a fortnight his heart and mind were in conflict, until at Moody's last meeting in the Dome at Brighton in December 1882, D. E. Hoste went forward, assured and happy, in open confession of faith.

He made no bones about his faith on returning to his battery in the Isle of Wight and began to feel that he ought to throw up his commission and go out as a missionary, a course to which his father, though sympathetic, strongly objected. At Cambridge meanwhile, among William Hoste's friends, interest was growing not only in the Church Missionary Society but in a smaller and younger body, the China Inland Mission, the only protestant society to have penetrated into the interior.

Founded in 1866 by a Yorkshireman, Hudson Taylor, who had already spent twelve years in China, the China Inland Mission was run on unusual and effective lines. Hudson Taylor believed that the vast need of millions of Chinese 'utterly and hopelessly beyond the reach of the gospel' was equalled by the resources of God. China had a claim on Christians and Christians could 'lay hold on His faithfulness Who has called us into this service.' The Mission had no guarantee of funds, but Hudson Taylor's conviction, 'Depend upon it. God's work done in God's way will never lack supplies,' had not been disproved in nearly twenty years' steady growth. To overcome prejudice, Chinese clothes had to be worn. No Consular protection could be given. No fixed stipend was offered, and no funds were solicited. The missionaries went forward in apostolic faith: 'The dangers and difficulties will be neither few nor small, but with Jesus for our leader we may safely follow on.'

Montagu Beauchamp's uncle Lord Radstock had been one of the first sponsors of the C.I.M. Beauchamp, a close friend of Stanley Smith and Kynaston Studd, had been a somewhat formal Christian, in obedience to the dictates of his family, when he first went to Cambridge. Throughout the Lent term of 1881 Studd and Smith were praying for him together 'every day after hall.' Early in October he told Studd that he had 'yielded all to Christ.' On October 20th Smith could write, 'How marvellously changed he is! So full of zeal instead of his coldness and lukewarmness,' and together they launched a weekly Bible reading for members of the 1st Trinity Boat Club.

Beauchamp was still up at Trinity in 1883 and it was probably through him that Dixon Hoste in the Isle of Wight first heard of the C.I.M. and read Hudson Taylor's pamphlet, *China's Spiritual Needs and Claims*. As a result of what he read, so Hoste wrote later, 'the overwhelming spiritual need of the Chinese began to burden my heart.' He again raised his proposal to resign his commission; his father now consented and on 1st August 1883 Hoste went to offer himself, rather diffidently, to the C.I.M. Hudson Taylor, back for a while from China, looked for spiritual capacity in his candidates rather than wordly position and was not at all sure that the shy gunner subaltern, so young in his faith, was the stuff of which martyrs are made. Thus, though Hoste was the first to offer himself, it was Stanley Smith, some six months later on 1st April 1884, who was the first to be accepted by the Mission.

Stanley Smith, son of a West End surgeon, had come up to Trinity in 1879. Affectionate and happy in nature, he had wide interests though without striking intellectual ability, was something of a pianist and could sing well, and was a brilliant oarsman. As a boy he had attended a Bible reading and prayer meeting over the Repton tuck-shop, but before he reached Cambridge his religion had become mainly a matter of introspection. He would write in his diary a daily verdict on his spiritual state: 'Poor . . . wee improvement . . . a blessed day . . . very poor . . . character unChristlike and foolish.'

A term at Cambridge drove such thoughts away, until one Sunday in April 1880, after a talk with his Repton and Trinity friend Granville Waldegrave, Lord Radstock's eldest son, Stanley Smith could write, 'I decided by God's grace to live for and to Him. . . . Thank God for sending G. W. here.' His Cambridge life grew increasingly happy, as he rose from the Trinity Fourth Boat to be stroke for the Varsity in the race of '82, lost to Oxford in a violent snowstorm. The spiritual in him steadily deepened. 'May I be the instrument of leading many souls to righteousness for Christ's sake,' he wrote at the start of his second year. Later he and Studd determined each to speak to 'at least one unconverted soul (who must be an undergraduate) a month,' but it was not long before he was exceeding his limit.

In '82 he had come down, and in the autumn started work as a master at his brother-in-law's preparatory school in South London, spending his spare time in open-air preaching in the East End, in helping the infant Church Army and in any such work which crossed his path. In January 1883, while staying in Norfolk, he came into the deepest experience of consecration with the result well expressed by his words, 'Bless the dear Lord. He is in me and *fills* me! How good He is. Oh! that all Christians knew this full surrender.'

It was not until ten months later that he first sensed any sure vocation for work overseas. Years earlier he had thought about it, but had believed that God wished otherwise. On 30th November 1883, while staying at Brockham Vicarage near Dorking, he saw in the words in Isaiah, 'I will also give thee for a light to the Gentiles,' a direct call to missionary service. By January he had met Hudson Taylor—'a nice long talk about *China*; I hope to labour for God there soon'—and on Wednesday 26th March 1884 Hudson Taylor came to dinner with the Smiths, and Stanley wrote in his diary, 'Decided to go to China with Hudson Taylor'; five days later he was accepted by the C.I.M. Council.

During the summer of 1884 a sense of expectancy was developing at the C.I.M. headquarters. News had come in from China that Harold Scholfield, a brilliant Oxford man who had gone as a medical missionary to Shansi only three years earlier, had died of typhus the very day Hoste had applied, and had 'died praying.' The passion of his last months had been prayer for the Universities—that men of intellectual as well as spiritual power should give themselves as missionaries to inland China. His prayers seemed already being answered. Not only had Hoste and Smith applied, but Smith had been down to see William Cassells in his Lambeth slum-parish. 'Had an interesting talk with Cassells,' wrote Smith in his diary, 'he is much interested in China. May the Lord send him out with me.' Cassells had been considering joining the C.M.S. in Africa, but on 18th August, three weeks after Smith's first visit, the two had lunch together, followed by an hour's prayer in South Lambeth church, after which Cassells became clear in his mind that his place should be beside Smith in China.

There was also the Polhill-Turner family. Arthur Polhill (they dropped their second name later) had never looked back since that last day of Moody's mission which had so transformed him. He went to Ridley from Trinity Hall on taking his degree but already thought in terms of China. And just as William Hoste had seized the first opportunity after the Cambridge mission of taking his older brother to hear Moody, so Arthur Polhill's cavalry brother Cecil, while walking to church one Sunday during his winter's leave of 1882 found the conversation taking an unusual turn. 'My brother startled me by saying he thought of going to "preach in China" instead of settling in the country living at home. Of course I could not see the slightest object in such a wild scheme and endeavoured to dissuade him. Later he quietly tackled me as to my own relations with God. . . . ' During 1883 Cecil obediently struggled through a daily verse of Scripture, 'adding a brief collect as a prayer,' but he thought it 'too sad a business to be a Christian.' For his next winter's leave he went to Stuttgart, where his uncle was Resident, perhaps to avoid Arthur: but by the time 'I stepped into the railway carriage on my return to Aldershot, it was with a mind fully made up. I had yielded to and trusted in Jesus Christ as my Saviour, Lord and Master.' He at first felt he ought to remain in the army, cutting out racing and cards but aiming to show his faith by being the best man in the Queen's Bays at riding, drill, cricket and polo. China, however, which had called his brother Arthur, called him also, and before '84 was over Hudson Taylor had met them both.

On 4th November it was announced that C. T. Studd was to join Smith and Cassells. A stroke-oar and a gunner subaltern were unusual enough, to say nothing of the Anglican curate. But when the most brilliant all-round cricketer of his day also proposed to bury himself in inland China the world sat up.

C. T. Studd, younger brother of the Kynaston Studd who had invited Moody to Cambridge, was twenty-three when he offered himself for China. He and his two brothers were at Eton when their father had given up his life of idleness and pleasure after hearing Moody. But C. T.'s experience needs his own words: 'I used to think that religion was a Sunday thing, like one's Sunday clothes, to be put away on Monday morning. We boys were brought up to go to Church regularly, but, although we had a kind of religion, it didn't amount to much. It was just like having a toothache. We were always sorry to have Sunday come, and glad when it was Monday morning. The Sabbath was the dullest day of the whole week, and just because we had got hold of the wrong end of religion. Then all at once I had the good fortune to meet a real live play-the-game Christian. It was my own father. But it did make one's hair stand on end. Everyone in the house had a dog's life of it until they were converted. I was not altogether pleased with him. He used to come into my room at night and ask if I was converted. After a time I used to sham sleep when I saw the door open, and in the day I crept round the other side of the house when I saw him coming.'

It was not until a year later that Charlie Studd and his two brothers, home from Eton for the holidays in 1877, were all, one by one, without the others realizing it at the time, brought to the experience their father already enjoyed. Cricket, however, gradually absorbed all C. T.'s time, and although at Cambridge Kynaston combined his cricket and his Christianity to the mutual benefit of both Charlie Studd (the better cricketer) did not. During the Moody mission at Cambridge he was touring Australia with the M.C.C.,[1] and it was not until 1883, brought up short by the near-death of his brother George, that he saw that lukewarm devotion was not enough. 'The Lord met me and restored to me the joy of His salvation. Still further, and what was better than all, He set me to work for Him, and I began to try and persuade my friends to read the Gospel, and to speak to them individually about their souls.' He afterwards learned that all the while he was in Australia two old ladies had set themselves to pray for him.

C. T. now divided his day between cricket and Moody and Sankey's second London campaign. Most of the Test Team were taken to hear the evangelists, while the

[1] He had also played in the great match at the Oval in August 1882 which Australia won by 8 runs, at which the term 'The Ashes' was first used. At this match a spectator in his excitement gnawed right through the handle of his umbrella.

Studd brothers with other Cambridge men worked at subsidiary meetings. One of their converts, though they probably did not know it at the time, was the young medical student who became Grenfell of Labrador: 'I felt I could listen to them. I could not have listened to a sensuous-looking man, a man who was not master of his own body.'

When Moody and Sankey returned to America in June 1884, Studd sought to discover his life's work. 'I wanted only to serve Him, and I prayed God to show me.' Several months of uncertainty followed, including a momentary decision to read for the Bar and a brief period of nervous breakdown, before he concluded that in view of his ample private means 'it seemed thoroughly inconsistent to spend the best years of my life in working for myself and the honours and pleasures of the world, while thousands and thousands of souls are perishing every day without having heard of Christ.'

Studd's chief natural characteristic was thoroughness. He had become an outstanding cricketer more by thoroughness than by native genius, and the devotedness which had kept him hours before a mirror practising a straight bat was transferred to his spiritual ambitions. Half-measures were repugnant to him. His mind worked in broad, simple sweeps, making him, at whatever he set his hand, utterly single-minded. But he still had a further crisis before his future became certain. 'I had known,' was his account of it, 'about Jesus Christ's dying for me, but I had never understood that if He had died for me, then I didn't belong to myself. Redemption means "buying back," so that if I belonged to Him, either I had to be a thief and keep what wasn't mine or else I had to give up everything to God. When I came to see that Jesus Christ had died for me, it didn't seem hard to give up all for HIM. It seemed just common, ordinary honesty.' Helped by Hannah Pearsall Smith's popular book, *The Christian's Secret of a Happy Life*, he came to the position which she maintained was the Christian's inalienable birthright, 'an entire surrender to the Lord and a perfect trust in Him, resulting in victory over sin and inward rest of soul.'

A few weeks later, after Stanley Smith had taken him to
a C.I.M. meeting, he became convinced that China's need
was decisive, and at the beginning of November 1884,
C. T. Studd offered himself to Hudson Taylor: 'God put it
in my heart and made me long to go to China.'

He met immediate opposition, not only from his mother
but from his brother Kynaston, to whose example and
leadership he owed so much. 'I was round there last
night,' wrote Montagu Beauchamp, 'and never saw anything like Kinny's depression. He says he has never in his
life seen two such days of suffering and sorrow, referring
to his mother. Yesterday all day she was imploring
Charlie not to go up to Mildmay and at all events "just to
wait one week" before giving himself to H. Taylor. He
would listen to no entreaties from M[rs. Studd] or
K[ynaston], who look upon him as a kind of fanatic.'
Studd nearly wavered, but at the height of this emotional
conflict, while standing on a station platform at night under
a flickering gas-light, he took out his New Testament, and
on opening it read the words 'A man's foes shall be they of
his own household.' Seeing this verse as a message from
God, he became settled in mind and determined that
nothing should hold him back.

Montagu Beauchamp also discovered that he had
marching orders for China. He had become one of the
leaders at Cambridge, and the trial-boat which he stroked
was known as the 'tea-pot eight' being almost entirely
teetotal. On his coming down in '84 his Christianity had
cooled, until in October his sister Ida was the means of
bringing him to a vivid experience of re-consecration. On
the night of Tuesday November 4th, as he wrote the next
day to his mother, 'I realized His presence in a way I have
never done before.' On the Monday he had had a long
talk with S. P. Smith; on the Tuesday he had seen Studd,
but it was while he was studying his Bible and praying that
night that it was 'made quite clear that not only was I to go
but to induce others to go too.' He broke the news of his
decision to his mother with consummate tact. Having
described Mrs. Studd's opposition to C. T., and the conflict in the family, he wrote: 'Their sorrow is cruel to be-

hold. What would *you* do under similar circumstances? Wouldn't you rather encourage, for instance, me, to go than hinder? If I am not mistaken I have often heard you say it would be your joy and rejoicing to have a son go to the heathen to "preach the unsearchable riches of Christ." This joy is likely to be fulfilled in Me! . . .'

The excitement at Cambridge when the intentions of Studd and Stanley Smith, Hoste, Cassells and later Beauchamp, were known, was intense. It was heightened by the announcement that 'S. P.' and 'C. T.' were coming up for a week with Hudson Taylor. On Wednesday 12th November, two years to the day since Moody's last meeting in the Corn Exchange, they went to the Alexandra Hall and told why they were going to China. Moule was in the chair. 'Most remarkable missionary meeting,' he wrote in his diary that night, 'Lord bless it. Deeply moving testimonies.' Five more meetings were held, Hoste and Cassells coming up for the two last, while Studd and Smith also spent much time in the colleges. On the Monday afternoon Studd was taken by Moule for a walk in the country: 'his spirit blessed and experience most remarkable.' This impression of Moule's was that of all who met him. It was not simply that Studd and his friends were giving up worldly prospects, but they that were doing so with such gusto. 'Spiritual millionaires' was how one undergraduate described them. Though some of the more staid of the senior men felt them distinctly eccentric, while others suspected their lack of intellectual ability, the ordinary undergraduates were drawn by their balance of stolid purpose and burning enthusiasm.

Studd and Smith were less anxious to propagate the cause of missions, or the claims of the Chinese, than to share their own spiritual experience. They therefore welcomed a suggestion that the two of them should visit Edinburgh University in December. With 'a Bible and tooth-brush their kit,' they went to Edinburgh and Glasgow, and also Leicester, Liverpool, Manchester and several other towns in England.

Wherever they went the effect was astonishing. Theirs

was a twofold message: that 'the knowledge of Jesus is everything in the world,' and that those who profess themselves Christians not only should live entirely for Christ but have the right to be thoroughly happy, victorious and effective. Their method was that of simple testimony. Smith had a degree of eloquence, but Studd 'couldn't speak a bit' (as an Edinburgh man said), 'it was the fact of his devotion to Christ which told and he, if anything, made the greatest impression.' Yet they made no pretence of taking this speaking tour in their stride, and seemed to their hosts to spend almost as much time on their knees as later on the platform or in personal talks.

At Edinburgh the impression made on the students was such that the two were obliged to return for further meetings. Their visit brought to white heat the religious revival which had begun under Moody in '81. David Cairns, the theologian, then a young man, who had been absent from Scotland since 1880, found the whole atmosphere changed and the theological colleges full when he returned in 1886. At Leicester they were the means of launching F. B. Meyer on the path which made him one of the greatest Free Churchmen of his generation. At Rochdale the hall was packed. Through it all the two men kept humble. 'We daily grow in the knowledge of Jesus and His wonderful love,' Studd wrote to his mother, 'what a different life from my former one; why, cricket and racquets and shooting are nothing to this overwhelming joy.'

The climax came in the first week of February 1885, when all the Cambridge Seven (the Polhill-Turners having joined the others) spoke at farewell meetings in Cambridge, Oxford and, by special request of the Y.M.C.A., at the Exeter Hall in the Strand.

The Guildhall at Cambridge, on the Monday night, was full, both town and gown being well represented. The Seven had asked old Professor Babington to take the chair, 'because,' so they told Moule, 'he is so large-hearted, he loves all who love the Lord Jesus.' Each of the Seven spoke. Stanley Smith's address, reported the *Cambridge Review*, was 'delivered with great fervour and listened to with closest attention. He spoke of the great love of God and their duty to the Saviour. Nothing had won their hearts so much as the love of Christ upon the Cross. . . .' One by one they told their audience why they were going to China. Studd's words were particularly memorable—'a priceless testimony' said Searle, Master of Pembroke, 'to the reality of the Spirit': 'I want to recommend to you my Master; I have tried many ways of pleasure in my time, I have tasted most of the pleasures this world can give. I do not suppose there is one that I have not experienced, but I can tell you that these pleasures are as nothing compared to my present joy. I had formerly as much love for cricket as any man could have, but when the Lord Jesus came into my heart I found that I had something infinitely better. I wanted to win souls.' Such words sent men back to their rooms thoughtful and praying. 'I saw,' said J. C. Farthing of Caius a few days later, 'that we were to take up our cross and follow Christ; that there was to be no compromise, however small, that there was to be nothing between us and our Master.'

The final meeting, on Wednesday, 4th February, in the Exeter Hall, was unforgettable. Public interest was increased by the national anxiety for General Gordon, 'Chinese' Gordon, whose character also seemed to find an echo in the Cambridge Seven. It had been raining hard all evening, but 'long before the time announced for the meeting,' reported *The Times*, 'the large hall was crowded in every part, and an overflow meeting of some of the many unable to obtain admission was held in the small hall.' Men and women were sitting in the gangways and standing on the edge of the platform. Although the meeting had been arranged by the Y.M.C.A. for young men, they were lost in a miscellaneous mass of all ages and social ranks. Across the back of the platform hung a huge map of China and behind the speakers' chairs were sitting forty Cambridge undergraduates, all intending missionaries themselves.

When the chairman, George Williams, founder of the Y.M.C.A., came on to the platform, followed by the Seven, the enthusiasm was immense. Then came two and a half hours of speeches, hymn-singing and prayer. The audience was held from start to finish as the Seven spoke—'a band of young Englishmen,' in Lord Cairns' words, 'high bred, high spirited, highly cultivated—men who had before them at home everything that social position and personal capability could ensure.' Stanley Smith spoke longest, on the theme that 'we are under an obligation to spread the knowledge of a good thing . . . not the milk-and-water of religion but the cream of the Gospel.' He touched the emotions of the hour with a reference to General Gordon, not knowing he was dead—'a greater than Gordon cries from Khartoum—the voice of Christ from the Cross of Calvary'—and called for volunteers in the spiritual war. Beauchamp, Hoste, Cassells and the Polhill-Turners said a few words each, while J. C. Farthing spoke for the undergraduates. Studd followed with a straight, unhurried account of his experience: 'I want to recommend to you my Master,' he said once again, as at Cambridge. After Hugh Price Hughes, already famous as a Free Church leader and social reformer, had said a few closing words, the meeting ended with Frances Ridley Havergal's consecration hymn, 'Take my life.'

The following morning, when all London was agog with rumours, confirmed at noon, that Khartoum had fallen, the Cambridge Seven left Victoria Station for China. Not only relatives and friends saw tham off, but most of the former M.C.C. team. And such was Studd's popularity that some of the team came on to Dover and over the Channel before saying good-bye.

Comment on the Cambridge Seven, as might be expected, was mixed. There were some who considered their pretentions false and their faith misconceived. Others assumed that the Seven had been swept overseas by passing emotion or by the glamour of an exciting sacrifice; but when Studd and Smith offered themselves to the Mission no 'Seven' existed, nor any thought of Exeter Hall meetings or cheering university crowds. They were expecting to leave at the end of December. Studd at least had all the glamour he wanted, and was still in the full tide of cricketing fame. There would be no cricket in China; if the Chinese could have learned the rules, which was improbable, such games were considered beneath the dignity of the educated.

But there was criticism also among those in sympathy. Just as Kynaston Studd had believed at first that C. T. was wrong to leave their widowed mother, Mrs. Cassells, also a widow, had gone in great distress to Hudson Taylor, although eventually she wrote to William, 'May God not despise the feebleness of my faith in giving you.' Some were worried because Hoste and Cecil Polhill resigned their commissions, while Arthur Polhill left his theological course unfinished, though he was later ordained. There was justification in the fear that because none of the Seven were scholars, Oxford or Cambridge undergraduates would be encouraged to despise learning, for even George Pilkington of Pembroke, who was eventually Senior Classic of '87,[1] nearly gave up reading for his degree to follow the Seven. Fervid preaching of holiness—as expressed by Stanley Smith's postcard to his Trinity friend Granville Waldegrave: 'My all is on the altar. The fire has come. He has given me a clean heart. Hallelujah! I am longing to tell you all about it'—was so balanced among the Seven by essential sanity of outlook that it did not come in for much criticism, although it contributed to current difficulties at Cambridge. A further, half-hearted complaint that the Seven would do more in England for Christianity than they could hope to in the recesses of China was answered by the event.

Criticism, however justified, seemed trivial beside the effect of the Cambridge Seven on contemporary religious life. The interest aroused was enormous. Fifty thousand copies were sold of the issue of *China's Millions*, the Mission's magazine with a normal circulation of twelve thousand, which contained the reports of the farewell meetings. When these, together with letters from the Seven and much detailed matter on the world-wide need of foreign missions,

---

[1] Miss Ramsay (the second Mrs. Montagu Butler) in fact was placed above him, but as a woman could not be given the title of Senior Classic.

were formed into a book. *A Missionary Band*, fifteen thousand copies were sold within a few weeks, and the book was still selling years later in an expanded edition. Sir George Williams had a copy sent to every Y.M.C.A. in the kingdom.

The China Inland Mission itself was raised from comparative obscurity to an almost embarrassing prominence. Soberly reminding itself that 'the hour of success is often the time of danger' the society reaped the benefits of increased funds and applications for service. The unselfishness with which it encouraged the claims of other fields than China, and what Moule called 'the uncompromising spirituality and unworldiness of the programme of the Mission' presented a challenge to other societies, and the Church Missionary Society was the first to acknowledge the debt.

The most marked effect was on the Universities. Not only were undergraduates, with their respect for the muscular, faced with the Christian gospel by men they could understand and admire, but fresh missionary enthusiasm was engendered. The chief significance of this was not to be realized at Cambridge until the coming of the Student Volunteer Movement from America in the next decade. But the immediate appeal of the Cambridge Seven nowhere met with such response as in their own University.

Hugh Price Hughes, in his closing words at the great Exeter Hall meeting, had remarked, 'It is a glorious fact that the University of Cambridge has done so much for this work. We have had an Oxford Movement in our time, but I love this Cambridge movement, and it may yet do untold good to our country at home.' In this he recognized that whatever impetus the Seven might give it, they were not so much the creators of Cambridge missionary zeal as its product. Yet it was Studd's and S. P. Smith's C.I.M. meetings of November 1884 which brought the missionary movement in the University to its zenith. As J. C. Farthing said, 'When men whom everybody had heard of and many had known personally, came up and said "I am going out myself," we were brought individually face to face with the heathen abroad.' That week meetings were held in room after room, night after night, and at one over forty men stood up in decision or confirmation that they would go overseas. A few weeks later, on 1st December, a special meeting of the Church Missionary Union was held, with Westcott and the principal secretaries of the C.M.S., Wigram and Eugene Stock, among the speakers. Wigram, whose own son at Trinity was an intending missionary, felt that the awakened interest at Cambridge was neither unexpected nor a momentary excitement: 'the roots had been long growing downwards.' Stock paid generous tribute to the C.I.M. Some hundred and thirty men were present; Moule wrote in his diary, 'the Lord bless this gathering to solid and blessed results,' and Stock commented fifteen years later that it had started the movement 'which has given the Society a large number of the best of its missionaries in all parts of the world.'

Early in 1885 the Vice-Principal of Ridley, Philip Ireland-Jones, offered himself to the C.M.S., together with Douglas Hooper, former leader of the fast set. Then came the C.I.M. farewell meetings, with the crowded Guildhall and the forty undergraduates on the Exeter Hall platform. Shortly afterwards the Y.M.C.A. suggested a similar meeting for the C.M.S. At half-past seven on 24th March, therefore, with all standing room packed and an overflow meeting forming nearby, with fifty undergraduates from Oxford and Cambridge on the platform and a vast map of the world stretched above them, and with Lord Cairns in the chair, Exeter Hall was resounding to Haydn's *Austria* set to Sarah Stock's hymn, 'Lord Thy Ransomed Church is Waking.'

By now Handley Moule was finding it 'constantly my duty at Ridley Hall to press urgently on men the claims of the home field, so almost universal was the longing to serve the Lord in the ends of the unevangelized world.' During 1885 the Seven in China were followed by Webley Hope Gill of Queens' (dubbed 'the eighth man') strengthened by a message from the President of the C.I.C.C.U.: 'Prayer will be following you, the Lord will

be with you, what have you to fear?' Several more went
out with the C.M.S. Early in 1886 news came of Bishop
Hannington's murder in Uganda. Hannington, an Oxford
man and only thirty-eight, had spoken in Cambridge in
1884 before leaving England for the last time. He was
remembered as 'a man of fire' and it may have been the
news of his death which led thirty-one Cambridge men in
April 1886 to sign a letter making a prospective offer of
themselves to the C.M.S. if the way opened up. Of these,
eighteen were able later to make a definite offer and the
twelve who were medically fit went abroad. In the same
year Ion Keith-Falconer, who had gone out in 1885 to run
a mission in Aden, and subsequently been elected Professor
of Arabic at Cambridge, added the weight of his words to
the movement: 'While vast continents are shrouded in
almost utter darkness, and hundreds of millions suffer the
horrors of heathenism or of Islam, the burden of proof lies
upon you to show that the circumstances in which God has
placed you were meant to keep you out of the foreign
mission field.'

Thus the roll grew. When John Barton left Cambridge
in 1893, one hundred and forty offers had been made from
Cambridge to the C.M.S. alone, of which ninety-seven had
been accepted, since 1877.

But this missionary enthusiasm was only a part, if the
most significant as well as spectacular part, of religious life
and growth at Cambridge.

*The large hall holding
over 3000 crammed & the overflow 500
besides hundreds going away. We all
spoke & most of all in the small hall;
afterwards came up from the small hall.
when Charlie was speaking — I concluded
with Prayer — a most affecting meeting;*

The Diary of Stanley Smith, 4th February, 1885

CHAPTER VII

THE REMARKABLE PERIOD

WITHIN a few days of Moody's last address to the University in November 1882, the Cambridge correspondent of the *Record* was noting 'a marked increase in the attendance at the Daily Prayer Meeting . . . a higher tone of spiritual life among the men—greater prayerfulness, greater diligence in study.' Handley Moule afterwards described the next five years as 'a remarkable period of religious blessing.'

One feature of this remarkable period had its start within a week, when Moule held his first University Bible Reading in Holy Trinity vestry after the Sunday evening service. Only eleven were present. A week later, forty came. These Bible Readings, working from the Greek, were continued week by week, year after year, providing for undergraduates a consecutive course of careful, solid teaching not divorced from the realities of life around them. Moule's position as evening lecturer at Holy Trinity, the post for which he had first returned to Cambridge in 1880, further strengthened his influence. His fame had spread far beyond Cambridge: 'Mr. Moule's lectures will be a help, won't they?' wrote Lady Victoria Buxton to one of her sons, 'and you must pray for him.' Moule had no striking oratorical powers, and his voice was often weak and monotonous; the service was unexciting, and it came at the end of a long day. Yet he never failed to draw. Few undergraduates, in a church-going age, could have failed to have heard these lectures, and they centred round what he called 'the golden alphabet of the Gospel, the mighty first things—Christ for thee, thy acceptance; Christ in thee, thy life and power.'

Early in 1883, when memories of Moody were fresh, four

speakers of the Keswick Convention, led by Evan Hopkins, came to Cambridge and held 'a Convention for the deepening of Spiritual Life.' Hitherto, despite mutual connection with Broadlands, Keswick and its message of inward holiness and the victory of the Spirit through faith was little known in the University. Moule was doubtful of these doctrines, later writing a strong criticism of Evan Hopkins' book *The Law of Liberty*. Many of the undergraduates were deeply stirred by the Convention. Throughout 1883 and into the Lent of '84, Holiness and the possibility of a 'clean heart' were constant topics. 'Of course some have been inclined to oppose,' wrote Harry Mac-Innes of Trinity, an outstanding Christian, an M.P.'s son who had been invalided out of the Navy, 'but still a great many have been helped in one way or another and have thought over the subject a good deal.' There was discontent with half-measures or second-rate Christian life; an urge not only for utter consecration to God's will but for the beauty of Christ's character to be reproduced in everyday life. They braved the rigours of winter with early-morning prayer meetings; they sat up late in discussion and argument and searching of the Scriptures. Methods—and limits—of attainment were so much in dispute, that it was sometimes forgotten that, as MacInnes remarked, 'holiness is to be *lived* more than anything else.'

On 10th March 1884 two men, at the invitation of the C.I.C.C.U., came up for another Holiness convention. John Smyth-Pigott and W. E. Oliphant were both deacons in the Church of England, though Pigott was thirty-two and, since first leaving Cambridge, had passed a colourful career as sailor before the mast, soldier and coffee-planter before settling temporarily as an Anglican curate. They were unconnected with the Keswick Movement, which they considered did not go far enough. They were sincere and in earnest, but what was known of Pigott's career was unlikely to instil confidence among the more thoughtful.

'The watchwords of surrender and holiness were everywhere,' said Moule; 'there was an almost passionate desire for entire deliverance from the power of sin.' These aspirations were fanned into flame by this new holiness convention. But disturbing reports soon filtered through to senior men. Though Pigott's manner was quiet, he and Oliphant were teaching sinless perfection, the entire eradication of sin from the believer. Divisions were inevitable. 'I do not think they are right by the Bible,' wrote a Corpus man, 'but I am accused of lukewarmness. It may be so, but I *do* love regularity. My Bible reading has been for the time upset. Only these wildish though blessed hymns ring in my ears, not the strong solid, Word of God.'

Moule and John Barton were puzzled. There were definite signs of blessing, of men humbled and deepened, but Pigott's and Oliphant's message contained undoubted error, and it was accompanied by an orgy of emotion. Everything else was neglected and men were talking of flinging property and future to the winds in a desperate desire for unhindered sanctification. The two seniors had no desire to repress what they did not fully understand. Further, they were anxious for unity. They spent two and a half hours on Friday, 14th March, in discussion with Pigott and Oliphant. The following day Moule talked with four of the most affected of his Ridleians and rather to his surprise was reassured. On the Sunday both Barton and Moule preached steadying sermons, the latter freely admitting the help which the week had given him though he had not been to any of the meetings. Early on the Monday morning, in St. Bene't's Church, a Communion service was held. Moule, Barton, Lang, Dean of Corpus, and Pigott officiated and, to Moule's delighted wonder, one hundred and fifty undergraduates were present.

With the end of term the first wave of 'Holiness' receded. Musgrave Brown of Corpus and some of his friends went the whole way with Pigott. They held meetings lasting hours and Moule's young nephew, whose rooms were next to Brown's, used to find them prostrate on the ground ; a little later Brown threw up his College course, gave away his considerable worldly wealth and, with Pigott and Oliphant, joined the Salvation Army. At Cambridge, though all Christians worth their salt were anxious for the highest life, opinion was dividing dangerously over the meaning of 'Sanctification.'

Assistance came unexpectedly. Handley Moule had not disguised his sense of debt to the holiness mission, and a week later he wrote 'my heart warmed by recent expressions of the Saviour's presence.' Though certain of the error of some of Piggot's teaching, he was seeking for himself a true and lasting realization 'of the Lord's sanctifying presence,' and through the spring and summer of '84 he read books on the subject, eventually coming down heavily in the columns of the *Record* not only against Perfectionism but against Keswick. His diary meanwhile became a pathetic catalogue of depression and struggle, relieved by fitful phases of 'hope and peace and gladness.'

In the autumn the Moules went to stay with relatives in a country house near Edinburgh and their visit coincided with an annual convention arranged by their hosts. 'I wished to get away,' wrote Moule, 'but there was no opportunity to do this without breach of courtesy.' He went 'again as an act of courtesy' to the first meeting. 'It did not please me at all.' At the second meeting Evan Hopkins, whose new book Moule had recently castigated, was the principal speaker. At first relieved to find Hopkins' sober teaching in such contrast to the emotional perfectionism of Piggot, Moule soon discovered that what he had severely criticized was what he needed. As he sat in the barn where the meetings were held he realized how all his life had been a struggle to do what God alone could do, and to dictate his own conditions of service. That evening, in response to the speaker's call, he stood up—'a helpful act of *definition*'—and found that his wife stood also. The following day, 'My darling and I both publicly confessed blessing; a *blessed* trial. . . . What, *I* delighting in a convention?'

The Michaelmas term of '84, which began less than a month later, was stimulated by the visit of Studd, Stanley Smith and Hudson Taylor. It also experienced a return visit of Piggot, now a Salvationist and accompanied by Musgrave Brown and Bramwell Booth, the General's son and future successor. Although as Piggot expressed it in the *War Cry*, 'we had some regular blood and fire comrades in the University,' there was so much noise at the

Saturday night open meeting, to which crowds of under-graduates flocked, that 'all we could do was to get on our knees and cry to God for them while they stood around and threw hymn books and water at us.' For all these stimu-lants and excitements the most significant event of the term was the writing, and delivery at open meetings of the Church Society in St. Botolph's Church, of Moule's *Thoughts on Christian Sanctity*. These lectures, published the following year as a little book which the undergraduates used to carry about in their coat pockets, sprang straight from Moule's own experience. It steadied the aspirations of the men, anchored in scholarship and Scripture what was in danger of becoming glib undergraduate jargon, and opened fresh spiritual vistas for the ignorant or puzzled.

'It is the insatiable desire of the soul which has truly seen the Lord,' said Moule, 'to be made fully like Him by His grace. And this desire has in our own day come to be a leading and ruling thing. . . . Everywhere there is felt and found in our Christian word of today a deep, strong and growing drift of inquiry and desire after Christian holiness.' He first defined the aims of Christian sanctity: 'to be like Him . . . to displace self from the inner throne, and to enthrone Him. To make not the slightest com-promise with the smallest sin. . . . We aim at nothing less than to walk with God all day long; to abide every hour in Christ, and He and His words in us; to love God with all the heart and our neighbour as ourselves; to live, and that in no conventional sense, "no longer to ourselves, but to Him Who died for us and rose again."'

Moule categorically rejected sinless perfection—'to the last it will be a *sinner* that walks with God'—but went on to say that 'it is possible to cast every care on Him daily, and to be at peace amidst pressure. . . . It is possible to see the will of God in everything . . . to put away *all* bitter-ness and wrath and anger and evil speaking, daily and hourly. It is possible by unreserved resort to divine power under divine conditions to become strongest through and through at our weakest point.' This new life meant a daily denial of self, taking up the Cross, yet 'it does not absorb nor cancel personality. Rather this is the very thing to enrich the resources of personal being.' Furthermore it does not depend on wearisome struggle but on God's power to take the consecrated soul and to keep him. God is 'an eternal person undertaking for you.' He urged his hearers to 'read again, all through your Bible, the places that give you this view of Him.'

Reaching the core of his argument, Moule spoke of Christ as the Divine Master, Keeper and Friend. 'My Master, my possessor; absolute, not constitutional; supremely entitled to order me about all day, and if He pleases, not to thank me at the close. . . . How delightful the thought that hands or head or voice are indeed the implements of the faithful slave, kept at work for such an Owner—His property, and glad indeed to be so.' He pictures this in work and recreation, on holidays and in deliberate service, and goes on to quote Aristotle's definition of slavery: 'a chattel that lives.' But, says Moule, 'the Christian slave is capable of a true perception of His Master's mind, a sympathy, as true as it is humble, with his Master's will. And then it is his delightful privilege evermore to act as if free. . . . He can look in the Master's face and say, as one who is at liberty to go if he will, "I love Thee, I am well with Thee, I will not go out free,"' For this Master, Who in His own interest will keep His slave, providing for every physical, moral, mental and spiritual need, is above all a Friend. 'Profoundest reverence will look full into the eyes of unalterable sovereignty.' But the gaze will be the gaze of friendship. Therefore 'I would not for a moment be free, an independent agent, choosing work and bargaining for pay. I have no rights; I make no conditions. I am a "chattel that lives." But ah! with it, and in it, and through it, I am my Master's friend.'

Moule concludes by showing how this state of absolute loyalty and friendship may come about, how it is sustained and what is its effect. It depends on utter surrender of heart, emotions, will and ambition, and is essentially maintained by Christ dwelling in power in the trusting heart. Such a life must be cultivated by study of the Scriptures, by worship and the Breaking of Bread and above all by prayers. God is a Friend. Therefore, 'I shall care often to be alone with Him; and when alone to speak with Him.' The dominant of life will henceforth be not I but Christ— a fact meant to shine out. 'Our position, our secret as His slaves, His implements, His members, we must carry into everything.' It will govern thought, temper and words; govern the use of time, money and position; a life of true sanctity and therefore of continuous happiness.

Moule's lectures, and their widespread circulation as a book, consolidated his influence. He knew that under-graduates would not be driven and he had led them. In so far as they were prepared to respect the opinions of any-one over twenty-five they acknowledged his wisdom and appreciated his sympathy, even if 'Old Moule' was con-sidered in some quarters too cautious. The year that followed, therefore, was less marked by extravagances. The President of the C.I.C.C.U. for 1884–85, Walter Scott, Master of Polwarth, who was also elected President of the Union Society, defeating Austen Chamberlain, was steady and balanced as well as eager, and he and the Secretary, J. C. Farthing, kept the movement within bounds, while fostering the spiritual enthusiasm which had been generated by the Cambridge Seven, by the Exeter Hall meetings and by the evangelistic mission arranged by themselves in the Michaelmas term.

Walter Scott was succeeded in 1885 by Douglas Hamilton of Clare, a man exceptional even in that period for his devotion and holiness of life. In the Long Vacation Cambridge men attended the Keswick Convention in strength and during August worked together on seaside missions for children. At Llandudno, Tyndale-Biscoe and Sidney Swann, the rowing blues, Charles Harford-Battersby and several others decided to urge the C.I.C.C.U. to hold a special session of prayer before the start of the following term. Then came a courageous decision.

In the mid-'eighties feelings ran high. If traditions or conventions were outraged, University men could express themselves forcibly in language and action. Preten-tiousness was not tolerated and the unusual, whether in religion or art or anything else, disliked. The more seriously a man took himself, the more he might expect a rough passage. A proposal therefore for evangelistic services in the University, which should not be addressed by a visiting speaker or a resident clergyman but by undergraduates themselves, seemed wild in the extreme. Each speaker, it was suggested, should give his testimony to the reality of Christ in his own life, describing briefly how he had been converted and led to further experience. It was a leaf out of the Salvation Army's book.

To invite men to listen to their own contemporaries seemed to court disaster. There could be a force behind ungarnished testimony which might reach further than an older man's more polished and, as it were, professional address, and if an undergraduate wished to speak publicly to others on a subject which many considered best left to parsons, he was wise to restrict himself to a plain account of his experiences. But public words would be tested against all too-public character; a Trinity man might get away with it, but in small colleges every failing and inconsistency was common knowledge. And even if the actual testimonies were delivered successfully, there was no certainty that they would do more than arouse curiosity. All this was debated by the C.I.C.C.U. Executive in Harford-Battersby's rooms at the top of the kitchen staircase of Trinity Great Court, in the attics overlooking Bishop's Hostel. It was, he recalled, a 'very solemn meeting.' But Douglas Hamilton was not prone to play for safety, and it was decided to go ahead.

The upshot was remarkable. The Alexandra Hall, in Post Office Terrace behind Petty Cury, saw a series of Sunday evening meetings at which men broke through fear and indecisiveness. Further, their friends who were indifferent to the claims of the Christian life or ignorant of its possibilities found themselves, to their surprise, reached by this new approach. There were no disturbances and if occasionally some of the dangerous perfectionist jargon was heard, it did not seem to detract from the reverence or value of the meetings.

John Barton was invited to the Alexandra Hall from the first. Of the dons some gave a cautious welcome to the new effort, others tended to resent activities which might weaken loyalties to college chapel. There were two sides to the question, ably summed up thirty years later by one of the C.I.C.C.U. men of '84: 'No doubt we did not appreciate the college chapel as we might have done, but it would have been a happy thing if those who were our nominal spiritual leaders could have realized how much they lost hold of us through failure to sympathize with our joys and aspirations.'

The Alexandra Hall slowly won a place in Cambridge life. In summer the meetings were transferred to the open air. Similar outdoor efforts were known before, but regular Sunday services, held on a space on the Backs behind Clare and King's first started in Douglas Hamilton's year, 1886. They were conducted with decorum and listened to with respect by considerable crowds. Open-Airs for the townspeople on Parker's Piece or Midsummer Common, were sometimes less fortunate. In 1887 a party of undergraduates determined to break up the Parker's Piece service, and even formed up and charged the rostrum on more than one Sunday. Protests from John Barton and from the Captain of Boats, in letters to the *Cambridge Review* failed to end the trouble that term, though it was not repeated the following year.

Sunday was now more crowded than ever. 'Literally the whole of Sunday,' Moule reported, was sometimes used up in evangelistic work, teaching and conferences to the exclusion of necessary quiet and rest. Many men went to early Communion in their college chapels; morning and evening prayer were compulsory. At midday came the Daily Prayer Meeting. In the afternoon, the Varsity sermon in Great St. Mary's, still largely attended; after Hall, Moule's lecture at Holy Trinity, with possibly his Greek Testament class as well. Attendance at this could mean being late for the C.I.C.C.U. meeting at the Alexandra Hall, and after '85 was missed if friends were to be taken to 'the most important item of all.' On return to college important talks over coffee or cocoa might follow before bed could be thought of. One or more informal prayer-meetings might be included in the programme, and almost invariably Sunday School or mission work, while sometimes a Grantchester 'grind,' choral evensong at King's, or some college dean's study group might replace one or other event.

Such intense activity depended on prayer. The Daily Prayer Meeting was well attended, but adequate personal communion and quiet sometimes had been edged out until a Morning Watch Union was started, its members signing a declaration: 'I will endeavour, God helping me, to set aside at least twenty minutes, and if possible one hour, in the early morning for prayer and Bible study, and also a short but uninterrupted time before retiring to rest.' The idea was Douglas Hooper's, the former Newmarket man who within a few weeks of his conversion had been getting together his friends at Trinity Hall to hear Moule, and who had since gone on to Ridley. 'The Morning Watch Union has been started here,' Harry MacInnes wrote home, 'and men are feeling the importance of having a good quiet time first thing in the morning.' At Ridley they had the example of Moule himself, who could be seen early in the morning before chapel walking up and down in his garden, a shawl over his shoulders, praying; and here Hooper instituted a Morning Watch Roll, which involved a summary ejection from bed of any who did not respond to the first summons of the knocker-up, Hooper himself. A system of Bible reading was already at hand—the Scripture Union, founded in London some years before and publishing an annual card of consecutive passages, pledging its members to regularity. It came to be believed that consecrating the first hour or half-hour of the day to Bible study and prayer was more important than any meeting or conference; and Hooper's final word to his fellow-Ridleians as he went down was not, as they had expected, a call to follow him out as a missionary but four words they never forgot: 'Remember the Morning Watch.'

The background to this life was that of any healthy undergraduate of the period—athletics and academic work, the friendships of Hall and staircase. Though they might seem to crowd their days with other activities the Christian men delighted as much as their contemporaries in hard-fought rugger matches, and in the excitements of the racing on the Cam; they rode penny-farthings, high enough to see over the hedges and faster than anything on the roads, or took leisurely 'grinds' through the countryside, bathed from Grantchester meadows or punted on the Backs. Their college rooms were, as others, crowded with furniture and knick-knacks, the curtains heavy, a profusion of photographs on the mantelpiece and pictures on the walls, and a roaring fire in the winter grate. There also were certain to be texts or motto cards. 'I like having texts up in my room,' wrote a Caius man to his mother, 'they catch one's eye at lunch, perhaps, or breakfast and give food for thought.'

In the academic work of the men a perennial tension was especially apparent in the mid-'eighties: 'The first and ruling purpose of undergraduate life,' wrote Moule, 'is preparation, and many excellent and devoted men have tended to forget this and to seek, as if it were a primary duty, to influence others in a measure out of proportion to their work and discipline of preparatory study.' Devotion to the schools was not an outstanding characteristic of the contemporary undergraduate, many of whom would have no need to work for their living. Christians might have shown more sense of responsibility. But memories of the unlettered Moody (and a mistaken belief that he despised education), unceasing zeal and ardent longings for more faith and holiness combined to put intellect at a discount. Forgiveness of sins did not depend on it, so intellect was unimportant or even harmful. Time was short. The need of the unsaved was pressing. The only knowledge that mattered was of the Bible. This phase passed, but work was still often preferred to study, and though Moule could write after a while that 'this is decidedly less so than it appeared to be a few years ago, and this without any loss in Christian love and devotedness,' Robert Sinker, Librarian of Trinity, was careful to insert in his *Memorials of Ion Keith-Falconer* a reminder to undergraduate readers that his hero's interest in social and evangelistic work, 'however great, co-existed with his studies yet did not interfere with them.'

On the other hand, several ardent and active Christians gained academic distinction, such as Archibald Hyslop, Walter Moule and George Pilkington.

George Pilkington of Pembroke was one of the most noted converts of the Alexandra Hall. 'Pilks' was a pugnacious Irishman, tall and thick set, proud, autocratic and self-willed, and with a first-class brain. In previous years the more aggressive Christians of Pembroke had tried to win him. In his first term, four freshmen, christened by the college 'the four apostles' had systematically called on the fifty-two others of their year until they had obtained direct talk on spiritual matters with each one. Pilkington wrote them off as 'mad.' The following summer they asked him to an informal meeting in a Clare man's room. Someone spoke on 'When I am weak then am I strong,' and 'Pilks' stayed behind, and standing with his back to the fireplace 'rated us well for preaching such nonsense.' But during the Michaelmas term he was being taken to the Alexandra Hall, rather reluctantly, though afterwards grateful to the friends who refused to let him alone. When his religiousness, which was ample, and his intolerance, which was strong, enabled him eventually to listen with humility, he realized that the men whom he heard possessed something he desired, but several weeks of unhappiness followed. He shut himself in his rooms in Pembroke New Buildings, studied the Bible, prayed and worried. When light came, he championed his new faith with as much downright tenacity as he had previously attacked it. He seized every opportunity to take men to the Alexandra Hall and make his friends aware of their need of Christ. He refused to be silenced. 'I told him,' said one man, 'unless he could avoid the subject I could not welcome him. Consequently he, for a long time, would not come to see me.' 'Pilks' lost his self-conceit, though his hot Irish temper never left him. His impatience of anything that was not directly spiritual nearly cost him his First; his dislike of conventional restrictions made him difficult to work with. But no one who knew him could forget his happy sincerity and singleness of heart, and when after a few crowded years pioneering for the C.M.S. in Uganda he was killed on a battlefield, the meteoric pattern of his life seemed in keeping with his character.

Douglas Hamilton's year was not only to be notable for the Alexandra Hall. In January 1886 Pigott was back once more, hat in hand, having renounced the Salvation Army, to read for a while at his old college before re-assuming Anglican orders. Musgrave Brown, also returned, was in an acute state of nervous depression. In time he recovered, was ordained and did notable work at Liverpool. Oliphant remained in the Salvation Army and rose to high rank and honours.

With Pigott in Cambridge, Holiness was soon again the absorbing topic. A further visit in the Lent term from Keswick speakers, arranged by Moule, reawakened the strongest desires for purity of heart and loveliness of life and Pigott, a magnetic personality, stirred the men to reach for the highest. Douglas Hamilton determined that Holiness should be the aim and attainment of every man in his care. The tempo rose steadily, and the spiritual movement culminated in a convention organized by the C.I.C.C.U. in June 1886. Keswick speakers were on the platform, and Pigott. For the undergraduates his influence predominated. 'It is impossible not to record gatherings of this kind here just now without some anxiety,' wrote Moule, 'for beyond all doubt there is a distinct tendency to what is in fact perfectionism in the minds of many undergraduates.' At some of the meetings men stood up and, with utmost sincerity, proclaimed themselves free from all internal sin. They believed that God's Holy Spirit was solely responsible, but as Charles Harford-Battersby wrote, 'many of us were led into the use of un-scriptural expressions.' Despite the presence of Keswick speakers, the more heady were unable to distinguish the true from the false, while the lead in error was coming from the President and some of the Executive; Douglas Hamilton whose earlier good influence none denied, had taken a fatal turning. The urge to perfection which had made his character so beautiful and his influence strong, ceased to be tested and balanced by Scripture. Subjective experience became the sole criterion of spiritual state. Soon therefore Hamilton had brought himself—with others—not only to believe that no longer was he a sinner, but that the presence of sin in a life committed to the Holy Spirit was a contradiction of God's power and therefore impossible. He had passed into a new state, from time to eternity. The Holy Spirit which now possessed him was to be his sole authority. Direct guidance was given on the smallest points. Direct commands were to be obeyed even when contrary to Scripture and the laws of man. Thus the love of fellow-men which had been the admiration of Hamilton's acquaintance, fettered no longer by earthy values and inflamed by high religious emotion, led straight to sexual perversion.

Barton and Moule spent 'long and anxious' hours salving souls from the wreck. Some, such as Harford-Battersby, drew back in time. Others having worked themselves up to conviction of sinless perfection ended in nervous breakdowns, with loss of all faith. The climax came in the long Vacation when Douglas Hamilton joined the Agapemonites. This minute sect, 'The Community of the Son of Man,' founded by a renegade Anglican clergyman, held beliefs compounded of immorality, blasphemy and genuine spiritual desire. With their 'Abode of Love' at Spaxton in Somerset they resembled the Mormons. Hamilton took with him one or two others, and some years later they were joined by Pigott, whose roving ended at the Abode of Love, and who proclaimed himself the Immortal Messiah in 1902 and died in 1927.[1]

'But the whole result,' said Moule afterwards, 'I say unhesitatingly, was nobly good, and many a day since then I have almost prayed for the aberrations back again for the sake of the wonderful life.' By the end of the summer all but few of the extremists had seen their error. Although

[1] Hamilton spent the rest of his life with the Agapemonites at Spaxton, dying in 1942. 'He was a very nice man and to the end deeply religious and I believe realized, but too late, what a mistake he had made.' (The Rev. F. G. Graham, Vicar of Spaxton, in a letter to the author, 25th April 1952.) In 1952 the Agapemonites were reported a dwindling community of some fifteen elderly ladies.

at the first meetings in the Alexandra Hall in October some claims of sinless sanctification were heard, these soon died away. When Evan Hopkins, carefully briefed by Moule and Barton, held another series of meetings for the deepening of spiritual life in January 1887, perfectionism was no more scotched but killed. The C.I.C.C.U. Executive, with Klein, one of the 'Pembroke Apostles,' as President in succession to Hamilton, had already agreed that it should no longer receive their sanction. They also arranged for the testimony meetings to include occasional qualified speakers from outside. As term proceeded 'a growing tone of humility and balance' was reported. Prayer increasingly imbued the atmosphere. An early morning prayer meeting was held each Sunday in the President's rooms at Pembroke, at which from forty to sixty would be present. On 3rd December John Barton and Eugene Stock got up at 6 a.m. 'in bitter cold and pitch darkness' and went to this prayer-meeting at 6.45, and such was the atmosphere that Stock in after years was reminded all over the world, by men he had not then known, of what he said that morning before they turned to prayer.

The same evening, after he had spoken in the Alexandra Hall, Stock heard some twenty-five brief testimonies, given in the presence of three hundred men, but 'there was not the least excitement. The utmost quiet, simplicity and brotherly fellowship marked the proceedings.'

CHAPTER VIII

DOWN-TOWN THEATRE

MISSIONARY fervour and work amongst their own acquaintance were not the only ways in which the undergraduates of 'the remarkable period' were showing the faith that was in them. They gave their energies for those in Cambridge less fortunate materially.

The men of the 'eighties were building on the past, not only in the Sunday School work, which continued unabated, but in the most prominent of the many down-town activities of the time—the Barnwell Theatre. Barnwell's unsavoury reputation had not decreased with the years. Its men were rough, its houses overcrowded and its boys were reckoned wilder than any from the slums of Bermondsey or Bethnal Green. Little was understood, and therefore less was done to overcome these problems by social reorganization or long-term planning. Nor were young University men likely to be sufficiently ahead of opinion to suggest it. What they saw was the spiritual need. In 1874 W. R. Mowll of Corpus and his friends, stirred by Pearsall Smith's visit and the Broadlands conference, held services for men and women in Barnwell. William Mowll, whether as an undergraduate or later as an Anglican parson, was a highly eccentric figure of far-reaching influence. Son of a Kentish coal-merchant, he had something of the coal-heaver in both build and habits. His strength was inexhaustible and he was a great walker, invariably carrying an iron walking-stick ('I like to sweat more') which it amused him to invite unsuspecting friends to hold. As an undergraduate he once persuaded an engine-driver to let him drive a train from Cambridge to London, after which he walked to his home at Dover. He was said to eat crab every night of his life. His preaching was equally unconventional but extremely effective, never lasting less than an hour, abounding with alliterations—fourteen were counted on one occasion—and lit up with what were sometimes excessively racy stories. He could do what he liked with his audiences. 'Mowll had you laughing at one minute and absolutely struck with fear of Hell the next.' For all his peculiarities he had a devoted following among his fellow-undergraduates, while in the words of his friend Mitchell-Carruthers he 'exercised an extraordinary influence on the rough element of Barnwell' by his mission services.

In the summer of 1875, Moody was expected in Cambridge. As it was term-time the town's one theatre, a somewhat tumble-down building in Barnwell permitted by the Vice-Chancellor to function only in vacations, was closed. A committee of town and gown decided to hire it for the month of May, which for university men in the 'seventies was free from pressure of examinations. These services would break the ground for Moody's visit. Although Moody never came, Mowll's energy ensured that the four weeks were not wasted, for the theatre-mission reached people who had never been seen in any church, but who came again and again to these informal services. The committee therefore decided to continue them, once a week, in a Ragged School nearby in New Street.

The Theatre Royal, once noted for the excellence of its Shakespearian productions, had long fallen from its high estate; as Sir J. J. Thomson remarked of this time, 'some of the interpretations of Shakespeare's meaning would not have met with his approval.' It dragged on for a further three unedifying years until, in July 1878, the owner put it under the hammer. News of the forthcoming auction determined Mowll and his company to buy the place. They at first limited themselves to £1,200, an audacious and unlikely enough figure, but Ion Keith-Falconer, then in his fourth year and reading Semitic Languages persuaded them to increase their bid by a further £450 and set about for promises of money.

The day of the auction arrived. To the intense disappointment of the missioners the bidding rose past their figure by £225, and the theatre became the property of a Mr. Robert Sayle, who had admirable intentions of turning it into a respectable and profitable place of entertainment. Mr. Sayle, a substantial draper, and proprietor of the St. Andrew's Street store which bears his name, was a generous and warm-hearted man. On hearing whom he had balked by his higher bid, he offered at once to let them have it for their original sum, the loss to himself to be announced as his own subscription to the theatre-mission fund. Keith-Falconer immediately closed with the offer, paid over the money from his own account, called in his promised subscriptions, over half of which came from within Cambridge, tapped both his father and his future father-in-law for handsome cheques and gave a large sum himself.

The missioners do not appear to have had vacant possession, for some time later a disgruntled local actor at his benefit night at the theatre was complaining that 'poor players who have tried so long to raise the tone and purify the morals of Barnwell are to be supplanted by a company of religious hypocrites. Acting has not ceased in this place; there will be acting still.' To this Keith-Falconer retorted that 'there *is* going to be some grand acting in which lives will be changed and ennobled.' When the last curtain had fallen at Barnwell, after which Cambridge did without a full-size theatre for eighteen years until the New Theatre was opened in 1896, the mission committee set to, renovating and cleaning, and preparing for the grand reopening on Sunday, 18th November 1878.

The spirit of Keith-Falconer's riposte to the actor was seen in the missioners' preparations. When the undergraduates came up at the beginning of the October term, 'We found posters all over the town announcing that the Theatre Royal, Barnwell, would reopen under entirely new management.' Handbills were passed around in the slums in the shape and form of an ordinary play-bill—'a bait to catch certain fish,' said Mowll. On the opening Sunday night the theatre was well-filled, and again on the Monday, and on the Tuesday the chief inaugural mission meeting took place. Six hundred free teas were provided, after which a further four or five hundred thronged in, not all perhaps aware of what was on the bill. William Mowll was in the chair. Young Frederick Charrington, already a prominent philanthropist, Keith-Falconer and William Hay Aitken, who was up for a University mission, gave addresses, and a Miss Chater sang, 'with much good taste and a clear voice,' as the *Cambridge Express* reported.

All the speakers suited their words to the occasion. Hay Aitken, recalling Moody's use three years before of Her Majesty's opera house, told a delighted audience how a 'yah-yah sort of man' had remarked 'Dear me! What a desecration of a theatre!' He concluded with an impassioned appeal to the people of Barnwell: 'If there is one this night who is looking back upon a misspent life, upon a wife whose heart has been broken, upon half-starved and neglected children and upon a home of destitution and misery, I say to such a one, "Brother, where sin has abounded, there let the grace of God much more abound."' The text he quoted was later painted in large letters round the front of the dress circle, which, as in all theatres of the time was built well forward over the pit, with the higher tiers sheer above it.

Keith-Falconer spoke of the 'marvellous transformation this place has undergone.' 'Our theatrical friends,' he said, 'are familiar with transformation scenes, but they have got a novel one tonight. Who can deny that it has been a transformation from evil to good? . . . It requires no prophetic eye to see the time when men and women, now sunk low in vice and crime, will be constrained by the mighty power of a Saviour's love and the solemnities of a coming Eternity proclaimed from this place, to act the magnificent part of the champions of God and the followers of Christ.' He likened life to a drama—'a play once acted and only once' and concluded by urging his hearers to see to it that the next act was a renewed life, 'and then you will be able to testify that the new act is better than the old; for the old was selfish and brought you misery, but the new act is Christlike and brings joy unspeakable and full of glory.'

Thus the Barnwell Theatre was reopened. By the mid-'eighties it had a secure niche both in the life of Barnwell

and in the affections of successive generations of undergraduates. Some twenty Pembroke men, with their dean,
were working there every Sunday night in Pilkington's
time. A Caius man of the same period, Whitfield Guinness,
described something of the work. 'We go round before
the meeting and invite the people to come in, visiting
many houses and public-houses. Then a few of us give
short addresses in the mission-hall, after which we go on to
the Gas works and speak to the men congregated there.
We do not get back till ten.' A united committee of town
and gown organized the mission with the support of
successive vicars of Barnwell, and the services continued,
Sunday by Sunday, until the Great War. Once a year an
anniversary meeting was held, and W. R. Mowll would
come up to preside, his force and humour unabated, and
the affection of his patrons from the Barnwell streets and
alleys undimmed.[1]

Other enterprises were undertaken during the 'eighties.
Drunkenness was common and it was not possible to walk
about Cambridge streets at night without meeting it
frequently. Temperance meetings were therefore much
to the fore and the blue ribbon, sign of a pledged teetotaller,
widely worn—Victor Buxton on coming down from Trinity
even refused to work in his father's brewery or to draw
money from it; for him as it happened this decision did
not mean financial distress, for his father sympathized and
made him manager of his Essex estates. In 1886, as 'a
thank offering for definite blessing received' at the Alexandra Hall meetings of the C.I.C.C.U., a number of undergraduates founded a Rescue Home where prostitutes of the
town, a perpetual thorn in the side to proctors, could be
cared for, brought to faith in Christ and found honest
employment. Ten years later its name and scope was
altered into a Preventitive Home, but in 1897 it was
reported in financial difficulties and did not, apparently,
survive much longer.

Not far from Cambridge were a number of brickfields,
where Walter Scott, Harry MacInnes and others would go

[1] The building was sold during the Great War, being later reopened as the Festival Theatre.

to give out tracts, and speak as opportunity offered. Response among the hardened men was slow, but one brickworker was so impressed by Harry MacInnes that on hearing of his death from a climbing accident in the Alps in the summer of '84, he gave up drink on the spot, saying 'I should like to be prepared lest I am called away soon.' Another such service was done among the coprolite diggers who at that time worked the fossil-bearing green-sand between Barrington and Haslingfield, south-west of Cambridge, which was sent into Royston to become phosphate of lime for manure. A mission to these men was formed by W. J. Petter, a quiet, reserved Trinity man.

A work of a different kind, highly popular in Long Vacations, was that organized at the seaside by the Children's Special Service Mission.

This mission had been founded in 1867, almost through accident, by Josiah Spiers, who realized not only that well-to-do children often missed the influence of anything deeper than a formal Christianity, but that rightly approached they were particularly accessible on the beaches during summer holidays. This mission was little known at Cambridge until Edwin Arrowsmith, one of the organizers, came up to recruit volunteers in the May term of 1885. Known as 'Papa' or 'Ye Chief' he led a happy party of thirty Oxford and Cambridge men at Llandudno during the following August, the effect of which and of other C.S.S.M.s, was no less marked on the undergraduates than on the children. In the free atmosphere of a seaside holiday, with bathing, games and boating as part of the very work of the mission, men who had never put themselves to deliberate Christian service before could prove its worth. Individualists became team-workers, and confidence was given to shy men, such as Tyndale-Biscoe of Jesus, the diminutive cox of the Cambridge crew, whom Arrowsmith had netted with two of his friends by pointing out the attraction to boys of a Varsity blue's blazer. 'As August drew near; wrote Biscoe, 'my courage began to fail, as I thought of this children's mission and all its publicity. I hoped I should catch scarlet fever and rode a bobbery horse hoping that I might break a leg or something.'

The horse duly threw him. But no damage appeared and he arrived at Llandudno where he thoroughly enjoyed himself.

'What the C.S.S.M. has been to the Christian life of the universities,' wrote one of the Llandudno men thirty years later in 1914, 'it is difficult to measure. Its robust manliness, which showed that the simplest presentation of the Gospel message was compatible with a delight in every form of sport; its absolute allegiance to the Bible as manifested by the Scripture Union, the mainspring of its work, gave it an influence which was most remarkable.' From the seaside missions sprang, in 1892, the Universities Camps for Public School boys, which were held under canvas by the sea or in mountains, with an army officer in command and undergraduates as officers. The boys roughed it, doing their own chores and spending most of the day in games or expeditions. The spiritual work was done by informal prayers and through the friendships which sprang up between officers and boys. A further offshoot was the foundation in December 1886 of *Our Boys' Magazine*, as the result of a talk between Eugene Stock and four undergraduates, afterwards an M.P., a doctor, an archdeacon and a public-school headmaster respectively.[1] Editorship was undertaken by an older man, but the four undergraduates and another, afterwards a missionary bishop but then a freshman,[2] became assistant editors, and were succeeded in their turn by others, until in course of time it came to be run from the London offices of the Scripture Union. The expressed aim of the founders was 'First and foremost, to help boys read their Bible; the Bible ought to be the first book, not only on the shelf but in the heart. To give boys something very interesting to read; and to help boys to all that is good and right.'

[1] Robert Armitage, M.P. for Leeds Central 1906–22; Charles Harford, M.D.; Ernest Sharpe, Archdeacon of London; Archibald Hyslop, Warden of Glenalmond 1902–13.

[2] R. S. Heywood, Bishop of Mombasa 1917–36.

CHAPTER IX

THE EARLY 'NINETIES

AT the end of the eighteen-eighties the C.I.C.C.U. received a new and powerful friend and, shortly afterwards, a new place of meeting.

Henry Montagu Butler, who became Master of Trinity in December 1886, had been C. J. Vaughan's successor as headmaster of Harrow and then for a short year Dean of Gloucester before being appointed by the Crown to Trinity. A brilliant scholar and a great headmaster, and in his youth a great athlete and cricketer, he was a man of stately appearance, slow and dignified in speech, courtly in manner, generous in nature, if sometimes barbed in tongue, who won the affection of all who worked or lived with him. As an undergraduate in the 'fifties, coming from an evangelical home, he had been a teacher at Jesus Lane Sunday School, and as he developed had drawn much of his inspiration from Vaughan. He hated party strife. He refused any ecclesiastical label and his sympathies were always with the persecuted. Thus although he did not approve of the teaching of *Essays and Reviews* he disliked far more the outcry against its authors. His soul recoiled strongly from infidelity, though he sympathized with those who could not bring themselves to believe. At the height of the early controversy on the Bible which followed *Essays and Reviews* he quoted Christ's vindication of the Old Testament passages 'which testify of Me,' and said 'these are expressions to which I cling with my whole heart.' He held to the Virgin Birth and the Resurrection when, in their turn, they were rejected by leading liberal scholars: 'If I did not hold these beliefs in their literal and accepted sense,' he wrote to Hastings Rashdall in 1914, 'I could no longer act as a clergyman,' but he was careful to say also, 'I have no temptation to blame those who explain such phenomena as non-miraculous.' Towards the end of his life he was seen leaving a fellows' meeting at Trinity in tears because of the expressions of unbelief he had heard expressed.

When he came back to Cambridge Montagu Butler was known to the undergraduates principally as a steady supporter of all good causes, and as a deep expositor of the Bible. He was not at one with Handley Moule in all points of doctrine, nor did he emphasize the Atonement ('not from approach to disbelief but from not vitally grasping it'), but his expressed aim was 'to consecrate youthful ambition to the cause of Christ.' When he was appointed to Trinity he wrote in his diary, as among his aims, 'The Chapel should be made a great spiritual power.' He should 'throw himself heartily into all good moral and spiritual causes,' making much of the recently formed Trinity mission in South London, supporting Temperance and Purity societies and missionary enterprises. His first sermon in Chapel, on 5th December 1886, was a clear call to belief in Christ, Who speaks 'as always, not as a disputant but as a King, a King Who has a right to the allegiance of the human heart.' Within a few months of his installation he could write to Westcott: 'On the 20th we have a Bible Reading in the dining-room, where there will probably be some fifty undergraduates', and for a quarter of a century, until old age made him too infirm, he not only held such meetings in the Master's Lodge but was a frequent speaker at Bible Readings arranged by the C.I.C.C.U. And when in Trinity Chapel one May week, he told the story of Bishop Hannington's conversion through a college friend and asked, 'My friends, does not this true story of recent college life hit any of you? . . . Is there anyone whom you have known here of whom you can say with grateful truth, "He brought me to Jesus"?' it was at once a vindication of such endeavours and a spur to fresh effort.

The new place of meeting which the C.I.C.C.U. received was the Henry Martyn Hall. As far back as 1881, during the Martyn centenary, John Barton proposed building in memory of Cambridge's greatest missionary a permanent home for the University Church Missionary Union. The project was shelved. Early in 1886 a street-widening scheme brought into the market the quaint old house inhabited by a Mr. Ingle which stood next to Holy Trinity Church on Market Street and which with its large and famous chestnut tree was doomed to destruction. A fund was therefore started, the site bought and the house pulled down. On 2nd December 1886, on a bitterly cold, snowy day, the foundation stone of the new hall was laid. The following autumn, on Tuesday, 18th October 1887, the Henry Martyn Hall was opened. On the Sunday, Vaughan's University sermon had been suited to the occasion, and on the Monday evening Montagu Butler had preached in Holy Trinity. At the opening, with five heads of houses present, Westcott delivered a speech 'of great force and fervour,' lauding Martyn's character and work and, as a King's man, speaking also of Simeon. The hall was declared open by Perowne, Master of Corpus; Moule led in prayer; and Barton collected £180 towards the considerable sum still needed to defray the cost.

The Church Missionary Union, which shortly would have been homeless (after twenty years Carpenter had given them notice in favour of lodgers), thus came into possession of one of the ugliest buildings in Cambridge. Although honoured and loved for its associations, the mock-Gothic of the Henry Martyn Hall's exterior and the dingy walls and panelling of its interior have perpetuated a particularly unfortunate architectural period, which thought it a 'beautiful fabric.' The property of trustees acting for the Church Missionary Union, the Hall was also to be used, on payment of a low rent, by the Daily Prayer Meeting, the Church Society and other religious bodies of Cambridge. D.P.M. and the C.I.C.C.U. met there thenceforth, presided over by Henry Martyn's whimsical smile and surrounded by the names of a selection of Cambridge missionaries.

During the next years, until the mid-'nineties, the C.I.C.C.U. was reaping the fruits of the remarkable years that had gone before. Interest in matters religious seemed unlimited in the University. 'If you were in Cambridge' wrote a King's man to his mother in 1890, 'you would be quite startled at the host of religious meetings and mission services.' Men would tramp the courts on a Sunday night discussing, for and against, the things they had heard during the day; the attendance at Moule's Sunday evening sermon in Holy Trinity 'seems to increase each term; often there is scarcely standing room,' while at the University sermon the crush was sometimes so great that W. F. Reddaway, the historian, who came up in '91, remembers having at least once 'entered Great St. Mary's backwards and off my feet to the shout of "Scrum up Trinity!"'

The Church Society continued its discussions, but was losing ground. If a man belonged to that alone he was not considered by the C.I.C.C.U. to be sufficiently in earnest. 'We thought he was cold . . . it was the refuge for the man who wanted to be something but not C.I.C.C.U.' For the C.I.C.C.U. was indisputably the dominant feature of active religious life in the early 'nineties. The Alexandra Hall meetings continued, with a Freshmen's Sermon in Holy Trinity arranged in consultation with Moule and the Vicar. The early experiment of personal testimonies had served its purpose and was entirely displaced by invited speakers of maturity and experience. In the course of time most of the prominent evangelists of the day were heard—Sir (Stevenson) Arthur Blackwood; Wilson Carlile and Dr. Barnardo; Lord Radstock, back from his leadership of an outstanding religious revival at the court of the Tsar, Major Owen Hay, the redoubtable E. A. Stuart of Holloway ('an intellectual as well as a spiritual treat to hear him') and younger men such as Taylor Smith, Talbot Rice (a breezy, cross-eyed Welshman), J. E. K. Studd, and Douglas Hooper on furlough from Africa. Two of the most able speakers, William Hay Aitken and Hamer Webb-Peploe often had taken University missions in Great St. Mary's arranged by John Barton. Both were of striking appearance—Hay Aitken with a remarkably long black beard—and were particularly apt in reaching intellectuals. Webb-Peploe, Vicar of the leading evangelical parish of the day, Onslow Square, was noted for his rapid speech and an immense grasp of the Bible. A famous gymnast in his youth, who had even leaped the Trinity steps, he had learned the epistles by heart when kept to his bed for two years by a fall.

Every two years a mission was arranged, and none present could forget the visit of a rather eccentric Irish clergyman, George Grubb, in Lent 1893. 'I came nearer to Christ than ever before' wrote Theodore Woods of Trinity in his diary. 'I and many others got much blessing from these services. . . . Absolute surrender to God's will.' Twenty years later Woods recalled 'the strained faces of row upon row of undergraduates which filled the large Guildhall to its utmost capacity while the preacher with the utmost solemnity, flecked here and there with flashes of Irish humour, discoursed on righteousness, temperance and judgment to come. But most of all I remember a more quiet service in Trinity Church, in which the preacher described his own sensations and experiences when during a visit to the Holy Land he had stood on the "green hill far away without a city wall" and communed in spirit with his Lord and Master there. The result of it all,' continued Woods, 'was the quickening to white heat of a group of men, some of whom had been "keen"—that was the word we always used—before, but to many of whom the mission had been a lift into a new life and the beginning of a new experience.'

The Open-Airs also continued. 'A remarkable service,' wrote a reporter in the *Pall Mall Gazette* of 1st June 1891, unaware that this was their fifth season. 'Upon Clare Hall Piece, just at the back of the College, were gathered a band of undergraduates, drawn from the various colleges in the University, engaged in an evangelistic mission. They were in strict attire with cap and gown. The gathering attracted a good many of the townspeople, who took part in the singing of the hymns with which the addresses were interpersed. . . .' A choir of some thirty or forty would stand round a small harmonium ('all of them fine, athletic manly fellows,' commented the wondering reporter), the President of the C.I.C.C.U. would lead and two or three men would give the addresses—'short and earnest,' as Harry O'Rorke of Trinity assured Victor Buxton in London. Once, in 1894, there was an unfortunate scene, 'peculiary disgraceful ribaldry from gownsmen standing by,' but the very fact of this indignant contemporary expression is proof that interruption was rare.

In the colleges, weekly Bible Readings, organized and impromptu, were a mainstay of life. Trinity, where all freshmen were sent a personal invitation, could always expect good numbers, but some colleges, such as King's, 'noted for having more brain than soul,' were happy if a dozen were there. Deans and chaplains were often present, the Masters of Trinity (Butler), Corpus (Perowne), and Pembroke (Searle), and Ryle, President of Queens', were always ready to come, and even Augustus Austen-Leigh, Provost of King's, led his college group on occasions.

At the centre was prayer, 'the real secret of work up here. . . . Definite prayer for individuals is the way to win them for Christ.' These words of Harry O'Rorke, in a letter giving his brother-in-law, Victor Buxton, a detailed account of Christian work in January 1891, could have been echoed by any of his colleagues. The Morning Watch was carefully observed, and the Daily Prayer Meeting, though having its ups and downs, could generally expect up to fifty men each week-day, despite late work in laboratories and early appointments for 'tubbing' on the river. Both in the Henry Martyn Hall and in the colleges, such meetings for prayer were open to all and were considered an indirect means of evangelism. 'I remember,' writes G. T. Manley of Christ's, 'how one of my friends called to get me along week after week until he wore out my patience and I went.'

The C.I.C.C.U. at this period was led, in Theodore Woods' phrase, by 'men of great force and character and brimming with enthusiasm.' Some rose afterwards to high office: Theodore Woods himself becoming Bishop of Winchester, Rennie MacInnes Bishop in Jerusalem, and L. F. D. Blair Bishop of the Falkland Isles. Others spent lives less celebrated but of equal worth and devotion, abroad or at home. But the most outstanding man of his generation was Douglas Thornton, who came up to Trinity in 1892.

'My grandfather, Spencer Thornton, was traced to have been the means of the conversion of thirty undergraduates when at Cambridge. I went up, knowing that, to do likewise, D. V.' Spencer Thornton, whose influence at Rugby School was so remarkable that Dr. Arnold told the boys 'to thank God for His goodness in having given you such a friend,' was one of the most attractive personalities at Cambridge in Simeon's last years. He died at thirty-six after a ministry in Buckinghamshire as outstanding as it was brief. Forty-two years later the grandson came up, 'the desire for souls' already born in him. During Douglas Thornton's first year he became conscious of incipient capacity to lead men, but it was not until the Keswick Convention during the Long Vacation in 1893, that he became sure of himself. At Keswick 'God showed me that the power of the Holy Ghost was needed in my life. I became conscious of His power, and proved it at Llandudno,' where he worked with the children's mission. 'My second year,' continues Thornton, 'was one of discipline. Loneliness, hard work, constant dealing with souls, and a few deep friendships were found.' But in spite of what he says, he had taken his natural place among his Cambridge generation. He was, as his great friend Woods put it 'the sun that warmed the circle.' His fiery, restless brain continuously sought outlets for the love of God and man which absorbed his whole being, and his organizing genius made a success of everything he did, secular and spiritual. 'When Thornton organized a picnic, it was a picnic such as had never been organized before by mortal man.'

Stories of Thornton abound. How he was missed during an open-air service in a Cambridgeshire village and later found kneeling in prayer with the barmaid in the local pub, how he seized a baby from its mother's arms at a service on Parker's Piece and riveted the attention of the crowd by lifting it high and shouting out the text, 'except ye be converted and become as little children, ye shall in no wise enter the Kingdom of heaven,' how he was quite capable of kneeling in the open street to wrestle in prayer. 'He had,' writes G. T. Manley, slightly older than himself, 'a strength of will and purpose which some took for wilfulness, but which interpreted itself to him as the Divine "I must."' His eccentricities were the outcome of utter devotion and complete disregard of consequences. Thus some members of his circle occasionally found their sun's rays inconveniently hot. This merely spurred Thornton to win them over to his plans, whatever they were. He loved a fight—almost sometimes for its own sake—and cared not at all when things were thrown up at his windows by antagonized members of his college.

Behind it all was a life of severest discipline. 'Thornton would have made a good monk,' was the verdict of another older man, Phil Armitage. An earlier generation had sacrificed comfort for the sake of foreign missions; Thornton pressed self-denial to its limit. He ate starvation lunches, stripped his room bare, the ornaments, pictures and even the sofa being sold and the money sent to the C.M.S. He would not 'hesitate a moment at what seemed a defiance of common sense if he felt the call.' To ensure a prompt obedience to the demands of the Morning Watch, he invented for himself a fool-proof curer of laziness, the fame of which spread wide. It was a Heath Robinson affair. At 6 a.m. the vibration of an alarm clock set fishing tackle in motion. Sheet and blankets, clipped to the line, moved swiftly into the air off the sleeping Thornton. In the long, bitter winter of 1893-4, when Cambridge was the coldest place in England and it was possible for weeks to skate on the Cam from Cambridge to Ely, Thornton's contraption must have been unbeatable. The wonder of beholders, it could be seen strapped to the roof of the cab carrying its inventor to the station at the end of each term, but the idea did not, as far as is known, catch on.

In Douglas Thornton's first term his friends had a glimpse of the urge which was to give him world-wide fame—the conversion of non-Christian races. Within a few weeks of his arrival he had gathered at his rooms (having called on men senior to himself, in defiance of contemporary etiquette) a party of Englishmen and orientals from all colleges, whom, to their astonishment, he then led off on his own version of a Grantchester 'grind,' each white man with a coloured man, 'paired like the young ladies of a school out for an airing.' The urge grew with the years, and it was with foreign missions that Thornton's name was to be imperishably linked.

The C.I.C.C.U. fold was wide. There was as yet no definitive membership, with signature of a card or payment of subscription, and therefore the lines of loyalty were loosely drawn. Not everyone was moulded in the pattern of Thornton and Theodore Woods, with their flaming evangelism and inexhaustible exuberance. Quieter men were no less in earnest. The comment of a King's man, 'Men seem so ready to talk on deepest matters if only one keeps one's mouth shut till they begin,' might have seemed rank heresy to Thornton, but both attitudes had their place. One power, much in the background, was Forbes Robinson of Christ's. Always delicate in health, and shy and retiring in nature, he had five University prizes to his credit. He had come up in 1887, became chaplain of Christ's and remained a fellow until his early death. Though seldom at public meetings, or even at college Bible Readings, he influenced his friends and acquaintance. His desire was to win souls; his stress was on prayer. He once said that in his younger days he had taken every opportunity of making personal appeal to men to come to Christ. 'But as I grew older I became more diffident, and now often when I desire to see the Truth come home to any man, I say to myself: if I have him here he will spend half an hour with me. Instead I will spend that half-hour in prayer for him.'

One approach to a clear view of the Christian Union at this time is through the eyes of freshmen. Some came up from thoroughly Christian homes. One such was W. D. Monro. He had been told by friends to get in touch with Thornton and Woods, and ten days after his arrival in Trinity he met them. They asked him to call on them— they were both on the same staircase in New Court—

whenever he liked, and a few days later he did so, finding Woods with another old Marlburian. Half an hour of music followed, until the third man left, and Thornton arrived. 'At 9.45 the two friends told me that this was for them a regular time of prayer. Would I care to stay? Nothing could have pleased me better.' From then on, he and they, and sometimes others, would meet every day at that time for devotional Bible reading and prayer.

In contrast, C. F. G. Masterman, the future Liberal statesman, coming up from a somewhat rigid home with a hot-house faith and an incipient rebelliousness, refused to join in at all, and would even profess to be an agnostic. Yet when, during one of their arguments together in Christ's, Manley said to him, 'Look here, Masterman, I can't understand why you don't pray: O God, if there be a God, show me the truth,' Masterman replied, 'My dear Manley, I pray that every night of my life.'[1] The 'nineties in England were littered with the discarded faiths of men such as Masterman, Reginald Farrar the novelist, Robert Morant, or Sir Arthur Blackwood's famous son Algernon, all brought up in strongly evangelical homes. Despite failures the Cambridge Christian Union rescued many, giving substance to lip-loyalties and absorbing doubts in satisfying service.

Nor was it concerned only with those who came up with faith, brittle or firm. Manley of Christ's, Senior Wrangler in '93, is an example: 'I entered the University,' he told some students in India a few years later, 'with an idea that evil companions would surround me on every side; a prospect which at that time filled me rather with pleasurable anticipation than alarm. I was disappointed; for in a year, I found myself for the first time believing in Christ as my Saviour.' For Manley the process was slow. He was taken to various activities in his first term, was much impressed with an address from Sir Arthur Blackwood, and in course of time found that most of his friends were in the Christian set. 'I was then only feeling my way to the truth, though I had had a real experience of pardon and

---

[1] Masterman did eventually again make open profession of faith, largely through the influence of Charles Gore at Westminster.

assurance of sin forgiven,' and it was not until his second year that he 'plunged in further still,' as he expressed it, and attended D.P.M. On the other hand, a freshman of King's, taken by a scholar of his college to hear Frank Webster of Birmingham preach on the first Sunday of the October term, 1893, found himself at the end of the service singing with utmost sincerity, 'O Jesus, I have promised to serve Thee to the end.' They went back to talk it over, the freshman was 'most pleased to hear about college Bible readings and prayer meetings,' and the scholar wrote home, 'more than enough was said to show that he was in genuine and living communion with the Great Master.'

Although the Christian Union was at the height of its influence and comparative popularity, there were tensions enough. Once again, as in the 'eighties, neglect of academic work was a temptation. Douglas Thornton and Theodore Woods both got poor degrees; Thornton in after years frankly confessed his belief that 'two or three men have to sacrifice themselves in a generation' for the sake of Christian work, but Woods deeply regretted his failure. This undoubted slackness was not entirely representative. Although Moule found it necessary to utter grave warnings at a Bible Reading in February 1892, and Chavasse of Oxford, in a University sermon the following year, called on young men 'not to neglect university work for too many meetings,' Moule could write by 1895 that the 'tendency among earnest Christian men to discount reading in favour of Christian work' was 'largely ancient history.' High places in the Tripos lists were taken by Christians— Manley, first Smith's Prizeman in '95 as well as Senior Wrangler two years previously; E. T. Whittaker of Trinity, later Astronomer Royal of Ireland, J. A. Wood and Stephenson of Christ's, the latter afterwards headmaster of Felsted; and C. V. Hawkins of King's, 'a little sharp-nosed fellow' with 'an extraordinary sweet nature and a most keen intellect,' who not only was the first freshman to win the Lightfoot Scholarship in Church History but took a First Class in History and a Second in Law the next year, when already ill of the tuberculosis which killed him in August 1894. Hawkins himself, in an article in the *English Churchman* the year before he died, went so far as to claim, with the sweeping assertion of youth, that 'a vast majority of the most brilliant undergraduates are known to be decided and fervent Christians.'

Whittaker of Trinity, writing forty years afterwards and from an opposite view-point to that of his youth, criticized the Christian Union of his day not for lack of intelligence but for 'their tendency to belittle the intellectual element in religion.' In so widespread a union this criticism could find its mark. Yet there were other sides to the picture. A Religious Discussion Society was started at this time by C.I.C.C.U. men, its object to discuss the antagonisms to Christianity and to equip its members to meet them; several groups in the University made thorough studies of missionary problems, while Hawkins and Manley, to take only two, sometimes spent hours together on such subjects as 'the worthlessness of ethics without definite religion, and the problems of heathendom.' There were C.I.C.C.U. men who were as excited as others at the discovery in 1892 in the University Library of the apocryphal Gospel of St. Peter. Charles Hawkins, a great believer in 'the union of spiritual and intellectual in the service of Christ,' throws another light than Whittaker's on the tension between the two: 'For my own part,' he wrote in a letter early in '92, 'my danger is to be lost in books and history, and I often find it necessary to humble myself from the proud thoughts which study and its worship are apt to bring.'

Another prevalent temptation was insularity. It was easy for some to be indifferent to the world outside and dead to much of University life. Such attitude was merely a version of typical undergraduate absorption in one or two special interests—whether the boats, academic work or, in this instance, Christian activity. A further mark of youth was censoriousness—often with a blind spot in the critic to his own failings. 'It is not often that we undergrads, can so easily forget to criticise, and listen with awe,' wrote one of them, after hearing E. A. Stuart's 'sweet, piercing voice, power of language and vivid earnestness of speech.' Christian faith and love might have softened harshness and intolerance more, but the undergraduates of the 'nineties were human, and young.

Where tension was not felt was in matters of Christian doctrine. Although as early as 1889 complaints of destructive higher criticism were voiced at Cambridge, the ordinary undergraduate and divinity student of the early 'nineties, unlike their Oxford brothers, were scarcely affected. Attacks on what was to become known as Modernism were heard from the University pulpit, and even after Westcott's departure for Durham in 1890 the Cambridge School was adverse to extremes of liberalism. Nor were the new anglo-catholics, at Oxford on the increase, much seen at Cambridge, though Swete, Cunningham and Peter Mason were high churchmen of the older way. C. F. Andrews of Pembroke, afterwards 'apostle of reconciliation' in India, a man of unusual religious background and of deep emotions, who had at first been attracted by the 'open, ardent courage, the passionate fervour' of the C.I.C.C.U.'s devotion to Christ, later broke with them and found his way through Basil Westcott to the small group of ardent anglo-catholics around Little St. Mary's. But little conflict, though no sympathy, was apparent between the Protestant and high church parties at Cambridge.

The conflict was with the Agnostics, though even they were more noisy than their strength warranted. At King's and Trinity the high intellects, centering on Bertrand Russell and the Apostles, were convinced beyond all doubt that Christianity was exploded. 'Nobody believed in it really among the young and advanced,' they told Maurice Baring. Less exalted persons also felt, as Masterman expressed it, 'the impossibility of belief. We were faced with ultimate challenges of thought without any outlet in service either for God or man. And in consequence we worried and turned and tortured ourselves over the bare intellectual affirmation, hard duty, defiant pieces of dogmatic assertion as they seemed to us then.' Against this agnosticism, which was not as widespread as Masterman implies, the average undergraduate still being open-minded, the Christian front was firm. No attempt was as yet made to reach a compromise of thought; consequently there was no undue sensitiveness on the part of the C.I.C.C.U. to shades of truth—not through uncertainty or an easy tolerance of conflicting beliefs, but because the essential message was understood and accepted by the preachers and teachers invited, however much their outlook on lesser matters might vary.

Strength meant unity, and a wide circle of older men in the University or from outside could be at home with the Christian Union, as the Christian Union with them. Thus Montagu Butler, Frederick Temple, Handley Moule, Herbert Ryle and F. B. Meyer could each preach happily from the C.I.C.C.U. platform.

CHAPTER X

THE STUDENT VOLUNTEERS

BACK in 1883 a young American at Princeton, Robert Wilder, had formed a small society among his friends, each signing a declaration of purpose: 'We are willing and desirous, God permitting, to become Foreign Missionaries.' They met at Wilder's home, and each day Robert and his sister Grace would pray that a thousand volunteers be found for the foreign field.

Three years later Wilder attended a conference of two hundred and fifty students from the United States and Canada at Mount Hermon School, Massachusetts. The school had been built by D. L. Moody, from the profits of *Sacred Songs and Solos* ('Sankey sang it up,' was Moody's phrase), and Moody presided at the conference. It was an informal affair, with talks, singing and plenty of leisure in the hot July sun. America had been deeply stirred by accounts of the Cambridge Seven the year before, but when the conference of 1886 opened little more than twenty-one of the men were settled in their minds for over-seas service. By the time it was over one hundred had signed a pledge to do so, and what had begun with no further object than, as Moody said, 'to stir you up and get you in love with the Bible' had ended in the rise of the Student Volunteers. 'Quietly, without forcing as I can. see,' reported a journalist, 'the Mission spirit has spread Each man has settled the question "shall I go?" by himself with his Bible and his God.' Robert Wilder was the man chiefly responsible.

Little was heard of this in England, nor of the 'Student Uprising' which followed when Wilder and his friend Forman, fired by the Cambridge Seven's example, toured American universities with such effect that over two thousand men joined the missionary volunteers within a year. Forman visited a few British colleges in 1887; and in 1889 Hudson Taylor's son Howard, studying medicine at London, formed a small Union on Wilder's pattern. This did not spread, and the annual Inter-University Christian Conference, held by Oxford and Cambridge men each March since 1877, remained the only effective link between British students.

In July 1891, Mrs. MacInnes, mother of Harry, so influential at Trinity until his death in the Alps five years before, and of Rennie, then up at Trinity, found that her house-party for the Keswick Convention was one person short. She asked Eugene Stock for a recommendation and was sent Robert Wilder, who had landed in England a few days earlier. The MacInnes family having expected a 'venerable saint with a long white beard' were agreeably surprised to find a young man of twenty-nine, who in the manner of his race immediately asked where he could get a typewriter and a stenographer. Wilder became great friends with Rennie MacInnes, whom he described as 'a student of a most attractive personality.' At Keswick Wilder so impressed the Convention with his brief but vivid account of the Student Volunteers in America that MacInnes and Trevor Horan, President of the C.I.C.C.U., immediately asked him to Cambridge, which was just what he wanted.

It was January before Wilder was able to start touring British universities. He came to Cambridge on 6th February 1892, gave a Bible reading in Corpus on 'the state of the heathen,' spoke at the Sunday evening C.I.C.C.U. meeting and later in the week addressed the Church Missionary Union in the Henry Martyn Hall, with Moule in the chair. He brought with him a packet of the North American Student Volunteer declaration cards, and after the main meeting had closed some dozen men signed them. Even more important were informal talks in MacInnes' rooms in New Court, Trinity, when the possibility of a British version of the American organization was discussed. 'We used to sit round and bombard Wilder with questions as to the way the new movement was to be run,' recalled MacInnes, 'as well as with numberless objections showing him the ways in which it might fail to catch on in England.' But Wilder soon won them round, and left Cambridge well content: 'I found the men there,' was his final verdict, 'more responsive to the appeal than in other British universities.' They had, in fact, immediately formed a Cambridge Student Volunteer Missionary Union.

In the Easter vacation two small conferences were held of men from Oxford, Cambridge, London and the Scottish and Welsh universities, the first in a house in North London and the second in Edinburgh. Howard Taylor's earlier missionary union of 1889 was absorbed, and the Student Volunteer Missionary Union of Great Britain formally inaugurated.

The secretary and organizer of the new Union was Louis Byrde of Corpus. The movement therefore was sure of support at Cambridge, for Byrde was a man of action and prayer, whose whole heart was in the project. Since Wilder's visit sixty-eight Cambridge men had joined the volunteers, fifty-four of whom had signed a letter informing the Church Missionary Society of their hope of service overseas. Byrde's rooms in Corpus also became the national headquarters of the Union. There he wrote and received some two thousand letters—the Corpus college porters must have regretted the loss of their ancient right to a penny a letter delivered—to and from students all over the world. So thorough was he in his methods that some men in Cambridge thought he went too far. Manley, who was later one of the leaders of the movement and a missionary in India, remembers him 'standing with his back to the fire in my rooms and producing every conceivable reason why I should sign the declaration.' Charles Hawkins, whose firm intention was 'to flog new life into the church at home,' wrote on 1st May 1892, 'This movement has gone rather too far; a large number of men have signed a written declaration to go out, several of them when they have mothers and sisters dependent on them. It is very foolhardy . . . Cambridge men are very apt to think of foreign missions so much as to forget what work lies at home at our very doors.' To such criticism the leaders replied that the Declaration was an expression of willingness, not of obstinate determination, and that the executive phrase was, 'God permitting.' Yet their emphasis was on deliberate purpose, and in the summer of '92 the Declaration was shortened and strengthened to 'It is my purpose, if God permit, to become a foreign missionary.'

In July 1893, the first students' conference was held at Keswick in the week following the annual convention, at which a strong party from Cambridge had attended, the larger part remaining for the conference. For some years each successive convention and conference at Keswick marked the stages in the new student movement. In '93 the Inter-University Christian Union was formed, parallel but separate to the Volunteers, though with the same General Secretary. In '94 the name was changed to the British College Christian Union, thus preventing the exclusion of scattered provincial colleges. From this grew the World's Student Christian Federation, discussed at Keswick in '95 and later formed at a conference in Sweden.

It was at Keswick in 1894 that Cambridge gave the student movement one of its foremost leaders. Robert E. Speer, a young American, was giving a powerful address on the Evangelization of the World in this Generation. Douglas Thornton, at the end of his second year at Trinity and already determined on foreign service, sat there dazed. 'Never shall I forget the bewilderment of that night when I first heard that Christians were responsible for the evangelization of the world in this generation.' The call, he felt, was to him personally. His eyes were opened and he was 'to lead the hearts of men.' 'It was an awful time,' runs the entry in his diary. 'B and I had to get away quietly three miles out on the hills from 9–12 p.m. to let God speak to us face to face. But then came the stillness of resting on Him, and casting the world-wide burden on Him.' On the Cumberland hills, where so many men had heard divine calls in the past twenty years, Douglas Thornton saw what had already been seen by Louis Byrde, and by men from the universities of the three kingdoms and the Continent, that the response must be as universal as the need.

The call thus given drew out Thornton's character. There were many who contributed much to the new student movement—Byrde, Manley and L. B. Butcher of Cambridge, Temple Gairdner, Willie Holland and J. H. Oldham of Oxford, Harry Duncan and Rutter Williamson of Edinburgh, W. R. Miller of London—but Thornton's volcanic energy, his breadth and depth of vision, together with an almost ruthless determination and streaks of harshness and impatience, made him the most formidable protagonist the Volunteers ever had.

Theodore Woods was now President of the C.I.C.C.U., and back at Cambridge in the new academic year Thornton and Woods (Dogger and Togger to their friends) pressed the Volunteer cause to the uttermost and once more there were protests that the movement went too far. Senior men, wary of the romance of missions, doubted the ability of immature undergraduates to choose aright. Some of the younger men objected to the aggressiveness of the Volunteers, their pestering of the less missionary-minded, their extremes of self-denial which led them, half-seriously and half in fun, to put in the missionary box the exact number of pennies spent on each sweet cake eaten. Woods' tact and level-headedness and the charm of his nature kept the balance. Thornton ('the only absorbing passion to press on') prayed and fought. 'Had we not learned to pray,' he wrote, 'the battle had been lost.'

The same year Cambridge had seen something for the first time of John R. Mott, who since Wilder's departure for the mission field had been foremost in the American volunteer movement and was to have more influence than any other man of his generation on students throughout the world.

Mott, tall, strong, square-faced with a penetrating eye, was a contrast to the fragile, gentle Wilder. Wilder had been bred from birth to a missionary ideal, Mott had left his school early, finding it too religious, and had gone to study law at Cornell University 'with a money-making motive,' only to have the course of his life changed by a talk from Kynaston Studd, whom Moody had invited over in 1885. Wilder inspired more love than Mott, but lacked his intellectual brilliance and qualities of statemanship. Both were men of profound faith and singleness of mind, but worked in different ways. As a mutual friend put it, 'Wilder was a delicate tool, Mott was a sledge-hammer.'

John R. Mott's first visit to Cambridge was as a learner. Theodore Woods has described his surprise when Mott walked into his rooms at Trinity, asked if he was President of the C.I.C.C.U. and sat down at the table, a man of thirty facing a boy of twenty, and said he had come to gain all the information he could of their ways of doing things at Cambridge. 'Note-book in hand, he proceeded to submit me to one of the severest cross-examinations that has ever been my lot to undergo. Might he come to our meetings and see what went on? Of course he might.' For several night, therefore, at Bible readings or prayer meetings in various colleges, 'this unknown American would steal in and take up his position in the corner, saying nothing, but noticing everything, and slipping away as unceremoniously as he had come.' During his visit Mott also learned, in a talk with Moule, the Cambridge secret of the Morning Watch, and thenceforth used the morning for the time of prayer which had previously competed at midday with interruptions or with wandering thoughts at night. At the end of his stay Mott described to a meeting which Thornton arranged the progress of the American Volunteers.

On New Year's Day, 1896, the early student movement reached a climax. Nearly a thousand men and women, the large majority students, with twenty nations represented among the seventy-seven from overseas, met at Liverpool for a five days' missionary conference. Preparations had continued for over a year, and the energy of Thornton, Woods, Manley and L. B. Butcher of Sidney Sussex brought ninety-nine Cambridge men. 'I can see now Woods and Thornton, in their B.A. gowns, standing somewhere in the Backs on a Sunday evening,' wrote G. H. Moule of Clare over fifty years later, 'and accosting me as a freshman and asking me to come to Liverpool. I refused on the score of expense. Their reply was that my ticket was taken and paid for, and lodgings booked.' Twelve women also came, eight from Newnham and four from Girton.[1] Among the senior members of the University were the Deans of Christ's (T. C. Fitzpatrick) and Emmanuel (J. O. F. Murray) and J. H. Moulton of King's. The aim was to inspire students with fresh fervour for the missionary cause, to link intending recruits with the societies and to catch the attention of the churches. J. C. Ryle, Bishop of Liverpool, gave the opening address: 'If you go forth in the name of the Lord Jesus, armed with the Word of God and holding the truth of the everlasting gospel, lifting up the Cross and saying to all to whom you go, "Behold the Lamb of God which taketh the sin of the world," I cannot doubt that the good seed will bear abundant fruit, although you may not live to see it.' In that spirit of consecration the conference proceeded, without extremes of emotion and with clear sense of aim. C. T. Studd and George Pilkington were among those who brought reports from the Field, and Theodore Woods was master of the music. 'I can never forget,' said Philip Armitage, 'the way Woods made the whole hall of us sing "At the Name of Jesus, every knee shall bow."'

From the Liverpool Conference came the next development. In the small hours of one morning that week, after a long session in a room at the Mitre Hotel, the executive of nine men and three women had decided 'in humble dependence on God's power' to adopt the watchword—'The Evangelization of the World in this Generation.'

This Watchword had its origin in an expression used nearly twenty years earlier by Robert Wilder's father, and had been adopted in 1884 by the Volunteers in America, becoming, in Wilder's view, undoubtedly one of the principal causes which brought so many to join. To its

[1] The composition of the party, which throws some light on comparative college strengths at the time, was as follows: Trinity 18; Corpus, 16; Christ's, 10; Emmanuel, Pembroke, 9; St. John's, Selwyn, 7; Clare, St. Catharine's, Sidney Sussex, 4; Caius, 3; Magdalene, Peterhouse, Queens', 2; Jesus, Trinity Hall, 1; Newnham, 8 and Girton, 4.

originators, and to those who adopted it at Liverpool, the Evangelization of the World in this Generation represented not an ideal but a programme. In 1885 a convention of ministers and laymen at Moody's New England home had outlined possibilities and opportunities in an open letter to the churches: 'The whole world is accessible. . . . If but ten million out of the four hundred millions of nominal Christians would undertake such systematic labour as that each one of that number should in the course of the next fifteen years reach one hundred souls with the Gospel message, the whole present population of the globe would have heard the glad tidings by 1900.' The barriers had fallen, they pointed out, and there was scarcely a region in the world that could not be reached by determined men; 'the last of the hermit nations welcomes the missionary.' In 1896 the Liverpool Conference adopted the Watchword as their own 'because they believe that He Who said "preach the Gospel to every creature" wishes His followers in every age to do it.'

Neither the originators of the Watchword nor those who adopted it at Liverpool expected every human being 'in this generation' to become Christian. They did not advocate a hurried or superficial presentation, nor deprecate the value of educational missions, and they denied strenuously the worth of mere Christianization. 'What is meant,' explains Wilder, 'is simply this: the presenting of the Gospel in such a manner to every soul in this world that responsibility for what is done with it shall no longer rest upon the Christian church, or any individual Christian, but shall rest on each man's head for himself.' 'Is it possible in this generation?' asked Manley in the *Student Volunteer* in 1897. 'Most distinctly we answer, Yes.' He estimated that thirty-three thousand Westerners volunteering in the coming five years would be sufficient to lead the Native Churches to the evangelization of their lands. Britain's share would be one in a hundred of all regular Communicants, and the cost per annum one-fourteenth of what Christian England paid for alcohol.

By 'this generation' the early volunteers meant their own lifetime. Their vision stretched into the future as far, approximately, as the early nineteen-fifties, when as old men they would be able to look around on a world open in every corner to the gospel, with a flourishing church in each country and province bringing, as Mott put it, 'the knowledge of Christ within the reach of all men that they may have an adequate opportunity of accepting Him as Saviour and Lord.' It seemed, at this time of the Diamond Jubilee, in a world of peace and plenty, when in Europe no Englishman even needed a passport except for Spain and Russia, and more distant quarters were coming nearer each year, that it was only a matter of consecrated effort.[1]

To this effort they set themselves. The response of Liverpool was not enough. It would take more than students to evangelize the world. And an opportunity for launching their programe on the widest scale seemed about to present itself.

In July 1897, the Bishops of the whole Anglican Communion would be meeting for the Fourth Lambeth Conference. The Liverpool report, *Make Jesus King*, with its emphasis on the Watchword had roused considerable interest. Furthermore, the new Archbishop, Frederick Temple, was known as a warm friend to Missions and to the Student Volunteers, of whom most high ecclesiastics were suspicious. Temple, a broad churchman, but unfriendly to the new Modernism, on several occasions came at the invitation of the Cambridge Volunteers to give strong appeals for foreign service, and Manley recalls Temple and Montagu Butler kneeling with him on the dusty floor of the room under the stage at the Guildhall before entering a great missionary meeting, Temple having responded to Manley's timorous invitation to lead in prayer with an emphatic 'Certainly!' The Student Movement, though

[1] cf. Archbishop Temple's speech to the S.V.M.U. conference 1900. 'It seems now as if . . . the young men who are now joining this new union . . . shall before they die be able to say, 'The whole race of mankind is not yet Christian, but nevertheless there is no nation upon earth where the faith is not taught if men will accept it. There is no place upon the whole surface of the globe where men may not hear the message of God and the story of the Cross if only they are willing to listen. It is brought home to them everywhere at their very doors.' (Quoted Wilder, *The Great Commission*, p. 86.)

with considerable hesitation, decided in December 1896 to approach the Archbishop and request that their Watchword be adopted as the official missionary policy of the Lambeth Conference.

The method of approach which they chose was that of a Memorial 'to the Church of Christ in Britain,' to be drawn up and presented to the Archbishop, and to leaders of the Free Churches. The Memorial, some twelve hundred works, was sketched out by O'Neill of Belfast, and drafted by him, Rutter Williamson, Douglas Thornton and G. T. Manley, in Manley's rooms at Christ's. After four hours, Thornton had to return to Ridley to be in by midnight, but the others worked at it till four in the morning.

A few weeks later Thornton, aglow with his plans 'to capture the Church,' went with Manley to be received by the Archbishop at Lambeth. Temple read the Memorial through and promised to put it before the bishops. 'Will you adopt the Watchword?' asked Manley and Thornton. 'I've been trying to do it for years,' replied Temple; 'the bishops are hard to move. They will say it's impossible. Most of them after all are over fifty and haven't a generation to live!' 'If everyone thought and felt as we do, would they not do it?' he was asked. 'Yes, they would. You may be able to rouse the Church but . . . I can't.'

'What a confession!' was Thornton's verdict, 'and what an inspiration! And now to prayer,' During April and May missionary societies and committees of different denominations gave favourable notice to the Memorial, and Thornton wrote, 'We shall try see the whole Church moved to a great advance. We must expect this.' But when the Lambeth Conference came, their disappointment was extreme. 'They patted us on the back,' as the Volunteers expressed it, but they did not accept the Evangelization of the World in this Generation as a practical programme. 'We are beginning, though only beginning, to see what the Lord would have us to do. He is opening the whole world to our easy access, and as He opens the way He is opening our eyes to see it.' Thus ran the Lambeth encyclical letter. The Foreign Missions committee mentioned the Volunteers and their Watchword, but limited themselves to a fatherly hope that such zeal would find outlets 'in earnest, sound, wise work,' and to the lame comment that 'the time seems ripe for a forward movement.' Nothing specific concerning the Watchword was found among the sixty-three formal Resolutions of the Conference.

The Watchword continued to be urged and expounded by the Student Movement after 1897 but with slackening emphasis and with decreasing expectancy.

Douglas Thornton, meanwhile, as Educational Secretary of the Volunteer Union, began to work another tack. The rebuff from Lambeth opened his eyes to the extent of the prevalent ignorance of missionary facts. He believed, and Temple Gairdner with him, that the Watchword would not be adopted unless 'floods of light' were thrown on the subject. He seized on the Cambridge idea of missionary study circles, prepared an ambitious scheme for their use by Christian Unions and in support of it amassed in a short space of time a vast knowledge of African problems for a text-book he thereupon wrote.

At this time also the question of reorganization arose. The Student Movement had begun with the sole purpose of raising forces for the Mission Field. Since men and women without faith, or depth of spiritual life, were useless, the promotion and strengthening of Christian Unions became a part of the programme. By 1897 both the British College Christian Union and the World's Student Christian Federation, for which John R. Mott had undertaken his first world tour, had developed widely, while a less successful approach had been made to another likely recruiting ground, the theological colleges of all denominations. Tissington Tatlow, a Dublin man who had discarded engineering ambitions to become Travelling Secretary for the Volunteer Union, suggested the amalgamation of the two parallel British unions. He was backed by John R. Mott and strongly supported by Thornton and Gairdner on the Executive Committee. Manley, though not against reorganization, was wary of the new constitution which Tatlow proposed. Three departments were to be created, one for the theological colleges, another for the Volunteers, and the third to carry on the work of the British Colleges Christian Union, the title of which was to be assumed for the whole movement. Manley feared that it would shift the emphasis from missionary recruiting. He believed that this should be the primary, as it had been the original, object of the Student Volunteer movement, and that a constant drive for volunteers would ensure the growth and health of the Christian unions. If the unions became the first interest, the Volunteer movement would lose its impetus, and might even change its character.

Thornton, too utterly absorbed in the cause of world evangelization even to contemplate such dangers as Manley saw, was determined on better, smoother organization, and nothing should brook it. The question was long debated in committee but in 1898 the two student unions formally became a united movement.

Some months later Manley, anxious to make way for a younger man, and to devote himself to his work as fellow of Christ's before leaving for India, gave up his place on the committee. In the autumn of '98 after another effort, of limited success but with far-reaching effect, to unite the theological colleges behind the S.V.M.U., Douglas Thornton left for his seven brief, intensive years in Egypt,[1] where he was joined in 1899 by Gairdner. With the departure of these three, the first phase of the Student Movement was over.

[1] He died at Cairo in 1905.

CHAPTER XI

FIN DE SIÊCLE

AT Cambridge, meanwhile, there was a hardening of the arteries.

This process was scarcely perceptible at the time. Nor at first did it seem likely. The religious life of the nation was slackening. Ecclesiastical politics were increasingly bitter, and routine complaints in church newspapers of the decline of religion among the young were finding more substance in facts, but at Cambridge the Inter-Collegiate Christian Union was at the height of popularity. The Church Society petered out, University sermons were more sparsely attended by undergraduates, yet the average attendance at the C.I.C.C.U. meetings was reported in 1896 as 'nearly twice as good as the year before.' Eighteen months later in December 1897, a similar comment was heard, the 'excellent attendance and high tone at the Inter-Collegiate Christian Union meetings' being pronounced in the *Record* the most satisfactory feature of the Michaelmas term.

The clearest evidence of this popularity was provided in 1895 by the episode of Anthony Deane.

A. C. Deane, afterwards Canon of Windsor and a gifted writer, had gone down from Pembroke in 1893 after taking a Third Class in law. He had come to some note as an amateur actor and as a writer in the undergraduate magazine *Granta*, and, as he later admitted, had found his friends from a set which took agnosticism as 'almost the necessary accompaniment of intellectualism.' He had been once 'cajoled' into attending a prayer meeting and resolved never to go to another. His closest friend, probably C. F. Andrews, had linked him to the little St. Mary's coterie, fervent anglo-catholics, but when he went down he was still not quite decided in his mind. Shortly afterwards he proceeded to Cuddesdon and was ordained.

In the *Nineteenth Century* for October 1895 Deane wrote an article on Christianity in Cambridge, a long, prosy and self-conscious condemnation of University life. Religion was at the lowest ebb. Compulsory chapel trained men 'to look upon the worship of God as an obnoxious duty or as a relic of schoolboy discipline,' and the picture he painted of lounging undergraduates, irreverent dons and impossibly intellectual preachers might have come straight from Gunning's *Reminiscences*. Most of the younger dons were not merely agnostic but took a 'misguided delight in disturbing and unsettling the faith of others.' Undergraduate religion was no better. 'A few misguided enthusiasts of the evangelical type' preached in the open air, but that was the best that could be said.

His attack provoked immediate outcry. The *Cambridge Review* printed a long answer castigating Deane. While admitting grains of truth in some of his remarks, the *Review* suggested that it was 'really preposterous for any member of the University with such limited experience to pretend to a knowledge of the undergraduates as a whole,' and concluded not that Cambridge was decadent but that 'Mr. Deane has been singularly unfortunate in the choice of his university friends.' A reply to Deane was printed in the next number of the *Nineteenth Century*, the *Granta* made fun of him and the Cambridge correspondent of the *Record* hastened to reassure his readers.

The strongest criticism of all was reserved for Deane's strictures on the few misguided enthusiasts of the evangelical type. The *Cambridge Review* suggested that 'few who have seen the enthusiastic meetings of the Inter-Collegiate Christian Union and know anything of the strength of the Missionary Unions' could doubt how wide of the mark was Deane's disparagement. Armitage Robinson, the Lady Margaret's Professor, in a University sermon on the 3rd November, claimed that he was happy to have been one of Deane's misguided enthusiasts in his youth, while the *Granta*, in a leading article on 'The Deane of Cambridge' said 'there is one thing for which we can never forgive the Deane. I mean the slighting way he alludes to the "Evangelical type."' The *Granta* continued to scoff and tilt at him—'a vain and foolish youth. . . . *The Granta* at least hopes to hear no more of him for a very long time'—and together with a humourless rejoinder from Deane himself, printed a string of letters. One of the last of these, signed 'Fresher,' made a fitting epilogue to the controversy. 'I think I can safely say,' wrote 'Fresher' in his schoolboy language, 'that in all the five years I was at my public school I never heard so much religious talk and met so many religious fellows as I have done in my five weeks here.'

Not only was the C.I.C.C.U. popular. It had sought to strengthen its hand by reorganization. Since its foundation the Inter-Collegiate Christian Union had not been a union in the normal sense. It was still a committee, composed of representatives from the colleges, each appointed by his predecessor, and directed by the small executive chosen equally informally from among its number. There was thus no membership of the union as such, except for members of the committee; if in the 'eighties a man called himself a member of anything it was of the Daily Prayer Meeting. In 1877 the initiative had lain with the D.P.M. committee and the college unions, whose humble servant the new-born Inter-Collegiate Union was happy to be, but in course of time the missions which the Union arranged, the Alexandra Hall meetings and the annual Inter-Varsity Conference which it organized, had shifted the leadership from the college representatives to the President and his executive. The term 'C.I.C.C.U. men' had come into common parlance, to denote those whose loyalties centred round the Henry Martyn Hall. The Daily Prayer Meeting and the Inter-Collegiate Union had reversed positions in the consciousness of those to whom both were important. But still there was no ordinary membership of the Union.

Suggestions for constitutional reform were first voiced early in 1891. The Union was criticized as 'a head without a body,' and some members—a term already used—wished to see it properly organized, its committee absorbing that of the D.P.M. and co-ordinating the various activities of Christian undergraduates. Such a proposal was not unopposed. Those who recalled that the C.I.C.C.U. at first was merely a committee were not certain whether this plan to make it a society was 'practical or judicious . . . It seems rather to attach a kind of work to the C.I.C.C.U. which that body was not originally intended to fulfil.' A further danger lay in the power which would be given to 'a body of men whose existence might not be found so helpful as it is at present anticipated would be the case.' The discussions of 1891 were inconclusive and the matter dropped. A year later, with the rise of the Student Volunteers, came the idea of a card membership involving a signed declaration. In 1893 the formation of the Inter-University Christian Union, constitution and all, seemed to encourage reorganization on similar lines at Cambridge. During the academic year of 1894–95, Theodore Woods being President, proposals for change were again debated, and were adopted.

An executive, as before, of President, Vice-President, Secretary and Treasurer was to be responsible to the general committee of college representatives. Henceforth, undergraduates and graduates could be enrolled, each signing a declaration, 'In joining this Union I declare my faith in Jesus Christ as my Saviour, my Lord and my God.' Members were asked 'To spend a definite portion of each day in Bible reading and Private Prayer, specially remembering the members and objects of the Union.' They were to attend, when possible, one of the two Daily Prayer Meetings 'to unite in prayer with members from other colleges,' these meetings each lasting twenty minutes and beginning at five past one and five past two. Thirdly, they should also try to attend the Sunday Bible Reading of half an hour; and were asked when they could to contribute to expenses.

The object of the Union was, 'To unite men whose definite aim in University life is to extend Christ's Kingdom, whether in seeking the conversion or spiritual help of men around them, or in promoting work for Home or Foreign Missions, or the like.' This statement was printed on a small coloured card, together with the names of the committee, the obligations of membership, and a list of specially commended 'meetings or branches of work'—the Alexandra Hall, ('members are asked to invite other men and to make it known in their colleges') Sunday School, Open Air and Mission Hall activities; the Inter-University conference, the Children's Special Service Mission and the schoolboys' camps; the Church Missionary Union, the Student Volunteers, and the Missionary Bands. Slipped in at the end of this annual manifesto was a promise that speakers' lists for the Alexandra Hall would be distributed separately each term (on a coloured flimsy tastefully printed in at least ten different types) and a tart reminder to members that 'the Union consists first and foremost for Christian work amongst University men.'[1]

The new constitution worked well, and about a year later 'a stronger consciousness of fellowship and co-opera-tion' was reported. Two hundred and fifty members had enrolled, and a number more were in alliance though not taking out cards of membership.

In the same year the C.I.C.C.U. received further strength in the creation by its senior friends of the Cambridge Pastorate. At Oxford in 1893 F. J. Chavasse, Principal of Wycliffe and his friends had conceived the novel scheme of a Pastorate—two clergymen 'whose single aim shall be to take up the spiritual side of the ideal tutor's work, and by frequent and affectionate intercourse to seek to win to Christ, or to build up in Him, the large number of Univer-sity men, who . . . are more than ready to welcome their help.' They were to be accessible at all times and given to hospitality, a combination which prompted *Punch* to inquire, under a picture of a parson in academic dress, rather tipsy but affectionate, with a bottle and a Bible beside him, how this accessibility could be combined 'with perpetual festivities.' When the two pastors began work they proved staunch allies and wise counsellors to the strug-gling and rather friendless O.I.C.C.U. which the Cam-bridge men regarded 'as a very tender plant.' The Pastorate idea seemed to invite imitation, and in 1895

[1] A C.I.C.C.U. card for the first year fortunately survives.

Handley Moule wrote to Phil Armitage, a tall and athletic Trinity and Ridley man, inviting him to become ordained as first Cambridge pastor. Moule gave him a nominal stipend of £25 and he was given an equally nominal title at Holy Trinity, but in fact was self-supporting and his own master. Three years later a Pastorate council was formed, the Principal of Ridley and the Vicar of Holy Trinity being members, and at the first council meeting, on 23rd May 1898, Armitage was formally reappointed, and with him as second pastor A. G. Dodderidge, very recently ordained but an older man, who had not come to the University until he was thirty.

Armitage and Dodderidge were a contrasting pair, differing in background, wealth and temperament and tending to work independently. They made much use of games, Armitage making friends with freshmen through racquets, squash, tennis and fives, and Dodderidge (universally known as 'Doddie') forming a hockey team, the Dodos, strong enough to take on college first elevens. Armitage soon found parents writing to commit to him the spiritual oversight of their offspring, often with an awkward plea that he should not reveal they had written, and he gathered about him what he called his Cave of Adullam, where, to quote the spiced comment of one of the more serious, 'he strove to bring Christian influences to bear on rather headstrong and flighty young men from evangelical homes.'

The principal work of these chaplains to the Pastorate was among Christians, helping them in difficulties, teaching, encouraging and restraining. They reached also beyond the Christian circle. Armitage's first convert, as it happened, resulted from the introduction of the first motor-car to Cambridge. For when in December '95 C. S. Rolls, an undergraduate of Trinity, became the fourth man in England to own a motor, he sold his tricycle to Armitage. They became close friends. During a Student Volunteer mission in February 1896 led by the American A. T. Pierson and by C. T. Studd, Rolls told Armitage that he had become a Christian. Motor-cars remained his first passion. His Christianity in course of time became lukewarm, and when the joint founder of Rolls-Royce, already famous for making the first non-stop double air crossing of the Channel, became in July 1910 the first Englishman to be killed flying, few were aware of his once-active faith.

On the surface the late 'nineties seemed halcyon. If the magnificent aggressiveness of former years appeared to have slackened, it was felt to denote a deepening and building-up of faith. Others would deny the slackening. The C.I.C.C.U. meetings continued, moving from Alexandra Hall to the Assembly Rooms in the Market Place, and sometimes to the Guildhall or Holy Trinity. The Open-Air services on the Backs were less favoured. In 1896 only four were held, the meetings on the other Sundays being arranged in the Church. In March 1901 the committee discussed their abandonment, but Edward Woods, Theodore's younger brother, afterwards Bishop of Lichfield supported them strongly, with others, and they were saved by twenty-one votes to six. Missions were held frequently, and John R. Mott began his series with a week in 1896 and another in '98. The latter was especially notable. Mott was tireless in the interminable round of personal interviews, 'among the most varied and absorbing in all my experience.' His frank speaking on sexual matters and on the dangers of self-abuse caused much stir, while thirty-five senior members were invited to Queens' by the President, Ryle, to hear Mott, and the two hours' meeting led to the formation of a dons' Christian Union, the subsequent history of which is obscure. Mott's visit was voted a success, and he himself could report 'I have reason to believe that many undergraduates were led to accept Christ as their personal Saviour.'

Cambridge men were equally active. 'We felt we were not doing our job unless we were hauling the ungodly along to our Sunday meeting,' writes Edward Woods, 'and then, by long personal talks, endeavouring, under God, to get them converted. I find constant references in my diary to going round, especially on a Friday and Saturday, trying to scoop up undergraduates for the Sunday.' There were notable personalities in the Christian Union: Edward Woods himself, W. G. Hardie, afterwards Archbishop of the West Indies; Charles Werner, a brilliant scholar of King's—later a master at Harrow and killed in the Great War; Henry Hodgkin and Joseph Barcroft—both Quakers, the former afterwards one of the most eminent of pacifists and the latter outstanding as a scientist; Tom Inskip of King's the future Lord Chancellor, and John Stuart Holden, small, dapper and a born orator.

For all these names and activities, it was at root a period of decline. One trouble was the steadily increasing challenge of liberal protestantism. Direct agnostic attack was still little known. Among Cambridge teachers who believed personally that science had destroyed the reasonableness of Christianity, a 'conspiracy of silence,' as it was later called, had grown up. A further strong bulwark was the undoubted faith of most of the scientific professors. Four were actively engaged in spare-time Christian work and three others were seen to preside at distinctively Christian meetings, and G. T. Manley once harnessed the Professors of Anatomy, Chemistry, Engineering, Mathematics and Medicine[1] to take the chair at a week of Christian Evidence meetings. He would meet each of them, as he told his Indian students a few years later, before going on to the platform. 'As we bowed our heads in prayer for the success of the meeting, I shall not easily forget my feelings as I listened to the simple prayers of these men, the fame of whose researches resounds through the civilized world.'

These men were of the older generation, and were no longer sure prophets to the young. Moreover many difficulties were not the product of scientists or other laymen, but of theologians. Cambridge had known varieties of theological teaching and had given birth to much of the best constructive criticism, but nothing had effectively disturbed faith in the reliability of Scripture or the Divinity of Christ. To the Christian undergraduate of the earlier 'nineties, with his vivid inner assurance of faith, such

---

[1] Alexander Macalister, a Presbyterian; George Liveing, (Sir) Alfred Ewing, Sir George Stokes, Sir George Humphry. (Sir) Michael Foster, Professor of Physiology, who was a Baptist, was prevented by illness from taking part.

higher criticism as there was, when he was aware of it, seemed to carry no menace. Ryle, a leader of the moderate higher critics, was welcomed by the C.I.C.C.U. as a speaker, for he preached a clear evangelistic message. Bethune-Baker, five years Ryle's junior and more extreme in his views, earned their tolerant amusement. Whilst emphasis remained on evangelism, and growth of mind was set in the context of continuing spiritual experience, the young Cambridge man was not often conscious of conflict. In the early days of the Christian Union it was rare for men to take an intellectual path such as Armitage Robinson's, steadily more divergent from that of his early views and friends. But as the decade unfolded fledgling theologians increasingly found the latest books and up-to-date thought demanding that they throw all their ideas into the crucible.

In their perplexity they turned to the men they most trusted, and were often left unsatisfied. The chaplains to the pastorate were true fathers-in-God, yet not over well-equipped to clarify intellectual difficulties. Handley Moule, with his majestic powers of scholarship, though he helped many, seemed too wrapped in saintliness to give always adequate answer to honest doubts. Infidelity of any sort repelled him. He had sufficient certainty for himself, which no fluctuating verdict of science or scholarship could assail, for it was founded on Christ's own recognition of the Scriptures as 'the decisive utterance of God, even in their minor features of expression,' but he was not always able to convey this assurance to pupils or questioners. C.I.C.C.U. men began to find men a few years senior to themselves—Theodore Woods, or Edmund Whittaker, though not Douglas Thornton—feeling their way towards views which, in so far as they had given them thought, they had decisively rejected at Cambridge, and coming to regard their C.I.C.C.U. affiliations with detached forbearance.

Inevitably this unsettling atmosphere had its effect, though men were scarcely conscious of it. There was as yet no discord around doctrine. Shades of opinion found their common ground in the unhesitant aim of evangelism—'bringing rebels to the feet of a crucified Saviour,' as one speaker put it. But beneath the bold exterior were symptoms of defensiveness—less willingness among some to increase in knowledge, for growth seemed a road to disaster; a tendency to rely on jargon and pet phrases without that inner certainty of their meaning which had made them fresh and real in the days of Moody; a shallow attitude towards foreign missions, with the Volunteer card signed as proof of keenness, thus making a hasty promise too often unfulfilled; a stridency which, if it did not quite echo the O.I.C.C.U.'s shouts of 'Hallelujah!' and their banner-marches down the High, tended almost to make an obsession of bearing witness to Christian joy and separation from the world. The salutary discipline of speaking in the Open Air when a rowing friend, amused or sardonic, might saunter up to the crowd, could and did achieve much. Equally valuable might be such adventures as that of 29th October 1899, when a party of undergraduates was invited to the Salvation Army Citadel, and sat on the platform, the Army band behind nearly blowing them off it, and then took over the service. 'There were about four hundred present,' wrote Edward Woods in his diary, 'we all gave our testimonies . . . There was an after-meeting with several coming up to the penitent form . . .' But sometimes these things were done with an eye to reputation, or in a scarce-confessed belief that such overt acts of witness were the only means where by faith could be declared.

University men at the turn of the century tended to be flamboyant and rowdy. Cambridge, always slow to respond to contemporary moods, was flooded by the back-wash of hedonism, 'decadence' and the *Yellow Book* school. Christians were not untouched. The line between church and world in a University is drawn close, and as the Varsity world grew more raucous, so in its own way did the Christian Union. Personal habits indicate spiritual state, but values change with the years; thus problems of right conduct were thorny, the balance between individual freedom and collective pressure could sometimes work uneven, and genuine consecration be threatened by the imposition of rules. Blood ran high once when the right of a man to smoke was debated, if he claimed to be a Christian. Since in the 'nineties undergraduates who did not smoke stood out as oddities, opinion sharply divided. Somewhat later the same problem perplexed Eustace Maxwell, a young Pembroke man of marked beauty of character, killed in a railway accident after only one term. As a schoolboy he had longed to smoke, but had come to believe it was an indulgence he should deny himself. On coming up, he heard the suggestion that not to smoke would weaken his influence over others. He consulted an older man of another college, who pointed out that 'separation to Christ comes before sympathy with the world; surely it will not be you and your pipe but Christ in you Who will enable you to point others to Him,' and left him to decide as he would. Unworldliness sometimes earned respect, sometimes displeasure, but Douglas Thornton has the last word: 'I pray God,' he wrote from Egypt, 'to keep alive a band of puritans, for they are the ones that make the best missionaries the world over.'

At the turn of the century the Christian Union suffered a grievous loss. Handley Moule who two years earlier, on election to the Norrisian Professorship, had left Ridley for the Divinity School, was in Switzerland in August 1901 for a two months' holiday. He came back to his hotel at half-past eight on the evening of Tuesday, 14th August, to find a letter awaiting him and in it, as he wrote in his diary 'the solemn surprise' of Lord Salisbury's offer of the bishopric of Durham. Three days later he wrote accepting. He was consecrated bishop on the 18th October and enthroned in Durham Cathedral on All Saints' day. On the previous Sunday he had preached in Cambridge, his first sermon as bishop, and Edward Woods wrote in his diary: 'I went to the C.I.C.C.U. 8.30 service in Holy Trinity. Church packed. Handley's first utterance as Bishop an absolutely simple and personal testimony to Jesus Christ. Praise God for such a man.'

It is fascinating, though profitless to speculate whether Moule should not have refused Durham as he had once refused the bishopric of Sydney. His record as a bishop was not all that his friends desired, and had he remained in Cambridge until his death in 1920 it is possible that the troubles of the intervening years might have found happier solution.

The gap left by Moule was never quite filled. His departure seemed to reveal the weakness which lay beneath the bold exterior of the Christian Union. Yet though attendance at sermons in Holy Trinity was slackening so that when the gallery was used it was worthy of note, though the Daily Prayer Meeting was weak and the sessions of the Executive seemed dry, yet few were so very conscious of decline until, two years after Moule went to Durham, a change for the better threw the past into sharp relief.

CHAPTER XII

THE NEW AGE

IN November 1903 old Cambridge hands were delighted to read in the *Record* of stirring events at the University. Prebendary Webb-Peploe, by then well over sixty, was conducting a mission which recalled the days of Moody.

There was no very evident reason why a mission at that time should have such effect. Large posters had been placed throughout town and University, all undergraduates and many senior men received personal invitations, and the list of C.I.C.C.U. speakers for the earlier Sundays of term was described as formidable. This was as in previous mission years. Some five hundred cards requesting prayer had been sent all over the world by the C.I.C.C.U. president, Gilbert Barclay, but similar cards had gone out before Mott's mission in '98; Webb-Peploe was older than Mott and the more experienced, yet both were able and spiritual men and Mott, being younger and already so much travelled, was the one more in touch with the mind of youth. Webb-Peploe's earlier missions at Cambridge, though competent and useful, had not been remarkable.

What was fresh was the spirit of prayer and expectancy. The Daily Prayer Meetings were better attended than for years, and in the week previous to the Mission groups were meeting in nearly every college each night. Such faith was rewarded. On the very first evening in Holy Trinity, full but not crowded, Webb-Peploe worked close in to the sympathies and consciousness of his hearers. His sermon —'clear, incisive and forceful'—was on the text from Romans, 'The wages of sin is death; but the gift of God is eternal life through Jesus Christ our Lord.' Webb-Peploe seemed in spite of his age to have an uncanny insight 'into the lives and needs of young men,' and whereas Mott had sometimes repelled by his vivid elaborations of the sins of the flesh, Webb-Peploe's less detailed but equally pungent preaching daily widened his circle of hearers. It was essentially a Scriptural presentation. With his unrivalled command of Scripture and his rapid speech, he had the knack of piling text on text to strengthen and clarify his argument. He neither shirked the Bible's view of sin, nor hesitated to proclaim redemption. 'Remarkable messages in the evident power of the Holy Spirit, with a clear and full unfolding of the plan of salvation.' Thus wrote the *Record*'s correspondent, T. W. Drury, Principal of Ridley, and he added: 'This is just what we need here.'

The missioner, tall and broad, with long grey side-whiskers, and prophet's eye and voice, would speak for some thirty-five to forty minutes. After the closing hymn those who wished could listen a further ten minutes on the way to become a true Christian. It was remarked how few left before this second address. A time of prayer followed, and then Webb-Peploe, who believed in being definite, invited men to stand in open confession of new-found faith. The men were then asked to come forward to the chancel steps, to give their names and colleges, and to receive a memorial card which they could sign in token of their decision and which with its text, 'My grace is sufficient for thee,' they could and did display in their rooms.

Comparisons with Moody's mission were soon heard. Three points of resemblance especially were noted. As in 1882, many who had already been identified with the Christian Union discovered a new and enriching experience. Again, 'all sorts and conditions of men came out on the Lord's side,' and what is more Webb-Peploe's converts, like Moody's, displayed immediate interest in the needs of their friends; men who had been unbelievers at the start of one night would bring others with them on the next. Doubts were expressed on the depth or durability of such conversions, but before the end of term the evidence was clear that 'those who took their stand . . . are identifying themselves with Christian work and workers.'

The spiritual life of Cambridge was visibly deepened. The Daily Prayer Meeting took on a new lease of life and a year later, in reporting 'a wonderful term; almost unparalleled in spiritual blessing—harmony, Christian love and sympathy, absence of self-assertion, an intense spirit of prayer have been the features of life in Cambridge,' Drury could state that 'Prebendary Webb-Peploe's Mission last year was the inception of a great wave of blessing which has come upon us.'

The C.I.C.C.U.'s freshly robust health was soon felt not merely in Cambridge but beyond.

In September 1904 the Student Volunteer Union undertook a Missionary Campaign in the North of England. The plan was to invade a large city, with the support of the local clergy, and win volunteers for the mission field. Huddersfield was chosen, and twenty-six Cambridge campaigners worked in over thirty parishes. Two hundred and sixty meetings were held in the ten days, culminating in a mass rally at the City Hall with the Bishop in the chair. The Campaign was judged a success, evoking 'not mere surface enthusiasm but earnest determination,' as Oswin Bull of Jesus wrote, and the following year was repeated at Nottingham. Here, in a Campaign 'steeped in prayer,' so the *Student Movement* reported, 'the Volunteer Watchword was brought into great prominence with God's hand very evident, guiding and controlling,' and forty-six parishes were worked. The Missionary Campaign became an annual event until the outbreak of war.

An even more enterprising feature of 1904 was the Cambridge University Missionary Party. The idea sprang from the Missionary 'Study Bands,' by then nearly twenty years old. It was proposed to form a party of Cambridge men for work in some hitherto untouched region of the mission field, those remaining at home to supply the financial needs of the others and support them in prayer, contact being maintained through a secretary in England. Northern Nigeria was chosen, in view of the Moslem advance among the pagan tribes. The Church Missionary Society offered a virgin field in the Bauchi Province and the pioneer missionaries of the C.U.M.P., Jack Lloyd and G. T. Fox, went out in 1906. Four other Cambridge men joined them and two tribes were occupied, and though the two pioneers died of blackwater fever and in course of time the close link with Cambridge was lost, the Missionary Party of 1904 had lasting effect both on Nigeria and at the University.

But the most outstanding venture of the period at home was the Cambridge Medical Mission in Bermondsey.

In the late 'nineties a young business man in South London had been invited one Sunday by the Rector of Bermondsey to come over and speak at an evening meeting. As Harold Salmon walked through the neighbourhood, squalid, tumble-down and wretched, he was so horrified that he resolved to do what he could for it in the future. At first he gave his spare time; then he threw up his business and went to Cambridge in order to take a degree, be ordained and start a University settlement. There were already College missions in various quarters, but these not only left scope for further effort, but were varied in aim and therefore drew an uncertain loyalty from Christian Union men. Watts-Ditchfield at Bethnal Green had his Ridley House, where undergraduates could stay for a while and help, but this was scarcely an organized activity; Cambridge House at Camberwell limited itself to social amelioration. Salmon, however, was not so much aiming to provide possible opportunities for Cambridge men as to meet the crying need of the slums to which he had given his heart.

As an undergraduate he had tried to procure someone to launch his Settlement, but it was not until 1906 that a committee of Cambridge men headed by the Bishop of Durham formed a trust, raised funds and appointed Salmon as Honorary Head of the new venture—the Cambridge Medical Mission Settlement. He bought a house in Jamaica Road and moved in with one undergraduate.

The neighbourhood was debased and drunken, a vast unrelieved expanse of mean dwellings, yet containing numbers of respectable though struggling families whose attempt to keep above the prevalent level seemed to

Salmon one of the strongest pleas of the place. The mission aimed to reach the boys of the area, catering for mind, body and spirit, and working in partnership with St. James' Parish Church. A boys' club and a public dispensary were provided and the doors opened in October 1906. The club was soon full and the dispensary never lacked cases, but the gambling in the streets, the usual obscenity, free fights and prostitution went on as before. 'When we came to the district,' wrote Salmon a few years later, 'we were convinced very strongly that the only remedy for this evil was the power of Jesus Christ. . . . We determined that we would put our belief into practice and start from the very beginning with knowing nothing among them but Jesus Christ and Him crucified.' But for eighteen months they lacked result. 'At last a lad of seventeen made a stand for Jesus Christ before his fellows, and his stand brought upon him a terrible persecution.' This was the beginning. In course of time, despite frequent disappointment, Salmon saw several of his boys active Christians. He even educated some at his own expense, sending them to public school and university in order that they might enter the ministry; he lived to see one become a missionary bishop. Others gave up their jobs to train for ordination, or helped in their spare time at their own or similar missions.

The Settlement, small and frequently beset with difficulties, slowly took roots and prospered. From the start the closest touch was kept with the Christian Union at Cambridge. Undergraduates would spend vacations in Bermondsey or help at the club's summer camps, old C.I.C.C.U. men living in London would give their free evenings, some living there while training at hospital or working in business, and the Settlement's name, which was changed after the Great War to the Cambridge University Mission, thenceforth appeared on the C.I.C.C.U. card. 'It attracted to it,' asserted a leaflet issued about 1917, 'the keenest men of Cambridge, and the result has been a very wonderful work done in Bermondsey.' A similar work began among girls in 1916, and in both branches the spiritual basis of the Mission continued to be honoured. 'The ideal and ambition . . . has been to prove that spiritual regeneration is the threshold of social regeneration.' The youth of Bermondsey were told, and were able to prove for themselves that 'the happiest life of all is the life spent in serving Jesus Christ,' and within a few years the friends of the Mission were able to claim that the story was 'of changed lives, changed characters and changed manners.'

Back in Cambridge, a brief week-end in January 1905 brought to the Christian Union an experience beside which Webb-Peploe's mission of '03 looked trivial.

In the previous year two Americans, R. A. Torrey and Charles M. Alexander had emerged as a latter-day Moody and Sankey, Torrey's speaking and Alexander's singing so stirring Edwardian England that, surprisingly, the days of the 'seventies seemed back. After working the provinces the two evangelists came to London for several months of meetings in the Albert Hall, the City and in South London. They were due for a visit to Oxford but could not find time to come to Cambridge. At the end of January, however, it was learned that Charles Alexander was coming up for a week-end visit to an undergraduate friend, Arthur Bradley; shortly afterwards he telegraphed to the President suggesting that he should bring with him his pianist and another soloist. The Executive called an informal meeting on the Saturday evening, and some twenty-five men came to the Henry Martyn Hall to hear Alexander speak and sing. From this casual arrangement sprang far-reaching results.

Charles M. Alexander, a thirty-eight year old Southerner from Tennessee, tall, with a radiant face and a light-hearted charm of manner, was not only a baritone of force and feeling but a born choir-master, who could extract music as easily from a few self-conscious individuals in a room, or from eight thousand untrained voices in the Albert Hall, as from his own chosen choir. His warm expansive nature balanced the rather cold, severe preaching of his partner Torrey. Not only was he a singer, but a speaker whose addresses were straightforward, simple and from the heart.

The twenty-five Christian Union men soon found themselves under his spell. First his assistant, the tenor Paul Gilbert, a large man with a baby face, sang 'My Soul crieth out for Thy Spirit' with its refrain of invocation in which all joined. Then Alexander spoke on service for Christ. He talked frankly, his soft Southern accent and affectionate nature giving added persuasiveness to his words, telling them that 'if any of you are not trying to win individuals for Christ, it is a sure sign of sin of some kind in your life.' Many had been ignorant of such personal responsibility or indifferent, and as they listened they could contrast their own easy-going Christianity with the life to which God called. The atmosphere became charged with emotion as past failures and future possibilities were faced: 'the prevailing longing of all our hearts was for the baptism of the Holy Spirit and victory over sin.' Alexander called for deliberate dedication. 'It was a time of deep heart searching and consecration,' one of those present wrote a few days later, 'when man after man stood up and expressed a determination to yield their lives wholly to God for personal work amongst others.'

On the next day, Sunday January 29th, the effect of Saturday night's meetings was evident. The normal C.I.C.C.U. meeting was to be held in the Victoria Assembly Rooms in the Market Place, opposite Great St. Mary's, and had been adjusted to enable Alexander and his team to take part. Some five hundred men were present, a crosscut of undergraduate life. Alexander soon had them singing, teaching them a new tune to 'Stand Up! Stand Up for Jesus,' and the 'Glory Song,' a solo with chorus which he had popularized and which London barrel-organs were even then grinding out as they once had Sankey's tunes. After prayer, he sang a solo and was followed by the preacher, a retired army officer, prosy but with his text, 'Prepare to meet thy God,' able to make effective use of the atmosphere generated by the music.

Then came the strangest and most impressive incident of the evening. Paul Gilbert the tenor sang a solo, 'Tell Mother I'll be there.' This simple ditty, with its picture of the backwoods prodigal leaving 'the old roof-tree,' breaking his mother's heart and repenting at her death-bed, seemed scarcely suitable for an audience of British undergraduates, nor its refrain, 'Tell Mother I'll be there, Heaven's joys with her to share,' likely to evoke response. It riveted the attention of the audience. While Gilbert was still singing, Alexander stepped forward, urged men to give their lives to God, and asked that as Gilbert sang and all bowed their heads in prayer, those who wished to meet their mothers in heaven, to be answer to their mothers' prayers, should rise in their places. When the hymn was over and eyes were opened, men were standing all over the hall.

Then Alexander continued. 'I reckon you under-graduates are not afraid. I want you to come up to the foot of the platform and shake my hand.' With every eye upon them two brothers, soccer blues, came forward, and thirty-one others followed, including Rowley Nelson, stroke of the Varsity boat. Alexander spoke to them from the steps of the platform and then made them repeat in unison 'I accept Jesus as my Saviour, my Lord and my God.'

There was no excitement, and the meeting had been reverent in spirit throughout. The tension however was too much for one C.I.C.C.U. man who had seen his friends go up to the platform, for when after they were crossing the Market Place together and happened to meet proctor and bulldogs his exuberance overcame him and he seized a bulldog's top-hat and ran off uncaught. More sober thoughts were in the minds of others. 'One of my chief recollections,' wrote Gilbert Barclay, 'is of much prayed-for souls who did not go up.' Yet there was an unfettered sense of thanksgiving for what was done, as forty or fifty men met Alexander that night for praise and prayer in Dodderidge's rooms in Trinity Street; and 'after Chapel on the following Sunday,' continues Barclay, 'I met some of the Trinity men who had been converted. What had before been to them a dry and irksome compulsory service had become full of life and interest. "Did you notice this in the Lesson?" And so on. . . .'

The following week the work done by Alexander was

furthered by John R. Mott, up for his third mission to Cambridge. Once again he spoke of sin, 'its subtlety, its variety, its enchanting and corrupting power' and showed how Christ can 'take a man just where he stands.' Once again he emphasized the call of world evangelization, made men face its challenge and secured recruits for the Student Volunteers.

Through the two Americans, Alexander and Mott, the one simple, persuasive and genial, the other intellectual, forceful and stern, Cambridge had been reinvigorated. A return of the great days of the 'eighties was expected.

CHAPTER XIII

CONTROVERSY

WHILE the Cambridge Christian Union was enjoying new lease of life the national Student Movement to which it was linked was changing in character, and soon was to present its parent University with problems and controversy.

The early Student Volunteers, with their missionary emphasis and their Watchword, 'the Evangelization of the World in this Generation' had stood in no doubt of their purpose nor of the beliefs from which it sprang. To win the Church of England and the Free Churches to the Watchword became Douglas Thornton's consuming ambition. This ambition had taken him with Manley to Lambeth, made him negotiate with the Junior Clergy Association of the Society for the Propagation of the Gospel, content that conflicting views on the nature of the Gospel should not hinder hope of its wider propagation, and had sent him on his vigorous if unsuccessful attempt to capture the theological colleges.

Thornton's vision meant much to the infant Student Movement. But it was accompanied by a determination which almost resented criticism or questioning. His passion could make him impatient of delay and blind to danger. 'If he had got an idea,' said G. T. Manley, 'he could not see that there might be another side. He did not see things you would have thought someone ought to see.' In his zeal for the programme of world evangelization Thornton urged that theological students especially 'should be praying and working for the extension of the common ground between them, both for their own sakes, and for the sake of the Churches at home and abroad.' With this plea, so rare for the day, he sought to merge denominational differences in unity of purpose. His own faith was plain, and he scarcely paused to consider whether the urge to evangelize and the desire for unity, blended so closely in his own mind, might not one day come into conflict. Nor did the times demand such a verdict. Neither the new Anglo-Catholicism nor the new Modernism, each holding beliefs widely divergent from those dear to Thornton and Temple Gairdner, had as yet revealed their strength. The first leaders of the Student Movement saw no need for careful definitions of doctrine. Manley was more alert to dangers than any, yet in the debate of September 1897 on amalgamation of the unions it was he who argued that fusion would cramp the Volunteers' Campaign since 'the British College Christian Union was very distinctly committed to a doctrinal basis, while the Student Volunteers Union was free from this.' Though they did not define it their own position was clear; when in 1897 the annual Students' Conference was moved from Keswick, a decision dictated partly by expense and difficulties of accommodation, partly to avoid appearing a subsidiary of the Convention, there was no question of disagreement with the principles of Keswick, and clash of dates was carefully avoided.

Three years later, at the second Quadrennial Conference of the Student Volunteers at London in 1900, 'speakers of quite opposite ecclesiastical types' were on the platform. But though veterans of Liverpool '96 missed its fiery spirit in London, the purpose and programme of the conference was similar and as a delegate commented a few weeks afterwards, 'the interpretation of the term *evangelization* accepted by the Conference was eminently sound: "Evangelization is the offer to sinful men of Jesus Christ the Saviour King through the lips and lives of redeemed men and women."' Yet already the conference chairman, Harry Duncan of Edinburgh found himself uneasy lest the Movement's distinctive message be lost in desire for a broad platform, and remonstrated privately with the man he considered chiefly responsible, Frank Lenwood, the Oxford congregationalist who had succeeded Gairdner as chairman of the Theological Colleges committee.

The Student Movement stood at the cross-roads. Seeking the sympathy and support of high churchmen and liberals for its programme of world evangelization, it might find their price a blurring of the evangelical gospel; once unity amongst Christians became more urgent than the winning, at home or overseas, of those who were not Christian, the spiritual force of the Movement would weaken.

Thornton, Gairdner and Manley with their vivid experience and clear grasp of truth had gone. Tissington Tatlow, an able speaker and accomplished organizer, appointed General Secretary in 1898 at the age of twenty-three, and to be at the heart of the Movement for nearly thirty years was anxious to make it acceptable to a wider circle, and thus to increase its influence. 'I believe,' he said in 1902, 'that the B.C.C.U. is making for true catholicity. The Movement at its beginning consisted largely of men of one type, but now men of widely different personal characteristics are being drawn in.' In contrast, at the Conference of 1903 Temple Gairdner, Ruth Rouse, Mrs. Thornton and Manley, all back from the mission field, together sent a private message to the Executive 'urging them to keep more closely to the old lines, and to recapture the spirit of the time when increase of Bible study, Prayer, Personal Work and full consecration were our sole objectives.' 'Even then,' recalls Manley, 'we deplored the lack of the old evangelical *spirit*, rather than any change of doctrine.' Less then two years had passed since the official basis of membership had been strengthened to run, 'I desire in joining this Union to declare my faith in Jesus Christ as my Saviour, my Lord and my God,' and a year later, in 1904 at the Conishead Conference, after praying daily with others 'for spiritual awakening' Tissington Tatlow made an impassioned appeal: 'If it is vital for you to be in Christ, dare you conclude that it is not vital for any man or woman in your college? . . . It is a privilege to be allowed to share with God the work of saving men. It is a joy to see men saved. . . . Let us consecrate ourselves afresh today to this service for the sake of the men and women in our colleges. . . .' At the conclusion of this talk 'the whole conference,' records Tatlow, 'spontaneously knelt in prayer for a long period.'

Almost imperceptibly, the Movement's leaders were becoming less certain of their position and their aim. Further, desiring influence in the theological colleges and anxious to win the confidence of theological teachers, they were confronted with current trends. Already, before 1900, presbyterian and congregational students had been imparting the somewhat heady theological conclusions which they had imbibed in their divinity schools. As the new decade wore on, the tide in the country was running strongly against evangelicals. Ecclesiastically the initiative was passing to anglo-catholics; intellectually, to the liberal protestants. Belief in the Scriptures as the Word of God, belief in Miracles, in the Resurrection, and in the guilt of human sin was being dismissed by preachers who had the ear of youth because they seemed to satisfy the claims of science and of the scientific novelists. Against those who thus sought to reinterpret Christian truth so that, in Sanday's classic phrase, 'the cultivated modern man may enter the Church of Christ with his head erect,' the older evangelicals appeared to offer little but well-worn phrases and their own passionate convictions. Of the younger, many among the Nonconformists were swimming with the tide, though few so far out as R. J. Campbell, one of the most acceptable of the younger speakers at Liverpool '96, who was by 1905 formulating his sensational though short-lived New Theology.

The counsels of the Student Christian Movement—as it officially became in 1905—were divided. Some worked hard to keep it in its original path, however unpopular it might prove. Others, steadily growing in influence wished both to adapt themselves to the new intellectual atmosphere, and to make their Movement representative of all students who professed and called themselves Christians. The majority, in 1905, knew not where they stood nor where they ought to go.

Few echoes of these stirrings and tensions had reached Cambridge. At the meeting of the Executive of the Student

Movement on 22nd December 1904 Edward Woods, then Vice-Principal of Ridley, Gilbert Barclay and Jack Lloyd 'represented a strong Cambridge appeal,' as Woods' diary records, 'to make the Student Summer Conference more of a "Keswick" for students. Interesting and useful discussion and they quite met our desires. I believe the Conference will be very adequate for our many young converts now at Cambridge.' The future somewhat belied this; but while older men were thus contributing to Headquarters discussion, undergraduates were absorbed in their Christian Union work, busily reaping the aftermath of Alexander's visit and Mott's mission and during the Easter Vacation of 1905 working, a 'large band of Cambridge men,' for Torrey and Alexander in their London campaign.

The C.I.C.C.U. was still unrivalled. 'The majority of the devotedly Christian young men in Cambridge,' an anonymous contributor to the *Church Quarterly Review* had written the previous October, 'are probably evangelical in their views; certainly this party is most in evidence.' As the writer pointed out, Pusey House had no counterparts at Cambridge, there were no Cowley Fathers and 'the three "ritualistic" churches do not attract undergraduates.' Only in one respect had times clearly changed; Montagu Butler, Chase, President of Queens' and new Bishop of Ely, and the professor of Hebrew, R. H. Kennett, who combined an advanced higher critical position with an evangelical message, continued sympathetic, and with Drury of Ridley and a few other resident fellows were called on for occasional C.I.C.C.U. sermons. But the close support of Moule, Sir George Stokes, Lang, Prior or Perowne was unreplaced. 'This does not make any great difference,' judged the *Church Quarterly* in 1904, but before very long it did.

The first indication that rather than another five years 'remarkable period of religious blessing,' the Christian Union might find itself in flux was the affair of Father Bull in November 1905. Father Bull, a member of the Community of the Resurrection, a powerful preacher and an attractive personality who as a chaplain had ridden through many battles in the South African War, was invited by a number of dons to hold a mission in Great St. Mary's. The sponsors invited the C.I.C.C.U.'s support. 'It was represented to us,' recalls Ralph Taylor the President, afterwards Bishop of Sodor and Man, 'that he believed in conversion and would preach to that end.' Similar problems of co-operation had not previously arisen. The C.I.C.C.U. were inclined to accept the invitation.

There was, however, early indication that all was not well. The shape of the preparations showed that the mission's aim, whatever might be said to attract other parties, was unequivocal. The daily Celebrations were to be held in the six churches 'known,' as Drury wrote, 'for their extreme ritual.' Some of the mission cards mentioned midday Intercessions, others called these same services Daily Prayer Meetings.

The matter was settled when G. T. Manley, then on the Pastorate, delivered the Bible Reading for Sunday 29th October. Taking as his basis Luther's treatise on Justification by Faith Manley showed that Father Bull, if consistent with his beliefs, would preach much that the Christian Union would find unacceptable. The issues were clearly stated and left no room for doubt. The mission committee's invitation was declined and though Winnington-Ingram, Bishop of London, publicly criticized the C.I.C.C.U. as 'anti-Church,' the Union felt when the mission was over no cause to regret its decision.

The close of this Michaelmas term of 1905 provided a further surprise. At the annual Inter-Varsity Conference, the twenty-eighth and last, held at Cambridge on 9th and 10th December the Oxford leaders privately suggested that the Christian Unions be broadened to enable unitarians to accept membership. This proposal was strangely out of tune with the Student Movement's reaffirmation, in its new basis, of belief in Christ's Divinity. That it should follow closely the mission which the O.I.C.C.U. had arranged for Torrey and Alexander indicated confusion of thought. Yet it was not unsymptomatic of the urge to make common cause with all whose intellectual position could be described, however loosely, as Christian, and did nothing to strengthen Cambridge trust in the national Movement.

The following year arose a new Society in Cambridge, taking the name of the Church Society, though the founders knew nothing of the former society, ten years defunct.

It had its origin in a small Reading Party, mainly of King's men, in the Easter vacation of 1906. 'The Cambridge Church Society,' writes E. G. Selwyn, its first secretary and afterwards Dean of Winchester, 'was the Church's response to the active agnostic propaganda which was then being carried on among the undergraduates. To many men,' continues Selwyn, 'the methods of the C.I.C.C.U. were not congenial; they felt that the Church of England's spiritual heritage in the University was not fully appreciated and used, and that the agnostic challenge must be met on intellectual and theological lines.' The political controversy over Church Schools was at its height, and the Church Society provided a rallying point also against the claims of political Nonconformity which were echoed in the debates at the Union.

The decision to found the Society was taken in the May term and the response was rapid. 'Many senior members gave sympathetic support, but it was essentially an under-graduate movement. . . . Each college had its secretary to keep members in his college together and to organize "squashes."' The chief activity was to be a Sunday evening service, four or five times a term in Great St. Mary's, at which Anglicans of various viewpoints—the Bishop of London and Bishop Gore, Wilson Carlile and Talbot Rice, Dr. Figgis, Father Waggett, Canon Scott-Holland—were to preach.

The formal launching of the new Society was announced for Sunday, 28th October 1906, the Bishop of Ely giving the sermon. Gordon Selwyn went to call on Arthur Bradley, President of the C.I.C.C.U. to see whether the evangelistic service in Holy Trinity could be cancelled for that evening, so that the Anglicans in the Christian Union might support this opening meeting. Bradley, referring to the published aims of the Church Society, 'to promote and consolidate the work of the Church of England in

M 165

Cambridge,' suggested that whereas the Church of England could scarcely be said not to be promoted already in the University, the C.I.C.C.U.'s Sunday evening services existed for a definite purpose, as urgent as ever, 'and had been blessed of God to the salvation of many.' Bradley asked him whether 'if you were in my place you would be prepared to give up this meeting.' Selwyn replied that he would not, and Bradley said his answer was the same.

The Church Society, with its Sunday services, was launched. 'The large undergraduate congregations which these services drew,' concludes Selwyn, 'did not seem to have militated against similar services at Holy Trinity; it was a case of there being room for both. . . . Within two or three years of its foundation the Church Society had six hundred members and was the largest Society in the University after the Union.' The C.I.C.C.U. was no longer unrivalled.

In the early summer of 1907 R. L. Pelly of Clare became President of the C.I.C.C.U. The national directors of the Student Movement were now sure of their course. In November 1906 they had decided 'to adopt frankly' the modern view of the Bible, and although hesitant as individuals towards extremes of modernism were prepared henceforth to accept a consensus of the latest findings of scholarship as guide in matters of faith. They also committed themselves to a 'comprehensive' policy, a move symbolized by the appointment in July 1907 of Neville Talbot, one of the most gifted and respected of the younger anglo-catholics, to the Executive of the Theological College Department. The S.C.M. was now anxious, in Tatlow's phrase, to 'shake itself free' from the conservative approach to the Bible, and despite its expressed desire for 'comprehensiveness' was giving an impression of impatience towards those who held it. The C.I.C.C.U., official representative of the Student Movement at Cambridge had been unresponsive to the new winds blowing from headquarters, and to Tatlow, ignorant of or ignoring the intellectual ability of such men as J. R. S. Taylor and R. T. Howard, both of whom had won Firsts at the end of their year as President and Vice-President, its approach to the Bible merely stood for 'emotional appeal . . . sentimental;' nor did he forget Father Bull. It was therefore gratifying when on a hot summer's day, fitting up a new office in Chancery Lane, Tatlow left off to receive Pelly, and found him ready to bring his Union into line with the national Movement. At Cambridge, Pelly's intentions caused particular satisfaction to younger dons whose friendship the S.C.M. had won but who were not in sympathy with the C.I.C.C.U.

There were no striking changes. To Pelly the foundations were prayer, evangelistic zeal and missionary enthusiasm. 'Evangelism must not be allowed to decline,' he wrote later. Thus G. F. B. Morris, a freshman of Queens' threw himself 'into C.I.C.C.U. society and activities and found them a great help.' The Freshmen's sermon was preached by Talbot Rice and to it Morris took a school friend, countering the objection that another school friend had warned him against it by the shrewd suggestion, 'We are both freshers, let's give it a trial.' The friend found the sermon a turning point in his life.

Though evangelism should not decline, Pelly believed that 'the methods used may have to be changed.' On Sunday, 10th November 1907 in place of their evening sermons, the Christian Union and the Church Society held a joint missionary meeting in the Guildhall, an occasion which the chairman, Donaldson, Master of Magdalene, described in his opening remarks as 'historic.' United meetings however, were not enough. To make the C.I.C.C.U. acceptable to all who were ready to join the Student Movement Pelly would have to amend its constitution; all meetings were open, but honest membership implied willingness to support the Daily Prayer Meeting and the Sunday evangelistic services, and alternatives would have to be provided for those who preferred another way. But Pelly knew that the three-fourths majority on the General Committee necessary for such drastic changes would not be obtained whilst retiring College representatives appointed their own successors. His path therefore was blocked. By the end of his year no advance had been made, the ordinary member felt no obvious change of character in the Union and Alex Wood of Emmanuel, a Nonconformist friendly to the Student Movement was writing to Tatlow, 'it would be an enormous boon if we could broaden the C.I.C.C.U. . . .'

Harold Rodgers of Corpus, afterwards Bishop of Sherborne, the second of the Reforming Presidents, as they came to be called, continued his predecessor's work. The Union would not be truly representative of the Student Movement until united with the Church Society and with the Nonconformist Union, the growing body drawing loyalties of Free Churchmen not wishing to work with the Christian Union.[1] The Church Society took the initiative. Correspondence during the summer vacation of 1908 was followed by discussions on the C.I.C.C.U. committee. The scheme fell through, but Rodgers was able to encourage joint meetings, and on November 8th the evangelistic sermon was replaced by a Guildhall meeting on Christianity and Social Reform, the President of Queens' in the chair.

In December John R. Mott held his fourth and last Cambridge mission, and the preparation, course and results of this mission put the new C.I.C.C.U. to the proof.

John R. Mott, although his personal faith never altered had in matters of policy kept step with the changing Student Movement, as it with him. From his early outlook, well defined in his comment on the British College Christian Union in 1895, 'I am glad to report that the basis finally accepted by unanimous vote is thoroughly evangelical,' he had moved by 1905 to a position which had made him, without success, encourage D. P. Robinson to bring men of all schools of thought on to the committee which was arranging his third C.I.C.C.U. mission. In this he differed from Robert Wilder, who on his return from India had joined the staff of the Movement and was often in Cambridge and who, though friendly with anglo-catholics

---

[1] Although there were always men who were members of both unions.

as with all men, and appreciative of spirituality where-ever he found it, was deeply distressed at the new trend of the Movement.

What Robinson had refused in 1905, Rodgers was glad to grant in 1908, setting up an advisory council drawn from all religious bodies in Cambridge to help organize Mott's mission. Nothing was left to chance. The publicity, in Mott's own estimate, was 'the most effective I have ever known,' and a message of commendation was distributed signed by the Bishops of London and Ely. When Mott opened his six-days' campaign on December 3rd his power seemed unabated and the message which had moved students throughout the world as impressive as ever. He preached the gravity of sin with vigour and centred his addresses on the Person of Christ; and if the appeal he had used in 1898, 'to accept Christ as their personal Saviour' had now become 'to follow Jesus Christ,' he seemed to be expressing the same thought in more modern terms.

The Guildhall was filled night after night. Two hundred or more stayed to every after-meeting. 'After each evangelistic appeal,' wrote Mott, 'a large number of men accepted Christ.' On the last night, wrote R. L. Pelly, 'the Guildhall, including the gallery and the orchestra were filled to overflowing and still some were compelled to stand.' One hundred and fifty stood at Mott's appeal. One hundred and twenty-five gave in their names in token of decision. Even the religious unity, which Mott felt was merely skin-deep at the start seemed to grow with the progress of the mission, its strength symbolized the day after the close by the thankgiving service which a high churchman conducted, an evangelical delivering the address.

One of the leaders assured Mott that 'over three hundred men decided for Christ as a result of the campaign.' Term ended a few days later. In January 1909, in the first week of the new term, it was reported that 'the Inter-Collegiate Christian Union had probably never had a wider or deeper outlook.' A General Secretary was appointed, Ralph Taylor at Ridley, to follow up the work of the Mission and to keep the C.I.C.C.U. in touch with senior members and with Student Movement headquarters, and Robert Wilder came up for ten days at the end of the month.

Despite all this activity, disappointment was felt. Mott had undoubtedly made, as Taylor wrote, a 'really wide and deep impression' and among those who had stood in token of new-found faith were scholars and thinkers hitherto reluctant to attend such services; but the strength which Cambridge religion expected was not materializing. Of the three hundred who had handed in their names only a scattered few were giving active support to any of the religious societies, and although allowance could be made for men who were not readily persuaded, however deep their experience, to join open movements, it could not detract from the growing dissatisfaction. A larger party than for some years went to the summer Student conference at Baslow, now so timed to be an alternative to the Keswick Convention though not without its quota of evangelical speakers, but by the beginning of the Michaelmas term 1909 the new President, A. C. B. Bellerby of Emmanuel, the Varsity high-jump and President of Athletics, was as dissatisfied as any with the state of the Union.

Bellerby, whom many members did not consider a representative Christian Union man and who himself believed that he owed the presidency to his reputation as an athlete, felt that most of the C.I.C.M.U. were missing the point of the evangelistic sermons: 'We all turned out getting ourselves saved once a week.' He had no quarrel with the sermons, but 'somehow members were not very successful in persuading the non-Christian men to attend.' Seeking to analyse the cause he became 'quite convinced that the C.I.C.C.U. was too narrow in its appeal.' Remedies were suggested to the Executive. The platform should be broadened yet more. If possible, union with the Church Society should be effected, though Tait, Principal of Ridley, suggested that 'it is wisest and best for each society to do its own work in its own way.' Open Air meetings should be dropped. There was even talk of abandoning the Daily Prayer Meeting in favour of formal Intercessions.

Bellerby found support in the Union and among senior men, at Cambridge and away. Some were conscious, as Pelly wrote, of 'grievous faults in the C.I.C.C.U. . . . unreasoning intolerance, indelicacy in approaching others, disregard of the intellectual side of religion. . . .' Others, as Edward Woods afterwards expressed it, felt that the C.I.C.C.U.'s reluctance to co-operate with others was to a large extent due to the difference of language and vocabulary between those who thought in conservative terms and those who expressed similar beliefs in other ways. Deeper understanding and closer co-operation would resolve such difficulties. Junior dons—Angus of Trinity Hall, Mozley of Pembroke, Wood of Jesus—whose primary desire was to make the Christian Union faithful to the S.C.M., were anxious to see a steady infiltration of friends of the Movement gaining control by weight of numbers, and suggested that President and officers should be elected by popular vote.

By October 1909 no undergraduate could recall the days before Pelly. Most members of the Union, becoming increasingly indefinite in their beliefs and undecided in their minds were unable to offer a solution to a problem they did not understand. The C.I.C.C.U. sermons which they heard were no longer consistent. On most Sundays they listened to men true to the first aims of the Union— Stuart Holden, Taylor Smith, Robert Wilder or Eugene Stock; but on others they would be treated to the diverse view-points of Lionel Ford, headmaster of Repton, Tissington Tatlow, A. J. Mason, then Vice-Chancellor, or Wynne-Willson of Haileybury, or would join forces with other societies to hear the great Charles Gore himself, founder of the Community of the Resurrection, Bishop of Birmingham and afterwards of Oxford.

Bellerby's Vice-President, G. F. B. Morris, afterwards Bishop in North Africa, saw the C.I.C.C.U.'s problem differently. With Lionel Studd, Kynaston Studd's son, A. C. S. Smith, son of Stanley Smith, and an increasing body of others Fred Morris believed that the trouble lay in divergence from the original path of the Christian Union. It was not a matter merely of ill-attended sermons, or of reluctance to keep abreast of modern thought; nor, on the other hand, of indecisiveness, nor that they were forgetting, in words used five years before by Drury of Ridley, that 'in spiritual matters, to be truly broad one must be really deep.' It seemed rather that truths for which Simeon had lived and Henry Martyn had died would be discarded or obscured. Some of those favourable to Bellerby's broader way openly admitted that the C.I.C.C.U. as it had been had made a good starting-point, that unless a man learnt in early days 'something of a passionate and even reckless enthusiasm for the kingdom of God he is not likely to pick it up in later life.' Could the new atmosphere foster a second Thornton or turn the introspective, lukewarm piety of a Stanley Smith into vigorous faith and prepare him for China? Smith and Studd were still revered as spiritual ancestors of the Student Movement; it was hard to see the Inter-Collegiate Union of 1909 breeding a latter-day Cambridge Seven. As Morris and his friends thought and prayed they came reluctantly but assuredly to the conclusion that if the character of the C.I.C.C.U. was irrevocably changed they must form a new union on the old lines.

Compromise was discussed. Junior dons at Cambridge suggested that the Union should resign its position as official branch of the Student Christian Movement. In its place a committee of representatives from all the religious societies in the University, including the C.I.C.C.U., would be formed. This proposal was debated at length by the Committee of the General College Department of the Student Movement on 16th and 17th December 1909 on receipt of a letter from Bellerby. It was held that the constitution of the Movement allowed affiliation to one Union alone in each University, Pelly assured the committee that to his belief 'the C.I.C.C.U. was moving towards reform,' and that the next executive would be more representative of the Movement. It was questioned, in that connection, whether the Sunday evening services were any longer necessary 'when there were denominational societies doing evangelistic work effectively.' The conclusion was that when reform came the services should continue but be arranged by a separate sub-committee.

The General College Department's conclusions were transmitted to Bellerby, who was told that only two courses lay open to the C.I.C.C.U.: that they should continue affiliation and 'show their keenness' by amending the constitution in order that officers, at present nominated by their predecessors should henceforth be elected by majority vote of members, thus making it worth while for those who disagreed with the Union's principles to join it in the certainty of changing them by voting their friends into office. The alternative was to break affiliation, the Student Movement then to form a fresh society. A general conference was proposed, the General College Committee deciding that if it proved impossible to make the Union more representative they 'would next year consider whether it was not possible to form a new Society.' A second letter was sent to the C.I.C.C.U. committee 'sympathizing with their difficulties and encouraging them.'

Bellerby, more than ever convinced that the Cambridge Christian Union was keeping good men out of the Student Movement, was prepared to bring matters to a head. During the Lent term he pressed the issue on his Executive: 'Either we enlarge our views and adequately represent the S.C.M., or we resign our affiliation and allow the S.C.M. to enlarge its membership.' He was so emphatic that the Executive agreed to ask Tatlow to Cambridge to address a general meeting, after which Bellerby would put the issue to a vote. 'I had complete confidence that Tissington Tatlow would win the day for what I wanted—a bigger Christian Union reaching a bigger circle of men.' Oxford already had this,[1] and Cambridge was about to follow. Ralph Taylor, as General Secretary in touch with the Student Movement, but sympathetic to Morris and aware how strong were the conservatives, felt otherwise. He knew that they would break away to form their own union if Bellerby won his vote; and when Tatlow arrived in Cambridge Taylor advised him to accept disaffiliation.

[1] The O.I.C.C.U. had already (temporarily) accepted the S.C.M's change of policy.

Early in March 1910 the C.I.C.C.U. was summoned to the Henry Martyn Hall to hear Tissington Tatlow and to decide the issue. Tatlow's speech was able and Bellerby felt confident. A long discussion followed and Bellerby put the question that the C.I.C.C.U. broaden its basis. The voting was close. 'It was a complete surprise to me,' recalls Bellerby, 'and a great shock, when the point I had so earnestly wanted was lost.' Bellerby turned to Tatlow, on his left, and whispered that he proposed to resign then and there, since the Union 'could hardly have any confidence in a president who had so unmistakably urged them to a policy they were not prepared to adopt.' Tatlow agreed that there was no option. The Union refused to accept the resignation, and asked him to continue until the end of his year, which had not long to run.

Many members were now strongly in favour of disaffiliation from the S.C.M. Tatlow himself advised it. But when the General Committee met in Bellerby's rooms in Emmanuel for the final decision, 'a tremendous discussion took place,' as Ralph Taylor recalled, 'there was a real fight on the part of those desiring retention of affiliation to reverse the decision of the previous vote. For a long time the issue hung in the balance.' By the end of the meeting Taylor, Morris and those who felt with them had succeeded in 'persuading the Committee to stand by the vote,' and shortly afterwards the General College Department received formal notice that 'the C.I.C.C.U. decides to break affiliation with the S.C.M.,' in order that both should be free to work unhindered in Cambridge.

CHAPTER XIV

AFTER 1910

THE Student Movement set to work reconstructing its position in Cambridge. A committee drawn from the principal religious societies, the C.I.C.C.U. convening it to provide formal continuity and then withdrawing, decided after six months that 'the present aims of the S.C.M. in Cambridge be: occasional meetings for prayer and interchange of ideas; to urge every member to do his duty in the Church Militant.'

Tatlow was finding it difficult to reassure senior friends who feared that his Movement was going 'off the rails.' His own explanation of events, made in the committee discussions of December 1909, and in the General Report of 1910–11, concentrated on his belief that 'the C.I.C.C.U. had for some time been feeling the difficulty of combining the fuller interdenominationalism of the Student Movement with the traditions and ideals of which it was justly proud.' To him the Union was a predominantly Anglican body which could not stomach the new spirit of unity. In the Cambridge of 1910 Anglicans naturally outnumbered Nonconformists, yet neither the C.I.C.C.U. nor the S.C.M., as Manley retorted to Tatlow's charge, had been anything but interdenominational from the beginning.

In the University Tait of Ridley and other seniors who had been friendly to the Christian Union but sympathetic to the new policies of the Student Movement were grieved with the upshot of the controversy. Others already suspicious of the Union dismissed its action as presumptuous and expected an early collapse. Manley, who had left Cambridge finally in 1906, and Robert Wilder, both hoping for the Student Movement's return to former paths, felt 'keen regret' that the one Christian Union to have remained faithful should have been forced out, whoever was responsible. Many former C.I.C.C.U. men not closely in touch found the quarrel hard to understand. The Student Movement still sounded an evangelical note and the Volunteer Union steadily increased in membership. Perhaps the most balanced judgement came from Bishop Moule in Durham. 'Debate and difference between earnest Christian men in itself gives me pain and anxiety . . . and here and there I cannot endorse either side without much reserve. The thoughtful man . . . will ask his Lord for large patience and open-eyed sympathies. He will avoid to the uttermost, abiding in Him, the spirit and accent of mere prejudice and of an unhallowed liking for strife.' But, added Moule with his eye on the Student Movement, 'the Lord and the Apostles have amply warned us that popular drifts of religious opinion are no sure indication of divine leading . . . the winning of the nations to the Lord will assuredly not be done through modification of the apostolic Gospel, and the belittling of the written Word and an incautious optimism about non-Christian faiths.'

Undergraduates and fourth year men who had supported Bellerby resented the extinction of their hopes, and a division of loyalty which they considered had been forced upon them by a minority. Pelly thought that Tatlow had come with his mind made up and that patience might have provided a satisfactory solution. Bellerby 'watched rather sadly' from Ridley as the Union, to his mind, became once again '"A small select club of saved men." Its members,' he added, 'were magnificent Christians but I felt they had lost a great opportunity of really reaching the average Varsity man.'

But as Morris took over the presidency there developed also a widespread sense of liberation, an eagerness to go forward in the work of evangelism, with the Sunday evening sermons once more the focus of the C.I.C.C.U.'s life and the Daily Prayer Meeting its strength. In the long Vacation a considerable party from Cambridge pitched camp at Keswick, the first attendance at the Convention for some years. By Michaelmas the Union's clarity of vision was in marked contrast with the blurred outlook of the immediate past and already, as an Emmanuel man could say in after years, 'the Holy Spirit's endorsement of the break was apparent in a widening and deepening of influence in the University.'

To defend its policy the C.I.C.C.U. was obliged to define its doctrinal position more closely than before. The idea of definition ran counter to an age which abhorred dogma. Controversy therefore increased. Men who preferred neutrality found themselves forced to take sides; intolerance and lack of charity on the one hand, impatience on the other threatened to absorb the energies of Christian Union and Student Movement men. Discord was in the very air of 1910, with its Constitutional crisis, two general elections and Labour unrest, with the suffragettes, Ireland and international tension in the background. At Cambridge matters were made no better when the Master of Emmanuel, Chawner, 'a layman, unmarried and in ill-health, officially something of a martinet, a charming host and a delightful companion,' as Charles Raven, his young and brilliant Dean described him, determined that the 'conspiracy of silence' between agnostic science and Christianity should be broken, and distributed three rationalist pamphlets to all senior members and ordinands in the University, and to certain third year men. The pamphlets, not particularly impressive or original—'the Master of Emmanuel has condescended to lay aside his learning' was Professor Inge's verdict—but coming from the head of a college, set Cambridge in a ferment. The Rationalist Press followed them up. The Heretics Society was launched, the first in the University to be founded with an avowedly anti-Christian aim.

In this atmosphere the C.I.C.C.U. was taking up positions rejected by the majority of those whose pronouncements were held to be authoritative. Against the prevalent humanism it stressed the guilt and weakness of human nature. It reaffirmed its belief in justification by faith. The doctrines of creation and of the Second Coming of Christ, ancient hope of the Church, were asserted in face of theological opinions which dismissed them as untenable. Against those who preached a merely social gospel, 'our belief is that no amount of reform will raise a man one degree from spiritual blindness and degradation.' As to any interfusion of opposing convictions, the Union's attitude was already sufficiently indicated by the break with the Student Movement.

Argument centred round the Bible: 'the C.I.C.C.U. makes its first and final reference to the authority of Holy Scripture as its inerrant guide in all matters concerned with faith and morals.' It was more anxious to promote 'the reverent and devotional study of the Bible than discussions as to its authenticity and veracity,' and in face of the popular and, to the mind of 1910, convincing doctrine of Kenosis, the Incarnate Christ allowing Himself no further knowledge than that of a first-century Jew, the C.I.C.C.U. affirmed that 'it is sufficiently reasonable to hold that view of the Old Testament which Christ Himself held,' and preferred to maintain a respectful scepticism towards adverse theories of scientist or scholar rather than to adopt a view-point which seemed to infringe the full divinity of Christ, and which before long might be discarded by its own first exponents.

For young men defining their convictions in an unsympathetic intellectual climate it was easy to run to extremes, to condemn opponents as insincere or morally perverted; to play with catch phrases, ignore the differing interpretations which might be laid on a single word, or to make sweeping assertions without considering their implications. Definitions however positive were but poor expressions of what was felt, and the proof of them lay not in argument but in the character which they produced when argument was done.

Controversy came to a head a year later. When the Cambridge Christian Union had disaffiliated from the General College department of the Student Movement, the link with the Volunteer Missionary Union remained. Sympathies among the hundred Volunteers in Cambridge were divided but lay mostly with the Christian Union, 'and many of them,' as Tatlow recorded, 'were very restive about their membership of S.V.M.U.,' the national Executive of which strongly desired its Cambridge branch to be truly representative of its policies. When in October 1910 the new local committee proved to be in close sympathy with Headquarters restiveness increased. On the other hand, 'some of the keenest' of those Volunteers who were strong Christian Union men were opposed to any break, 'pointing out,' as Murray Walton of Pembroke has written, 'that in the first place membership of the S.V.M.U. did denote a dedication to missionary service, a dedication so far reaching that men and women of all types would find in it a common basis. And that further, once they got out into the mission field they would inevitably be brought into contact with others different from themselves.'

Those in favour of a separate Cambridge missionary branch were not so concerned with the future as with the present. They complained of 'chilling' changes in the conduct of Volunteer meetings, of 'absence of spiritual power' in their gatherings for prayer. The C.I.C.C.U. had already set itself against the new and popular policy of co-operation and unity, demonstrating by renewed vigour that whatever might be the merit of this policy in the international religious scene, in a student world it led to feebleness and indecision. During the Easter Vacation of 1911 four Volunteers determined to withdraw from the national Union. The following term they invited those whom they believed to share their feelings to a meeting at which a Cambridge Volunteer Union was formed. Some who were not asked resented what they supposed an unrepresentative decision; but the sponsors of the scheme had no thought that their action was binding on all Cambridge volunteers, and whatever a general vote might have showed, they were settled in their minds to withdraw.

Many who joined the new Cambridge Volunteer Union retained their membership of the Student Volunteers. 'I think my reason,' wrote Handley Hooper, son of Douglas Hooper of Moody's day, 'was that in spite of a lack of inspiring leadership the Student Volunteers presented a challenge of which the S.C.M. was sorely in need. Those of us who had come up committed to foreign service were ballast in the S.V. boat, and our withdrawal would weaken its witness and claims.'

At first the formation of the Cambridge Volunteer Union and the Bible clause which it inserted in its declaration of membership heightened controversy, encouraged wrangles on the meaning and definition of Inspiration and increased misunderstandings. But argument was giving way to strenuous activity, for November 1911 was drawing near and with it, Dr. Torrey.

Reuben Archer Torrey was fifty-five, an erect, impressive figure, with steel-blue eyes, and beard and hair prematurely white. He spoke in curt phrases, without emotion but with rugged assurance. 'You can tell at once,' ran a contemporary description, 'that here is a man who knows where he stands and is prepared to defend his position . . . no wavering, no compromise, no middle course.' Where Moody had been genial and expansive, Torrey was terse and stern; Moody's addresses flowed as if they were improvisations, Torrey's sounded sometimes almost as if learned by heart; both men felt deeply, were always gentle with those in distress and were happy in heart. But Torrey confined humour to occasional subtleties of speech.

Three factors made him peculiarly fitted to reach the Cambridge man of 1911. The first was his past. Moody, the New England farmer's son had sown no wild oats; his development had been comparatively smooth. Torrey, the New York banker's son had no sooner gone to Yale, at the age of fifteen, than he forgot the exhortations of his mother and the staid religiousness of his father and set himself during the next three years to blow away an ample allowance, for which his father asked no account— 'it would have been a good thing for me if he had.' A quick mind made him free of hard work; his skill as a dancer, a taste for the gaming-table, and an easy manner made him popular. 'I went in for a good time. Did I find it? I did not.' His assertion, 'I went deeper, deeper, deeper into dissipation and sin' might have been dismissed as the exaggerations of a Bunyan or a Cromwell were it not for the plain fact that 'one awful night, a mere boy still, with life fairly burned out,' he tried to commit suicide. He jumped out of bed and opened a drawer for the revolver kept there. 'For some reason or other I could not find it. God did not let me find it, and in my despair I dropped on my knees and said, "O God, if you will take this awful burden from my heart I will preach the Gospel."'

It was a year before he made good his vow. In course of time he entered the ministry, working first in an Ohio country town, and then in hard districts of Minneapolis, from whence in 1890 Moody invited him to lead his Bible Institute in Chicago.

The second factor was Torrey's intellectual ability. He was a thinker and scholar, who not merely read the New Testament in Greek each day but the Old Testament in Hebrew. He had spent seven years at Yale and one at Leipzig, could quote the classics or the poets in his sermons, could draw on science and history, was apt at repartee and had a memory which gave him an inexhaustible supply of anecdotes and incidents to illustrate his points.

Thirdly, Torrey had been for a while a thoroughgoing disciple of the higher critics and had gone to Leipzig expressly to sit at the feet of the aged Delitzsch. 'There was a time,' he said at Cambridge, 'when I was so wise that I believed so much of the Bible as was wise enough to agree with me.' But Germany had an unusual effect. Having sifted what he was taught, he abandoned his advanced position and returned with assurance to a belief 'in the Bible, the whole Bible, as the Word of God: an altogther reliable revelation from God Himself of His own character, His will, His purposes; and of man, his nature, his possibilities, his duty, his destiny.' Yet he could add, and the comment was salutary for Cambridge, 'I don't care for theories of inspiration.' He had his own theory, but if a man 'accepts the absolute authority of the Scriptures . . . I have no quarrel with him about theories of inspiration.'

Torrey was unknown beyond the United States until December 1901, two years after Moody's death, when he was invited with Charles Alexander to undertake missions in Australia which originally had been planned for Moody. In 1903 Torrey and Alexander had come to Great Britain, their work culminating in the London campaign of 1905. They had been to Oxford, and were invited to Cambridge, but were unable to accept. Early in 1906 they had returned to America. Before they sailed, Torrey had said to Bradley, shortly to become President of the C.I.C.C.U., 'I am convinced, Arthur, that God will yet bring me to Cambridge.'

In January 1911 Arthur Bradley, Fred Morris, who had handed on the Presidency a few weeks earlier, and the new President, Howard Mowll of King's, a nephew of the redoubtable founder of the Barnwell Theatre Mission, met in London and sent a cable of invitation to Torrey.

The issue between Christian Union and Student Movement, as Mowll, afterwards Archbishop of Sydney wrote in after years, had 'mainly turned upon what attitude was adopted towards Holy Scripture and how it was used in Christian witness. The C.I.C.C.U. Executive,' he continues, 'therefore planned for a Mission to be conducted in the University which would rely only on the power of the Word of God, without any other aids to attract an audience or to lead to the conversion of souls.' Alexander therefore was not asked. The Executive desired that 'nothing should compete with the preaching of the Word of God.'

There was nearly a year to run. Throughout 1911 the C.I.C.C.U.'s attention was focused on their coming opportunity. Howard Mowll was a vigorous personality, exceptionally tall, a man of iron will and marked administrative ability, with depth of spiritual understanding. Under his direction preparations were made on a scale and with a detailed care which surpassed even the Webb-Peploe or the Mott missions. One million prayer slips were sent out, printed on India paper to be placed in Bibles, and in Cambridge men were praying. In July seventy were at Keswick, and one of them wrote, 'the convicting power of the Spirit swept through the Camp and all the seventy came away definitely blessed.' In

THE GENERAL COMMITTEE OF THE UNION, 1911

Back Row — R. W. A. Ward — —?— — W. Hillbrook — W. A. Pitt-Pitts — H. D. Hooper — B. C. Corfield — J. E. Davey
Ordained — *Died Great War* — *Archdn. of Ruanda* — *Ordained, Kenya* — *Bp. Travancore* — *Professor, Ordained*

Centre Row — Graham Browne — W. Ayling — W. H. M. Walton — C. A. Herapath — F. L. Williams — E. F. F. Bishop — H. M. S. Taylor — W. E. Ovens
Bp. in Jerusalem — *Lawyer* — *(Canon), Japan* — *Industry* — *Uganda* — *Palestine* — *Ordained* — *Ordained*

Front Row — C. C. Kerr — G. F. B. Morris — H. Earnshaw-Smith — C. W. Jameson — H. W. K. Mowll — G. B. Sellwood — A. B. Buxton — R. P. Dalley — J. B. Leather — Rev. J. R. S. Taylor
Preb. St. Pauls — *Bp. in N. Africa* — *Ordained, Nigeria* — *Ordained* — *Archbp. of Sydney* — *Doctor* — *Congo, Abyssinia* — *India* — *Surgeon* — *Bp. of Sodor and Man*

September they were at Liverpool for the largest missionary campaign Cambridge had yet arranged. By the start of the Michaelmas term, a month before the Mission, the pitch of expectancy was high.

Every undergraduate in the University found on arrival a card which announced ('in very vague terms') the forthcoming visit of Dr. Torrey of Yale, Leipzig and Erlangen. Old Cambridge men together with C.I.C.C.U. members had raised a generous fund, and in a year when, with income-tax at a shilling, paper and labour were cheap, one hundred pounds was spent on printing and posters alone. Eight-foot posters were displayed behind the railings of King's and St. Catharine's, on the hoardings outside the half-finished New Court of Emmanuel, in the market-place and throughout the town. Small posters were on college screens and in shop windows. No one could escape being confronted with the news that Torrey was coming. As term proceeded a scheme was drawn up (an unconscious echo of 1873) whereby every man *in statu pupillari* was allocated to a supporter of the Mission, who undertook to invite him to an informal 'squash' and if possible to take him in to the main meetings. Special instruction classes were held to train men in helping those who should come.

But it was the spirit of prayer which most marked these weeks. A unity and intensity of prayer permeated the Christian Union. 'It was as natural,' said Colin Kerr of Emmanuel, 'to go into a man's rooms and suggest prayer as to talk about the boats or the debates at the Union.' Half-nights of prayer were not uncommon. One man wishing to attend such a meeting in another college asked his tutor for leave to stay out after midnight. It was refused. He was not defeated. 'Sir,' he said politely, 'you would grant it for a May week ball, wouldn't you . . .?' 'All right,' replied the don, 'you can have it.' 'There may have been some extravagances of adolescent zeal,' summed up one of the men of 1911, 'but I am convinced that ninety-five per cent of it was a definite, expectant outpouring of the hearts of students to God.'

The invitation to Torrey had aroused immediate antagonism in the University. His great Albert Hall campaign of six years earlier was remembered, his uncompromising views were well known. The announcement of his coming did nothing to mitigate the prevalent atmosphere of contention. Many senior men considered that to bring an 'American Revivalist' to Cambridge was thoroughly unwise, even a deliberately unfriendly action. C.I.C.C.U. men felt that scarcely a don was with them. They found difficulty in securing a hall, the Guildhall being already engaged, and were obliged to take the Riding School beyond Jesus Lane. Even this was suddenly closed to them within ten days of the opening night, for fear, so they were convinced, of senior disapproval and of undergraduate disturbances. The Christian Union, as members often recalled when it was all over, resorted to further prayer; St. Andrew's Hall was let to them by the Baptist Church, and the Guildhall at length discovered that it could make itself available for the fourth night and after.

Antagonism among junior members also was strong. A few Trinity Hall men even planned as a rag to kidnap Torrey on his arrival at the railway station and confine him, courteously but closely, in an hotel at Royston until his week was over. Rumour of this spread across Cambridge. It was reported that one of the kidnappers would personate Torrey and that while the C.I.C.C.U. were walking away with the decoy, others should welcome Torrey in their name and drive him to Royston. The Committee were waiting on the station at the appointed time, Colin Kerr suggesting that to make sure they were greeting the right man they should kick him on the shin: 'If he does not swear he is Torrey!' The train drew in and Torrey was soon safe in Selwyn Gardens, with his host the Bursar of Queens', W. M. Coates, the only don actively working for the Mission; but for several days he was given an impromptu bodyguard, and when he mentioned the abortive plot in one of his addresses a stamp of recognition went round the hall. The C.I.C.C.U. had rightly considered it good publicity.

The Mission began, as had Moody's, on the first Sunday

in November. And as in 1882 it was Guy Fawkes' night.
All seemed set for a repetition of the scenes of twenty-nine
years before. To the police this was a warning, and a few
constables were sent in readiness. To the Christian
Union men it was an augury.

On the Saturday, at an official welcome in the Henry
Martyn Hall, with the President supported on the platform by the Vicar of Holy Trinity and the Principal of
Ridley, Torrey had made plain the objects of the campaign: to win men for Christ, to cause Christians to live
nearer to Christ and thirdly, 'to stir up God's people to set
about in dead earnest the salvation of their fellow-men.'
This work, he reminded them, could only be carried out by
'dependence on God, on prayer, on the Word of God
and the Holy Spirit, and by personal work.' At midday
on Sunday in the Victoria Assembly Rooms he spoke once
again, stressing 'the joy and reward of winning souls to
Christ.' The C.I.C.C.U. therefore were alert. And
already, at the private preparatory talks which Torrey had
delivered earlier in the week a hint of possibilities had been
given, for a habitual drunkard had been brought by a
friend, and 'something Dr. Torrey said,' so Mowll recalled,
'was used for his conversion. He often declared that from
that moment all desire for drink left him. For many
years he has rendered devoted and outstanding service
as a missionary.'

On Sunday evening the St. Andrew's Hall steadily
filled to its limited capacity, each man being handed a
card giving names of clergymen and other graduates
available should he become anxious for a personal interview. In a room downstairs a small group was already in
prayer, to remain so throughout the evening.

The opening hymn over, the Chairman, A. J. Mason,
Master of Pembroke prayed ('and in his extempore prayer
seemed to voice the petitions of all earnest souls') and
introduced the Missioner. The audience had shown no
propensity to behave as their fathers had done; but Torrey
had no sooner begun his address when, to the Mission
committee's dismay, he appeared to be wrecking his own
meeting. His text was the vision of Isaiah, 'I saw also the

Lord, sitting upon a throne. . . . Above it stood the seraphims, and each one had six wings. . . .' And here the committee saw their evangelist, with his steely eye, and his reputation for paucity of gesture, begin to illustrate the passage by acting it, '. . . with twain he covered his face, with twain he covered his feet, and with twain he did fly.' Titters ran round the hall as Torrey touched his feet and flapped his arms; the committee shrank into their chairs. But the bad moment was soon over, and Torrey had passed to his main text, 'In the beginning, God' and the incident, which was never repeated and never explained, had been forgotten as he expanded his theme, 'God *is*, God is very great, is holy, is merciful, and saves men through Jesus Christ.'

Sunday's meeting gave little indication of the way the week would go. At five o'clock each following afternoon Torrey gave a Bible Reading, precise in teaching and vivid with illustrations, and when he spoke on prayer, 'the most effective form of Christian work . . . by prayer the bitterest enemies of the Gospel have become its most valiant friends, the greatest scoundrels have become true sons of God.' he sent men back to their knees with renewed determination. On Wednesday the Mission moved to the Guildhall. Numbers were increasing and already men for whom definite prayer had been made were telling their friends of decision. The rowdy opposition which had been expected had not materialized; the nearest approach to it was reported by two of C. T. Studd's daughters who told the C.I.C.C.U. 'that men sitting near them in the gallery had stink bombs in their pockets, but before they could throw them they had been converted!'

Since Torrey pressed for immediate 'acceptance of Christ as Sin-bearer, Saviour and Deliverer from the power of sin,' most of the dons were writing him off as 'intensely emotional.' His concentration on the vileness of sin and the terror of judgement made some of Torrey's hearers regret the absence of Alexander. But the strongest impression was of logic, earnestness and spiritual power. 'The addresses,' wrote the correspondent of the *Record*, 'have been very simple and searching; when a man has heard two addresses he has seen himself as he is, and cannot be in any fog about his bearings; he knows perfectly well whether he is saved or lost. If by refusing to change sides and take his stand for Christ he is lost, he has none but himself to blame.' Torrey had spoken on the Wednesday on 'What it costs to be Christian; and Not to be a Christian.' 'By a Christian,' said Torrey in no uncertain terms, 'I understand, any man that comes to God as a lost sinner, takes Jesus Christ as his personal Saviour, surrenders to Him as his Lord and Master, confesses Him as such publicly before the world and strives to please Him in everything day by day.' He followed this up on the Thursday with an address on Pilate's question, 'What shall I do with Jesus which is called Christ?' and on the Friday and Saturday dealt, as had Moody, with excuses.

By Sunday, 'the most powerful time we have experienced,' it had been decided that the Mission must continue a further week. Torrey spoke this Sunday night, November 12th, on Heroes and Cowards—'he who rejects the Lord is a coward. . . . When you and I stop to think what Christ has done for us; how He left Heaven with all its glory and came down to earth with all its shame; how He was scourged and crowned with thorns . . . spat upon and buffeted and nailed to the Cross for you and me . . . if, knowing that, you will not confess Jesus Christ because of the fear of man you are a coward. . . .' At the close of an address that gave five logical reasons, worked out with wealth of illustration and phrase, why men ought to accept Him, Torrey invited them to do so, 'All over the hall men sprang to their feet, singly and in groups, till those who were watching could not keep count.' Then came an after-meeting, when those who had stood previously rose again and 'publicly, by the spoken word,' wrote an eyewitness, 'confessed the Lord Jesus.'

Confession was not enough. A man might spring to his feet but was of no use to himself or to anyone if faith went no further. The C.I.C.C.U. men had therefore so divided the hall that there was always at least one of them sitting not far from anyone who stood up. 'His job,' wrote the

President, 'was to take his name and college and invite him to his rooms for coffee, personally escorting him there. He was to follow up this invitation with Bible study and prayer together until the individual was well grounded in the Scriptural basis of the Salvation he professed to have received, in evidence of it taking part audibly in prayer meetings and speaking in the Open Air, as well as strengthening the fellowship of the Christian Union in his own college.' As an immediate means to this the second week contained only two further evangelistic addresses. The other nights were devoted to Bible studies, while the Missioner spent much time also in private interviews.

On Sunday, November 19th Torrey gave his final address. 'At first,' wrote Barclay Buxton, one of the several from Moody's day who were present, 'there was a tendency to disturbance, but Dr. Torrey spoke most solemnly, and gradually the whole audience was subdued by the power of the Holy Spirit. I doubt if any man went away without facing in some measure the supreme question.'

Buxton's words summed up the whole Mission. Suspicion and cynicism had turned to respect or gratitude. 'The advent of Dr. Torrey,' wrote the *Cambridge Review*, 'is not to be passed over in silence. Whatever the general body of opinion may be as to the desirability of revivalism in Cambridge, there can be no doubt that Dr. Torrey's addresses have had an effect which is by no means negligible. It is not for the *Review* to analyse the process of conversion, but this much we say, that Dr. Torrey, by the use of perfectly simple methods of oratory, unembellished by any particular beauties of style, has definitely sent certain of his hearers away enriched by something which they did not possess before. It is a question of plain fact, which some may deplore, but none can disprove.' The stroke of the Cambridge boat and other athletes had professed their conversions, nor were reading men absent from the list. On the other hand a King's man, afterwards a prominent diplomat, was present to his friends' surprise at the opening meeting; stood up, still more to their surprise, at Torrey's appeal; yet never came again nor would have anything more to do with Christians in his college.

But 'I have reason to know,' Archbishop Mowll could sum up years later, 'that the conversions were not only numerous but lasting.' 'When I look at the College War memorials of the First World War,' wrote Mowll still later, 'I find there so many names of men who came to the Lord just before they gave their lives for their country.' 'A great affair,' was the verdict of C. T. Studd, who had worked as an assistant missioner, 'there were some wonderful cases. The Spirit of God was mightily present.'

And Torrey, as he returned to America, wrote to Arthur Bradley in China, 'I believe under God that my three weeks at Cambridge have been the most fruitful of my life.'

CHAPTER XV

THE LAST YEARS OF PEACE

WITH the Torrey Mission the Inter-Collegiate Union became once again numerically powerful, Sunday by Sunday packing Holy Trinity to hear Handley Moule or other stalwarts of former days, or Freechurchmen—F. B. Meyer or Graham Scroggie—younger parsons, or laymen such as Thomas Inskip the rising lawyer, or on occasions one of the founders of the C.I.C.C.U.

The missionary call was heard with renewed emphasis. The Volunteer Unions flourished and a steady stream of recruits flowed to the mission field. Hopes were high 'not merely for a Cambridge Seven but a Cambridge Seventy.' C. T. Studd was back for a short time from the pioneering in the Southern Sudan which had followed his work in China and India, and during the Torrey Mission he had spoken at the Guildhall, 'a most solemn meeting,' as Barclay Buxton, on furlough from Japan described it, 'and from what we have heard since, God's clear call was heard by many a man.' Buxton's own son Alfred was among them, and some months later Cambridge was startled by Alfred Buxton's decision to abandon his medical studies to go straight to the Sudan with Studd. His father strongly advised that such decision must be wrong. For months the issue hung in the balance. On Sunday 3rd November 1912, Alfred Buxton's twenty-first birthday, his father unwittingly gave him in the course of a sermon preached for the C.I.C.C.U., the certainty he sought. That night, thirty years almost to the day after his own conversion in Cambridge, Barclay Buxton listened with bowed head as Alfred told him he would go. Two months later, with Fred Morris, who had worked as Stuart Holden's curate, and Jack Batstone of Queens' and the London Hospital Alfred Buxton left for Africa with Studd.

For all the new vigour, controversy still clouded the Cambridge sky. The Torrey Mission had sharpened differences, several senior men feeling that further hope of unity was destroyed. The Student Movement drew wide support, including that of some whose outlook in no way differed from the Christian Union's and yet preferred not to join. A fruit of controversy was a booklet published in June 1913, *Old Paths in Perilous Times*. Written by six C.I.C.C.U. members and with a preface by Handley Moule, *Old Paths* gave a brief account of the rise of the Christian Union and then described the course and cause of the recent disaffiliation from the S.C.M., 'an amicable agreement to differ and not a quarrelsome parting.' The historical section suffered from being based on hearsay, and the rest displayed, as an otherwise friendly critic complained, 'a somewhat indignant spirit of vindictive apology.' But as the critic could also point out, the booklet was written 'at the climax of a time of severe criticism from friend and foe,' and its spirit of contention should not 'prejudice the reader against those essential truths which the authors have endeavoured to emphasize.' Whatever its defects, the booklet helped to clarify for a new generation the issues which had led to the break of 1910.

But a later and more ambitious literary effort of 1913, *Cambridge Christian Life*, was a sign of returning unity. A committee of former Christian Union men conceived the plan of a monthly magazine 'to keep alive and intensify interest in the Christian life in the University.' It aimed both to keep old Cambridge men informed of events and to reach the undergraduates with well-chosen religious articles. 'The winning of men for Christ's service,' wrote A. T. Phillips, one of its editors, 'was a never absent motive.' The first number appeared in December 1913 and the magazine was issued twice a term. 'Our journal,' Henry Orpen of Pembroke, its first editor wrote to some friends, 'is divided into articles and news. The articles which are all written by leading men in the country, are sanely evangelical. Our purpose has been to stand and work for just those principles for which the C.I.C.C.U. stands and works. . . . In the news part we . . . take a rather wider view. We do not, however, hold ourselves responsible for the views expressed in the various reports of meetings. Thus we report C.I.C.C.U. and Church Society, Christian Social Union and most missionary news of the University.' This magazine, which Orpen hoped would 'do a great deal towards forming the C.I.C.C.U. traditions' was to run throughout 1914 and survive into the War until the summer of '15.

Unity increased, and when the University went down in the cloudless June of 1914 arrangements were well ahead for a United Mission in November; Charles Alexander and Wilbur Chapman, an evangelist who stood where Torrey stood, were to be the missioners. 'Let us lay aside all private likes and dislikes,' urged T. R. Glover, fellow of John's 'and all criticism, and in humble dependence on God let Him work in His own way for His own glory.'

In July came the Keswick Convention. The Cambridge camp, seventy strong again and scarcely touched by possibilities of War, was on the lower slopes above the town: 'a mug of brown shaving water at 7 o'clock, then a dip, a quick dress and over the fence for a quiet time among the trees of Latrigg,' was one man's nostalgic memory, a few weeks later. 'The roll of praise which surges through the great tent . . . searching and powerful addresses . . . out on Derwentwater in a boat of an afternoon . . . singing hymns in a secluded spot under Charles Alexander's leadership . . . then on to tea at Lodore and back singing across the lake.'

On the last Sunday evening, 'while heads were bowed in prayer, one after another humbly thanked God for a fresh vision of Himself, for lives purified, for hopes renewed, for surrenders gladly made.'

Less than ten days later came August 4th 1914.

CHAPTER XVI

POST-WAR

THE War soon depleted Cambridge. In October 1914 less than half the usual number of undergraduates came up, to find Trinity a temporary hospital and the First Welsh Division camped and billeted across the town.

Each year the University decreased; by the end of 1916 a mere few hundred, unfit for service or maimed in action, were mingled with the officer-cadets who filled the colleges. The C.I.C.C.U. with other societies reflected the changing situation. At first its normal life continued. For several months also the Henry Martyn Hall was used as a troops' recreation room, closing each night with a short service: 'from the very first the one supreme aim has been to bring men to a saving knowledge of the Lord Jesus Christ. . . . It was very rare to find the hall not filled at this service. . . . Over two thousand Pocket Testaments have been taken by the men.'

At its lowest the Union was reduced to one registered member. By mid-1917 it had risen to ten and the Daily Prayer Meeting began once more, never to lapse again in Full Term. The weekly sermon was represented by short informal talks or Bible readings, in the vestry of Holy Trinity or sitting round the table, twelve or fourteen undergraduates or cadets, in the Henry Martyn Library. Clifford Martin, future Bishop of Liverpool, an officer with the cadets, found his faith rekindled by these small meetings, and opened his billet in Corpus for further Bible readings. A year later, in October 1918, the evangelistic services were revived by P. H. Potter, who had returned as curate-in-charge of Holy Trinity. But the Christian Union's affairs remained, in words of one of its few members, 'stationary and discouraging.'

In the early weeks of 1919 the flow back to Cambridge began. Numbers increased. And with them, the power and prestige of the Student Christian Movement. 'It rose up like a rocket,' was Norman Grubb's comment, an ex-serviceman who came up in January. Most of those whose religion was active found in the Student Movement's mingling of outlooks and in its lenient terms of membership an atmosphere congenial to the faith brought back from the trenches. When Edward Woods, a chaplain in France during the War, arrived to take up his appointment at Holy Trinity he found the S.C.M. already 'in a very flourishing condition,' and as the months passed the religious life of the University seemed, as he wrote, in sharp contrast to 'the sad tales going about, I fear some of them true, of the immorality then prevalent in Oxford.'

The Inter-Collegiate Union was small. A. G. Pite, Roland Pelly and many others who had worked with it before the War, had thrown in their lot with the S.C.M. Not more than fifteen men regularly attended the Daily Prayer Meeting in the Lent term 1919. 'But most of these fifteen,' writes Norman Grubb, 'were very keen men, whose faith had stood the test of the War experience.' The S.C.M. approached them. 'Many and urgent' representations were made that the Christian Union should 'link up and become a kind of devotional branch of the Movement.' Charles Raven, Dean of Emmanuel, the most active of the religious leaders and a man who wished to see a strong evangelical group in the S.C.M., told Grubb 'you have got the thing we want.' Others were less complimentary: 'Move with the times or the C.I.C.C.U. will be dead within a year.'

To settle the matter, a meeting of delegates from the two committees met in Trinity, Norman Grubb and D. T. Dick the President representing the C.I.C.C.U. Grubb and Dick had no wish to be factious. But they knew something of the issues of 1910 and they had seriously to consider whether the spirituality which the S.C.M. so much admired would survive fusion. The Movement reflected the strongly liberal tone of theology and the prevalent concentration on a social gospel. Only a few months earlier it had weakened the wording of its Basis in order, as its friends explained, to make easier 'the union of those who sought with those who believed they had found.'

The meeting took place early one afternoon; throughout it the Daily Prayer Meeting was continued, men praying on until the two representatives returned. 'After an hour's conversation which got us nowhere,' reported Grubb, 'one direct and vital question was put: "Does the S.C.M. consider the atoning blood of Jesus Christ as the central point of their message?" And the answer given was, "No, not as central, although it is given a place in our teaching." That answer settled the matter, for we explained to them at once that the atoning blood was so much the heart of our message that we could never join with a movement which gave it a lesser place.'

Relationships remained close and friendly. The contentiousness of pre-war years had disappeared. Student Movement men came to Daily Prayer Meeting from time to time; once a week or more C.I.C.C.U. representatives would go to the S.C.M. Prayer Meeting, though, as Clifford Martin recalled, 'the prayers seemed mostly social service prayers and were generally led as Intercessions.'

The Christian Union began to move, numbers slowly rising, but when Godfrey Buxton, still on crutches, returned to Trinity in the May term he found ignorance of basic truths and a tendency among members 'to consider themselves a Mutual Admiration Society.' Grubb, Martin and Buxton set to work. They took teams into the villages to do Open Air work, knowing that such activities would send men to their knees and to their Bibles. They urged them in the colleges to get out among 'the heathen'—of which there was no lack after four years of War—and to take parties to the evangelistic sermons, with coffee in their rooms to follow.

The Long Vacation was memorable. The Keswick Convention was to be held but no Cambridge Camp could be arranged. An invitation came from Mrs. C. T. Studd to form a house-party of University men. Twenty-nine went, including two or three from Oxford and Noel

Palmer, who while at Cambridge recovering from wounds had been brought into the life of the C.I.C.C.U. and was going up to Oxford in October.

The first few days were arid. Five men therefore met one evening in the drawing-room of their boarding-house for prayer and it was two in the morning before they separated. Hamilton Wilkes of Oxford took off his coat and, in Norman Grubb's words, 'hammered the heavens.' Before the impromptu meeting was over, recalled Clarence Foster of Emmanuel, 'we had a very certain assurance that God was going to work in the house-party. Indeed, when we stopped there was something of Pentecost in the room.' The burden they had felt had gone, happiness pervaded them and a new experience had come—'we had never before known assurance in prayer.'

'The blessing fell the next morning,' wrote Grubb, 'the atmosphere was so charged with His presence that men were getting alone with God, having things out and coming back transformed.' They went out each night in twos and threes to the woods and found themselves in this spirit of prayer. An overwhelming sense of the holiness of God gave men new standards for their lives, absorbed selfish ambition, and emphasized with fresh urgency the spiritual issues of the times. The danger that the C.I.C.C.U. would be a hard, barren, defensive clique was over; as Grubb put it, 'With the decision against reunion came Faithfulness; at Keswick came Fire.'

The spirit of prayer and assurance was carried to Eastbourne, where many of the men worked for a month on a Children's Mission. With Noel Palmer and Hamilton Wilkes it reached Oxford; there, on the lines of the old O.I.C.C.U., they launched a Bible Union, which after a somewhat chequered history was refounded nine years later with the original name restored, Oxford Inter-Collegiate Christian Union. Back at Cambridge in the Michaelmas term the C.I.C.C.U. seemed rejuvenated.

As in the eighteen-seventies, as in 1911, the most marked feature was prayer. 'A terrific atmosphere of prayer,' so Clifford Martin described it, 'the spiritual temperature was magnificient.' When men met for tea or coffee they would settle to prayer afterwards; the back-views on which visitors would stumble when calling unexpectedly on C.I.C.C.U. men became a byword. The Saturday night meetings would be extended beyond schedule; at the end of each D.P.M. for a while six or seven would join Norman Grubb to pray for his brother, an atheist, until prayer was answered. With this spirit abroad it was not strange that as Leslie Sutton of Queens' wrote, 'numbers of unusual men were won for Christ.' There was the dandy of Emmanuel, with his gold cigarette-case and well-cut clothes, and the Trinity soccer captain, brilliant also as a mathematican. There were men direct from school, such as Ivor Beauchamp, son of Sir Montagu Beauchamp of the Cambridge Seven, and John Eberstein, up from Welling-ton to Pembroke, who resisted invitations to C.I.C.C.U. sermons so long as courtesy allowed; was mildly interested by the sermon which eventually he heard, only to be shown, over tea a few days later that 'everyone had to choose between Christ and world. Somehow I felt,' as he recalled thirty years later, 'that this was the choice I had to make and that this was the time that I had to make it. As though it were only yesterday I can remember saying to myself, "for me it will be Christ."' And behind everything was prayer. 'I was taken along on Saturday night to the Henry Martyn Hall,' continues Eberstein, 'I had never been in a prayer meeting before, had never even heard of such a thing and it was a revelation to me to hear people around me praying—not formal prayers, but quite spontaneously.'

Problems, however, were not over. It had been clear from the start that a mission should be held; no plan, however, had emerged when in May 1919 an invitation came from the University Council for Religious Questions, a new body which had been formed by deans and chaplains with the hope of co-ordinating all efforts, to join a United Mission for the Lent term 1920. Edward Woods, whose saintliness of life and power of preaching had quickly made him a force in post-war Cambridge, but who now represented the Student Movement outlook rather than that of the Christian Union, was eager that all should take part.

C.I.C.C.U. counsels were divided. The united mission for November 1914 was to have been addressed by Wilbur Chapman, with Charles Alexander; men whom the Union could have backed to the hilt. That of 1920 was to be addressed by a team of missioners of widely divergent though, as the sponsors believed, complementary views. On the other hand the University would be awake and responsive; the mission would carry almost official status and the stigma which handicapped the preparations for Torrey in 1911 would be absent. And an independent effort, taking place afterwards, would find its message falling on surfeited ears. Yet to stand on a united platform might vitiate the earlier decision that 'the C.I.C.C.U. must remain,' as Grubb put it, 'absolutely separate, in order to give a clear witness in the University to God's way of salvation through Christ.' The undergraduate needed a message which could not be mistaken, and he might not get it. The C.I.C.C.U. would have its chosen Missioner; two of the others, Herbert Gray and Theodore Woods, who was now Bishop of Peterborough and whose doctrinal position had somewhat changed since Cambridge days, might preach a gospel akin to that of the Christian Union's man, but with distinct differences and omissions. Bishop Charles Gore, lately resigned from Oxford, would frankly offer another approach. And each missioner would have the same credentials in the eyes of the University.

After much prayer at Keswick, the Union decided to stand out. A month later the decision was reversed, after two further prayer meetings and not a little contention. But they came in on condition, readily accepted, that their 'clear witness' be maintained, and that their missioner should not join in any united definition of belief. Godfrey Buxton the President stressed their fear lest the University 'be edified with a code of morals to observe rather than enriched by a new life,' and defined once again the Christian Union's conviction 'that the Bible as originally given is, and not merely contains, the inspired Word of God, and is the only infallible guide to faith and practice; and that all are dead in sin and unable to please God until they have turned and received atonement for sin through the death of Jesus Christ and new life through His spirit.'

'Having decided to unite with us,' recorded the Official Report of the mission, edited by Charles Raven, 'they did more than any of the groups to call their members to prayer and to circulate prayer slips throughout the country.' Thirty thousand such slips were circulated, and sent by missionary societies or in personal letters over the world, while at Cambridge immense activity filled the days of ex-servicemen, who being required only to keep four terms without examination to qualify for a degree considered themselves unhindered by claims of academic work. They invited as missioner George Grubb, Norman Grubb's uncle, at whose mission in 1893 Bishop Theodore Woods had been converted. He was abroad and unable to accept. Barclay Buxton, the President's father and a distinguished missionary, then aged forty-nine, was chosen in his place.

On Saturday, 31st January 1920 the Guildhall was packed, many being turned away, for the opening meeting addressed by Bishop Gore and Herbert Gray. The Mission Committee had hoped to obtain Lloyd George to speak, or some other distinguished layman 'whom the University would get up in the middle of the night to hear.' But the President of Boats, Alfred Swann, made a chairman whose name increased the platform's drawing power. On the Sunday the four missioners each spoke at their own services, Great St. Mary's, Holy Trinity, the Guildhall and the Examination Hall being used. Edward Woods noted in his diary for that day an estimated total attendance of about two thousand four hundred. In the days that followed an average of two thousand were present.

On the day after the mission Edward Woods wrote, 'We are all gasping with wonder and praise at the events of last week, overflowing with thanks to God. All groups an unbounded success except the C.I.C.C.U.'

This disappointment was partly due to geography. Five or six hundred gave the Bishop of Peterborough a packed Holy Trinity; the same number could only fill three-quarters of the Guildhall, and the empty rows of seats were depressing in contrast and helped to lower numbers on subsequent nights. To some extent it was a matter also of personality. Gore and Woods were highly prominent with great reputations, Gray was a leading Student Movement speaker. Barclay Buxton had spent most of his working life in Japan and was unknown beyond his circle. He was a saint, deeply versed in the study and practice of Christian sanctity, and his influence had been felt mainly among Christians whom he was skilled in leading to lives of deeper blessing. Ten years earlier he had been offered the living of Holy Trinity and had refused it, to continue his work in Japan. Since then, Cambridge had become impatient of any who could not make their appeal primarily to the intellect.

But Christian Union men were conscious of a difficulty which lay deeper than geography or personality. Though happy to see several men brought into the Christian life and the faith of others strengthened, they were made only too aware of the principal weakness of a United Mission: as Godfrey Buxton put it, 'a man might receive strong convictions from one missioner and then go to another and find them dispelled.' Nor could they feel confident that Gore, Gray and Woods, the missioners whose influence predominated had broken through the optimism and even arrogance which characterized many of the men who had won the War, or had deeply satisfied the spiritual hunger of others. They regretted that except in the Guildhall the stress had been, as the Official Report claimed, 'rather upon social duty and corporate righteousness than upon personal conversion and individual salvation,' and they distrusted both the tendency of the mission's sponsors to rely on attendance figures as the measure of success and in their confidence that conviction of the 'reasonableness and practicability of the faith' would ensure 'a sincere and lasting judgement.'

Edward Woods remarked to one of them that 'the

prayers of the C.I.C.C.U. were answered in Holy Trinity.'
The Union hoped it was so, but doubted it.

Despite disappointments, the fourteen months since the
Armistice had seen the Christian Union securely back on
the map. 'Their fervour and assured faith,' commented
the Official Report of the United Mission, 'is an element
in the life of Cambridge that could ill be spared.' But these
months had also seen the launching of two new movements.

The first was among the women of the University. With
Girton and Newnham and the two training colleges
scattered in distant corners of the town, each more than
two miles from its neighbour, nothing approaching an
inter-collegiate union had ever appeared. In the 'eighties
Mrs. Handley Moule had arranged meetings for women
students and in the 'nineties Cambridge women Volunteers had been responsible for the founding in India of the
Missionary Settlement for University Women. The expansion of the Student Christian Movement before the
Great War had produced branches in each college, and
women sat on the local S.C.M. Executive, but in 1920 no
provision yet existed for those who, had they been men,
would have been members of the C.I.C.C.U.

In October 1919 Miss Dorothea Reader Harris, afterwards Mrs. Godfrey Buxton had come to stay in Cambridge at the suggestion of the C.I.C.C.U. Executive, 'to
see whether the usefulness of the mission could not be
extended to the Women's colleges.' In January she came
back for the mission, staying in Newnham as the guest of
Rachel Wingate, sister of the future General of Chindits
and one of the few girls thoroughly in sympathy. On
several nights of the mission Miss Reader Harris, who had
been a soloist with Charles Alexander, sang before the
address, for wireless had not as yet made audiences im-
pervious to such appeals. She spent much time encouraging the college girls to the Guildhall, and one, a
prominent member of an Atheists' Club, was brought into a
vivid experience of Christ through Barclay Buxton's
preaching, and immediately broke off her engagement to a
man who was not a Christian.

Several other women were reached by the mission, and at its close they came to Miss Reader Harris concerned at the absence of opportunity for the organized prayer and Bible study which they desired, and which they felt would not be adequately supplied by the Student Movement branches. Four days later, on Wednesday 11th February 1920 Miss Reader Harris and six Newnham girls and three from Girton met in the Henry Martyn Library and decided to form the Cambridge Women's Inter-Collegiate Christian Union, on a similar basis to the C.I.C.C.U. Two days later Miss Attenborough of Newnham and Miss Jacob of Girton, both converts of the week before and afterwards prominent as headmistresses of schools, were elected President and Secretary, and Miss Wingate, who was shortly going down, was made Treasurer. During the following week inaugural meetings were held at Newnham and Girton, the President being supported at the one by Godfrey Buxton and Miss Reader Harris, at the other by Clifford Martin. Efforts to carry the new Union into Homerton or the Cambridge Training College failed.

Distance prevented a united Daily Prayer Meeting for women; the two colleges each ran their own and came together once a week, generally to be addressed by the C.I.C.C.U. speaker. They were invited to make full use of the Sunday evening sermon at Holy Trinity and 'after much discussion' they accepted, encouraged perhaps by the assurance that four back rows of the nave would be kept for ladies only. No official contact or co-operation with the C.I.C.C.U. was provided; the Executive of the men's Union took grave warning from the number of S.C.M. Presidents who announced their engagements to lady members of their executives, and recognized also that the frequent presence of ladies at C.I.C.C.U. meetings might distract both sexes from the work in hand. But the men hastened to show their welcome by undertaking all initial printing expenses and by presenting the new Union with a handsome minute book.

Thus the C.W.I.C.C.U. started on its twenty-eight years' history.

· · · · ·

The second and the most significant contribution of the first post-war generation at Cambridge was their vision of an Inter-Varsity Fellowship.

'I cannot remember the exact day,' wrote Norman Grubb some fifteen years later, 'but it was sometime about the middle of the Michaelmas term 1919, that one day in my room, God gave me the vision of the Inter-Varsity Fellowship that was to be.' He had been reading a letter from Noel Palmer in Oxford reporting progress and asking for prayer. Palmer was building from the foundations, the old Inter-Collegiate Christian Union being by then the Oxford branch of the S.C.M., and in no other University was there any body with the C.I.C.C.U.'s basis and aim. 'I saw,' writes Grubb, 'that not only must there be this witness in every University but that God was going to do it.'

Grubb took his idea to his friends, Clarence Foster and Leslie Sutton. In the latter's rooms, looking out over the Cam and the wooden, steeply arched Queens' Bridge, 'we spent time in prayer and in waiting on God for His guidance.' They saw that the first step would be to arrange an Inter-Varsity Conference, 'at which we could get as many as we could from other Universities, and enthuse them with starting a branch.'

They worked quickly and on Monday, December 8th 1919 some sixty men met in North London at the headquarters of the Egypt General Mission. The largest contingents were from Oxford and Cambridge, a few came from London and one from Durham. Barclay Buxton and George Grubb, E. L. Langston and G. H. Lang gave Bible Readings and 'Convention addresses.' The emphasis, as in the twenty-eight pre-war conferences between Oxford and Cambridge, was on devotion, spiritual growth and the need to evangelize.

On the Thursday evening the Conference closed with a missionary meeting. 'One speaker after another,' wrote Ivor Beauchamp, 'told of the white harvest fields, with the few labourers overstrained, some in lonely stations the sole witnesses for Christ among millions who knew Him not. And the wonderful possibility suggested itself, "did He perhaps want me to help reinforce the thin red line?"'

Thus from the start the new movement showed that it was to be of value not only to the Universities but to the mission field.

The men returned to their colleges, as Grubb knew that they would, fired by their vision and with a new sense of responsibility. For the next nine years the growth of the new movement provided a background to the work of the Christian Unions. The Inter-Varsity Conference became annual and in 1922 a General Committee was set up and a Constitution drafted. By 1927, when one hundred and ten men and women met for the Conference, a more permanent organization was urged; in provincial universities new unions were finding it hard to extract recognition from official authorities without being able to point to a parent body. The following year therefore, 1928, the Inter-Varsity Fellowship was formed.

'The Fellowship has been firmly built,' stated an account issued some six years later, 'on the principle of local autonomy and the endeavour to ensure the strongest local leadership.' Such policy, fruit of memories handed down from the years when the Student Movement had pressed its branches to fall into line, made for 'slow and irregular growth,' but often a Union would come into being without prompting from the Fellowship. 'A feature of these societies,' one of the leaders could say to students at Cardiff as early as 1923, 'is the spontaneity of their formation,' and when the Fellowship spread overseas, to Canada, Australia and New Zealand, its travelling secretaries not only formed fresh unions but found small groups already active.

Working alongside the Student Movement the I.V.F. found itself obliged to define its beliefs carefully, and became at times, as one of its Vice-Presidents wrote, 'doctrinally self-conscious and anxious.' But basing its activities, as had the old Student Volunteers, on 'a deep conviction that the Bible is the Word of God'; its object continually 'to stimulate personal faith and to further evangelical work'; its officers bound by constitution to be clearly committed to its doctrinal beliefs but its meetings open to all, the Inter-Varsity Fellowship grew with its years. By 1939 in every University in the British Isles save one University College, a Christian Union had been affiliated, and the Technical and the Teacher Training colleges were feeling the Fellowship's influence. It was issuing its own magazine, *Inter-Varsity*,[1] possessed its own publishing house and had a staff of travelling secretaries in Britain and the Commonwealth. Alliances had been made with similar fellowships in Scandinavia and on the Continent and in 1934 their first International conference took place in Norway.

Cambridge men played a foremost part in the Fellowship's development and when in the summer of 1939 the fifth international conference, with a thousand students attending, was held at Cambridge and a conference service was broadcast from Great St. Mary's, it seemed to set a seal on the Inter-Collegiate Union's work. For all this had sprung from the prayer of one man, twenty years before, in a ground-floor room on Trinity Great Court, that autumn morning of 1919.

[1] The original title was *The Inter-Varsity Magazine*.

CHAPTER XVII

FIVE YEARS' UNCERTAINTY

IN the autumn of 1920 an unknown American arrived in Cambridge, Frank Buchman. Born in Pennsylvania forty-two years before, he had been ordained a Lutheran pastor, starting work in one of the poorer quarters of Philadelphia. For six years he was building up a new church, opening and developing a hostel for poor boys and a settlement for Christian work, until in 1908 disagreement with his managing committee made him resign and leave for Europe, resentful and 'harbouring ill-will.' At the Keswick Convention that summer, so he recounted later, at a small meeting in a nearby village church addressed by a woman, 'Something happened for which I shall always be grateful. . . . I had entered the little church with a divided will, housing pride, selfishness, ill-will which prevented me functioning as a Christian minister should. The woman's simple talk personalized the Cross for me that day.'

Like so many with similar experience at Keswick, he sensed an immediate urge to share this new understanding of how 'the love of God in Christ had bridged the chasm dividing me from Him,' and to pass on 'the new sense of buoyant life.' He returned to America, working as a chaplain at Pennsylvania State College. The high moral demand of Christianity, with the certainty that it could be met in the power of the Spirit increasingly impressed itself on him, as on so many who had heard the Keswick message, and early each day between five and six he kept his quiet time or morning watch. He began to find that he had an exceptional understanding of the thoughts and problems of those whom he met and an almost magnetic influence on them. As the years passed, two elements in this new life were especially emphasized: the guidance of God, in small matters as in major decisions, and the comfort and value of the open admission, between friends, of sin and shortcoming. To receive Guidance he would spend much time, note-book in hand, 'listening'; whenever he was conscious of sin he would seek to 'share' it and the experience of its forgiveness.

In 1915 Buchman began a four years' tour of India and the Far East which indirectly was to lead him to Cambridge and to the founding of the Oxford Group. For in China he met Bishop Molony, the Pembroke man of the 'eighties, whose stepson Theodore Goodwin had gone up to Pembroke after war-service and was Vice-President of the C.I.C.C.U. Molony wrote suggesting that Buchman, who was about to visit England, should be invited to address the C.I.C.C.U. pre-terminal 'quiet day', for he had been 'the means of much blessing at meetings for missionaries which he had addressed in various parts of China.'

Goodwin and Clifford Martin met Buchman at Brown's Hotel in London in September 1920—and found him 'a little frightening'—and early in October he came up to Cambridge. 'Quiet and restrained,' so the journalist Harold Begbie described Buchman shortly afterwards, 'the voice low but vigorous, with a sincere ring of friendliness and good humour . . . he strikes one as a warm-hearted and very happy man, who can never know what it is to be physically tired or mentally bored.' He spoke in the Henry Martyn Hall, telling the C.I.C.C.U. of his experience at Keswick, stressing God's demand for absolute purity of living and the benefit of absolute honesty and open speaking between Christians. 'He shook us,' recalled Clifford Martin, 'none of us liked it but we needed it.' When the meeting broke up many of the men went back, as did Willie Oswald and Guy Bullen of Queens', to 'talk it over.' Reserve was broken down and they had, as Bullen wrote, 'our first heart-to-heart talk about the things that matter.'

Buchman spoke of himself as 'Professor of Personal Evangelism,' and mentioned that he had worked with Torrey and Alexander. At first Christian Union men, 'all of us eager to learn all we could about soul-winning,' were his ardent disciples. But before long the C.I.C.C.U. was divided by Buchman as sharply as forty years earlier it had been divided by the Holiness movement. Some of its leading members were convinced that he held the secret of Christian living for modern times. His whole foundation was in the evangelical message and his emphasis they believed to be right. 'I knew him well,' wrote one of them later, 'seeing him under all strains and stresses, and I owe him a great deal and gladly acknowledge it.' Others were unhappy with him. He reported wonderful cases of 'Life-changing,' and yet they never seemed to see his converts. They feared lest when men were 'Changed' it was more by his personality than by the power of the Holy Spirit. They mistrusted his over-emphasis on sex; 'every intellectual difficulty or problem of any kind seemed to have its origin in sex.' At Daily Prayer Meeting Buchman would open his note-book, and while others were praying he would be sitting at the back 'listening'; some of his friends were soon doing likewise. Nor were matters eased when Buchman informed the President that he had been guided to speak at the Saturday night prayer meeting, at which no talks were then given, or when his followers appeared to spend their times of prayer being guided when to change their shoes or to have baths. And there was always the strange effect of his presence. As John Eberstein wrote, 'I was a bit scared of him and did not like his eyes. He seemed almost to have something hypnotic about him.'

Frank Buchman made Cambridge his base for nearly a year, staying at Westminster, the Presbyterian theological college. He hoped that the C.I.C.C.U. would work whole-heartedly with him, developing his discoveries of Sharing and Guidance. After some months he was disappointed and left the Christian Union to itself. But he was continuing to make friends, and the captain of University Rugger was among his converts.

In May 1921 Buchman visited Oxford, taking with him the captain of Rugger and two of the older Christian Union men. His effect on Oxford was immediate, and although he returned to preach the C.I.C.C.U. sermon for May 23rd, his interest in Cambridge soon slackened. During the summer he returned to the United States, touring universities with the two C.I.C.C.U. men. In the winter he arranged a house-party in Christ Church, Oxford and there founded his First Century Christian Fellowship.

At Cambridge, Buchmanism without Buchman declined, and by the close of 1921 any possibility that the C.I.C.C.U. might form the nucleus of a future Cambridge Group had evaporated.

Buchman had come from beyond Cambridge. Most of the C.I.C.C.U.'s problems at this time were indigenous.

After 1922 the flow of ex-servicemen dropped, though their maturity and steadiness seemed left as a legacy to the men of the next few years, fresh from school. It was, by contrast, an unclouded time, the fruits of victory still sweet, the economic depression as yet beyond the horizon. But religion and morals already were in sharp decline. Despite much activity the Cambridge churches were losing hold of undergraduates. College chapels, with few exceptions, were empty, depressing and ineffective. Cambridge theology was negative. 'You spent the first year of theological reading,' commented Max Warren of Jesus, 'on being told what you were *not* to believe.' Critical theories were still worked on the assumption that literary and historical criticism answered all theological problems. Sir Edwyn Hoskyns, already deeply influenced by Karl Barth, alone seemed to take a more positive line. Throughout the country many of the more thoughtful younger evangelicals, though detached from the extremes of liberalism, were influenced strongly by contemporary trends. The Anglican Evangelical Group Movement, outward expression of the new view-point, was growing rapidly, allowing itself 'with conscious purpose,' as Vernon Storr claimed, 'to be swept into the stream of modern knowledge . . . absorptive of the manifold new truths which God is revealing . . . adjusting itself to the changing conditions of modern thought and life.' For the liberal evangelicals,

Storr continued, the supreme authority was 'the mind of Christ,' and they sought to distinguish 'the essential message of the Bible' from the form in which the message was originally given: 'the form belongs to the past and has often to be abandoned.' They also rejected the 'substitutionary view of the atonement as that was interpreted by the older evangelicals.'

The liberal evangelical did not find himself at home with the C.I.C.C.U., nor it with him. Thus the Union found itself restricted in its choice of preachers and, although public reputation was not considered the first test of suitability, seldom able to bring men whose very names attracted attention. But two, coming regularly, who always commanded the widest hearing were Bishop Taylor Smith and John Stuart Holden. Taylor Smith, with his power to express spiritual truth in simplicity, his wit and aptness of phrase, and his ability to draw his hearers to Christ the centre of every message he gave, had for over twenty years been Chaplain-General. Stuart Holden, Vicar of St. Paul's, Portman Square and a prolific writer, had become one of the most able preachers of his day. If sometimes his force was spent in an excessive artistry and smoothness of speech, yet the wide range of his knowledge, his culture, his clarity of thought, and his faithfulness to the whole Bible as the Word of God even when tempted strongly to move into liberalism, made him of inestimable value to the Christian Union. Moreover he held the confidence and respect of senior men in the University.

Holden was often called on for advice in the first postwar years. But in 1923 a young Cambridge missionary, Harold Earnshaw-Smith of Christ's, invalided back from Nigeria, became Chaplain of Caius and brought an accession of strength to the C.I.C.C.U. which outweighed the indifference or even hostility of the Seniority of the University.

Earnshaw-Smith, as one President of this time wrote, 'seemed to know a liberty of spirit and a happy detachment from fear of man and bondage to tradition. His bright outspokenness could shock those with fixed ideas, but his influence was in the direction of true spiritual liberty and joy, and his counsel in time of problem was invariably helpful.' His rooms became the centre of the Cambridge Volunteer Union, he gave a marked impetus to Bible study and prayer, rallied the C.I.C.C.U. for weekly mission services in the Victoria Cinema for the townspeople, and soon seemed to be guide and counsellor to the whole Christian Union. In due course he joined the Pastorate, in 1925 resigning from Caius to continue his Pastorate work unchecked.

To Earnshaw-Smith, with F. H. Sheldon, who came as chaplain to Trinity Hall in 1924, moving later to Caius, the Christian Union owed much of its vigour. For though in some colleges—Corpus, King's, Sidney Sussex—representation was low or even from time to time absent, and in comparison with thirty years before and thirty years later the C.I.C.C.U. was small, it was not insignificant. Its membership was drawn from all Cambridge. Readers in arts predominated, many being future clergy or schoolmasters, but there were wanting neither scientists not a steady supply of medical students; and what was widely considered an old-fashioned, out-dated gospel was continuing to transform men, mould character and reorientate the purposes of life. Recruits to the Union in the early 'twenties were drawn as much from those coming up without personal faith as from those who sought out the Union on arrival, and although much was done in the freshman's term—'squashes', arranged somewhat casually, and a leading preacher on the first Sunday evening—the sense of responsibility for others was maintained throughout the year: 'it was looked upon as a disgrace to be at a C.I.C.C.U. sermon without at least one "fish" in tow. If you could walk in with a whole string it was very difficult to maintain due humility!'

The concern behind such activities did not end in Holy Trinity Church. Across Cambridge late on a Sunday evening Christian Union men and their friends would be facing the impact of truth; nor, when the sermon had been without apparent effect was that always the end of the story. Thus two men, one a Christian whose experience dated only from his first term, the other a scientist who was an agnostic and a dabbler in theosophy, were in casual conversation one Sunday night after a most unfortunate sermon. 'Nearer midnight than was safe, for my friend lived out of college,' recalled the Christian, 'the spiritual issue came up again. It was just this: sermon or no sermon, "What about Christ?" Yes, God was working, and the friend, agnostic and theosophist as he was, broke down, saying "I think I'm too bad."' 'I had been,' so the other man wrote, thirty years later; 'for many years under real conviction of sin and had wondered how bad one would have to be before God would shut one out of heaven. But I had no idea of the solution.' They were soon looking at the fifty-third chapter of Isaiah, 'For the first time in my life I began to see the real meaning of the *Gospel*. "The Lord hath laid on *Him* the iniquity of us all." I had never seen it before. Now light began to dawn. I saw that everything had been done when Jesus died on the Cross and that it only remained for me to accept it.' Then they were on their knees and, so the Christian could say of his friend, 'that moment he passed from death into life.' As for the former agnostic, who a few minutes later was running back to his lodgings to be in by midnight, 'it was as though my feet scarcely touched the ground, and I have the most vivid recollection of saying to myself over and over, as I ran, "I've seen Jesus! I've seen Jesus!"—words that I had certainly never used before, nor heard anyone else use.'

Friendships which led to such incidents deepened as men continued in the faith thus found. But faith sometimes burned low. 'Our duty is to get a personal talk and to deal straightly with all C.I.C.C.U. members in our college,' wrote Godfrey Webb-Peploe to the college representatives in 1922, 'so many of them are powerless and defeated.' Webb-Peploe of St. Catharine's, a man of great gentleness and beauty of life, in the tradition of the early Volunteers visited every man in his college to lay the claims of Christ before them. Yet he knew his own limitations, and did not hesitate to confess, though President, that 'in the past term I have not had victory.' The Keswick Convention of 1922, he wrote, opened his eyes to the possibilities of Christian living: 'I can tell you it is humbling to our pride to come back to Calvary in our nakedness, but it is a thousand times worthwhile.' This urge towards spiritual depth was widespread. 'O Jesus Christ take away from me my pride and conceit,' prayed Guy Bullen of Queens' and Ridley, afterwards Assistant Bishop in the Sudan, writing in his private diary, 'replace my own self-love with a pure, intense love of Thine own Self.' Such intensity was not unhealthy. 'We were a gay, happy lot,' as Max Warren could recall—a comment which might have seemed strange if the Union's indifference towards many undergraduate indulgences was misinterpreted—and their spirituality found expression in unstinted zest for living as much as in care for their neighbours or in personal devotion and discipline.

It found expression also in consciousness of missionary responsibility. In the first four years after the War ten Christian Union men and women left for the mission field. A new Cambridge Missionary Band of fifty members was formed, A. E. Vollor of Queens', their specially supported representative sailing for Africa in 1923.

The same year awakened an echo of the Cambridge Missionary Party of 1904. G. T. Manley, as Africa Secretary of the Church Missionary Society came up in the Michaelmas term and, addressing some twenty undergraduates in Earnshaw-Smith's rooms in Caius, appealed for a party to go out together to the Hausa of Northern Nigeria. One of Manley's hearers was Max Warren of Jesus, then a freshman. A few months earlier Warren and a London medical student had committed themselves privately to forming, if at all possible, a small band of missionaries to go out to some specific project. 'We had no ideas at all beyond that, and had decided to pray about it and wait to see what guidance we might be given.' Warren wrote immediately to his London friend 'to ask him if he thought this might be the answer to our prayers.' In the following vacation they met and became certain that it was the answer. Each had one friend to whom he spoke of the project. Two terms later ('it was on the last night of the Lent races, the Jesus boat was head of the river and there was a terrific bonfire in the court!') Warren was sitting in his rooms working with his door locked when, 'after a terrific knocking,' Guy Bullen, then at Ridley, and Willie Oswald entered, and said that they had heard of the Hausa Band and asked if they might join. Warren, excited, and 'rather overwhelmed,' for Bullen was far senior and had been in the War, had no hesitation in accepting. A few weeks later formal offer of the Hausa Band was made to the Church Missionary Society, and in due course four Cambridge men, with a number of London medical men and nurses, went out to Northern Nigeria.

The Inter-Collegiate Union had grown, it was held in higher respect and no longer could be dismissed as a coterie of diehards. Yet Harrison of Corpus, in his presidential letter of January 1925 had to write, 'Some of us have felt strongly that our Union lacks power and effectiveness as a witness in the University, and there is a deep need for greater unity of heart and purpose among us.'

The most pressing problem remained that of relationship to the Student Christian Movement. The S.C.M. had become, in C. E. Raven's words, a 'great debating society,' even cold-shouldering Raven himself for a while because he addressed them too directly on sin and, so they told him, preached the atonement 'emotionally.' The great Watchword of the Student Volunteers was 'dead, though a certain sentiment still clung to it.' Since 1918 the Movement's former basis of membership, 'I declare my faith in Jesus Christ as my Saviour, my Lord and my God' had been replaced by a longer statement in more general terms.

But the Student Movement was powerful, and well represented in the colleges, far outnumbering the C.I.C.C.U. It seemed natural that many who were in the one should have friends in the other, to hold membership cards for both was not uncommon, while some, such as Stephen Neill of Trinity, intellectually one of the most brilliant of his time, who was a college representative of the C.I.C.C.U. and President of the S.C.M., served on both committees.

The Student Movement leaders in Cambridge were

hoping continually for reunion, recognizing that the Inter-Collegiate Union provided an element which they were prone to lack. Clifford Martin, President of the C.I.C.C.U. for the Michaelmas term 1920 had been sympathetic to such suggestions and believed that the two movements could work in close harmony. As the direction in which the S.C.M. were moving became more defined, presidents were increasingly certain that hopes of reunion were forlorn. Clarence Foster, in 1921–22, had done much to shape and guide the policy, and as Fred Pickering of Queens', President two years later wrote, 'We were realists enough to know that amalgamation with the S.C.M. would mean the end of the definite evangelistic ministry that the C.I.C.C.U. exercised in the Varsity.' There was no bitterness or antagonism. 'We longed for and prayed for that unity of spirit between members of both societies which makes for a fellowship of love and prayer,' continues Pickering, 'but we knew from long experience that unity of organization would be impossible.' A year after Pickering's presidency the Oxford Bible Union, since 1919 the counterpart of the C.I.C.C.U., amalgamated as the Devotional Union of the S.C.M. in Oxford. And the three years before the experiment broke down were proof of what might have occurred at Cambridge.

Edward Woods at Holy Trinity who had encouraged every move towards unity, was distressed by the tendency in the Union, but he was losing the confidence of its leaders. His preaching, forceful, personal and abreast of modern thought, seemed increasingly to favour interpretations of truth which they could not reconcile with what they believed essential, and the relationship between the Union and Holy Trinity slowly became less close.

In 1925 C. J. B. Harrison of Corpus received further overtures from the S.C.M. and the two Presidents met for discussion. The Student Movement man, 'frankly puzzled' by the C.I.C.C.U., outlined to Harrison 'what the S.C.M. stood for.' 'A fellowship of students,' so ran the recently adopted basis, 'who desire to understand the Christian faith and to live the Christian life. The Movement seeks to set forth Jesus Christ as the supreme revelation of God and of the true nature of man . . . the one sure guide for all mankind in every sphere of thought and conduct . . . the source of power for the overthrow of evil and the renewal of human life. The Movement challenges students to recognize the urgent need of the whole world for Christ . . . and to respond by dedicating their lives to His service as He may guide them. It calls them to explore His teaching and to follow the guidance of His Spirit in the pursuit of truth, beauty and righteousness, to prepare themselves . . . for the future; joyfully to accept God's gift of deliverance and life for themselves; and to enter the fellowship of worship, thought and service which is the heritage of the Christian Church.'

'After hearing his account of what the S.C.M. stood for,' writes Harrison, 'I gave clearly the ground of our faith and experience of Christ.' Harrison spoke of the Bible as God's Word, of man's fallen nature, the atoning death of Christ and 'the necessity of a miraculous new birth by the work of the Holy Spirit that we may *become* children of God. . . .' The S.C.M. President seemed 'quite shaken' and remarked, 'the fact is, you have the thing we are looking for.' 'I told him,' concludes Harrison, 'that this knowledge of Christ was for him too, but he must come in God's way, which is very simple, very humbling—there is no other way. There we had to leave the matter.'

But pressure also was coming from another quarter, for an element in the Union wished to see it segregated from all other religious activities in the University, treating itself as a separate sect, to the exclusion of loyalty to college chapels or to town churches, Anglican or Nonconformist, in the manner of a closed meeting of the Brethren. Though not all those in the Union connected with the Brethren subscribed to such views this element was becoming stronger, and added to the problems of the Union's leaders in their search for a true course for the future.

By the summer of 1925 the Inter-Collegiate Union was thus hovering between two courses, each leading away from the path pursued for nearly fifty years. The party favouring close co-operation with the Student Movement and with other religious work in Cambridge was growing, and in the mid-'twenties such policy, if decisive, could scarcely fail to blunt the Union's distinctive thrust. The influence was equally extensive of the other party, who wished the Union to insulate itself from risk, thereby maintaining an isolation which though giving a measure of power would be severely restricting. In the new Executive which took office late in the May term the two parties were equally represented.

Within the next nine months the difficulties of the Union were to be intensified and then resolved in a manner none could have surmised.

It was five years since the United Mission arranged by the Council of Religious Questions. An invitation now came to the C.I.C.C.U. to take part in a second mission, to be held in February 1926, and the Executive, like their predecessors of 1919 were in doubt. 'No definite decision was reached,' recorded the minutes for their meeting of June 5th, 'but the committee were rather in favour of keeping out of it.' During the Long Vacation more details were released: the principal Anglican Missioner was to be the Bishop of Manchester, William Temple, already at forty-four a name with which to conjure. The Nonconformist would be Dr. Norwood of the City Temple, and the C.I.C.C.U. was free to choose its own. By October decision had still not been reached. The divisions in the Union were hardening, though Harold Earnshaw-Smith exerted a moderating influence between them. The President, who was of the party favouring isolation, was hesitant and a further difficulty developed from his increasing emphasis on the validity of Divine guidance received direct in prayer. On October 14th the President told the Executive that he now inclined towards joining the mission and it was decided to invite Stuart Holden to be C.I.C.C.U. missioner. Nine days later, at the Executive's prayer meeting, 'the President suddenly announced that "The Lord had mercifully preserved us from going into the Mission,"' for Stuart Holden on learning that Temple was to be a missioner felt 'very reluctant to appear in any way a rival to a bishop of his own church.'

Holden overcame his reluctance, but the indecisiveness

of the Executive and the increasingly emotional instability of the President were provoking disturbance. On Saturday afternoon, November 21st, the Executive met 'to consider the critical situation which had arisen in the Union. It was perfectly clear that something must be done if God's work through the Union was to go on unhindered.' The following afternoon a memorandum signed by twelve members was handed to the President, demanding the resignation of the entire Executive. Some days later the President announced his resignation, on the ground of 'pressure of work,' in favour of the Missionary Secretary, Hugh Gough of Trinity.

Hugh Gough, afterwards Bishop of Barking, held the confidence of the whole Union. The decision to join the United Mission was endorsed and preparations were pressed forward. But breaches were not healed and the future seemed uncertain.

CHAPTER XVIII

THE IRISHMAN

IN January, less than a week before the United Mission of 1926 was due, Hugh Gough at Trinity received a telegram from Stuart Holden: the doctor had ordered him a fortnight's rest and had forbidden the visit to Cambridge; Gough must come to London immediately to discuss what was to be done.

'We spent the evening together,' writes Gough, 'trying to think of some suitable substitute and making enquiries by telephone.' Man after man refused at such short notice. 'Suddenly we remembered that the next morning Mr. Nicholson was arriving at Euston from Ireland.' William Nicholson, an Ulster evangelist, was a minister of the Presbyterian Church of Ireland. Holden knew him as a man of force and fire, and had suggested that he should go up to Cambridge for the three days previous to the mission, 'to stir up the C.I.C.C.U. to prayer and service.' But Nicholson, who had spent a wild youth at sea, was a man of little culture or education; his impassioned oratory had swept the Irish working-classes into religious revival but he had scant experience of more sophisticated audiences. 'Was it possible,' thought Holden and Gough, 'that it was in God's plan that he should be the Missioner? The more we thought about it, the more we felt that it might be so.'

The following morning Harold Earnshaw-Smith arrived, with a few of the C.I.C.C.U. committee. The suggestion was approved, and leaving Dr. Holden's house in Hyde Park Square they went to Euston to meet the boat train. When Nicholson received their invitation, so he said afterwards, 'I nearly fainted. I would rather have entered a den of lions!' 'I can't talk to educated University men' was his reply 'I'm just a simple sailor fellow. . . . But let us have a wee word of prayer.' 'So there on the station platform,' recalls Gough, 'we formed a little circle and bowed our heads in prayer asking for guidance and grace.'

When the news of Stuart Holden's illness became known, there was consternation at Cambridge. One young senior member, however, Dr. B. F. C. Atkinson was quite sure that the matter was in Divine hands. Basil Atkinson, a Magdalene man who after a double First in the Classical tripos had lately taken a doctorate of philosophy for linguistic work, was to be intimately connected with the C.I.C.C.U. for years to come. He had, as he once wrote, 'more than once sought God's will with regard to work on the mission field but felt led from the first to remain in Cambridge,' and had accepted an appointment as Under-Librarian at the University Library. His little eccentricities endeared him to the Union, his Bible expositions influenced generations in the colleges, and though his frankness and strong views did not always commend him to his fellow senior members, his clear understanding of issues made him in course of time the C.I.C.C.U.'s valued adviser. And he was a man of prayer.

During 1925 Basil Atkinson had become disturbed lest Stuart Holden, for all his great reputation with the Christian Union, might submerge its distinctive message in his desire to be as warm as possible in co-operation with others. When, in October, Stuart Holden had signed a joint message in somewhat general terms with Bishop Temple and Dr. Norwood, Atkinson was even more concerned. 'I began to pray very definitely and urgently.' The news of Holden's withdrawal three months later and a few days before the mission, was therefore no surprise to him. His conviction was further strengthened by two apparent coincidences: when Nicholson, who was in great demand for missions all over the world, telegraphed to Ireland to ask if his arrangements allowed him the time required, he learned that he was due in Bangor, but that since he would be using his own mission hall this was the only engagement for many months which he could reasonably cancel. This seemed conclusive to Nicholson. 'There was no way out. I accepted, in great fear and trembling.' An emergency meeting of the Council of Religious Questions was called. Then followed the second coincidence. Only one man on the Council knew enough of Nicholson to have vetoed his name as clearly unsuitable, and this man had been called urgently to London. Nicholson was accepted.

The Christian Union proceeded to the three days' preparatory talks for which Nicholson had originally come. They soon saw what manner of man he was. 'We were faced with our responsibilities to our fellow students who were without Christ,' wrote J. B. Tupman of Corpus; 'the meetings were searching times.' It was impossible for the men to remain complacent under Nicholson: 'So few clean and strong hands prepared unto every good work, especially lifting men to Christ. This is the work that counts most. The one business of the Devil is to damn. The one business of the Lord is to save. Both are busy at this all the time. . . . We never succeed by compromise. . . . We can never win men to Christ until we show them we have something far better than they have and that we are enjoying it.' But with this went astonishing statements which made the men gape. 'Why are you fellows wearing those black things on your backs?' they would hear him ask, pointing to their academic gowns. 'Why don't you pawn them and go and buy Bibles?' As they sat listening to this quiet-looking, dark-haired man, so humble in character, so dogmatic in speech, with strong Irish brogue and Irish humour, they recognized the good to their own souls, but wondered what would be the effect on the University.

The mission opened on Saturday 31st January with a united meeting in the Guildhall, the President of the Union Society, Michael Ramsey, afterwards Bishop of Durham, in the Chair.

William Temple spoke first. Temple, who in 1906 had offered himself to the Church Missionary Society but in 1926 was not so closely identified with the evangelical movement, gave a scholarly and impressive speech, well-calculated to do much for any who were open to conviction of the reasonableness of Christianity. Norwood spoke next, somewhat lamely. Then the Chairman formally announced Stuart Holden's withdrawal and asked Nicholson to speak.

'I understand,' began Nicholson, 'that the purpose of this gathering is to introduce the Missioners to you. My lord bishop is well known, and so is Dr. Norwood. But I am an unknown quantity. Who am I?' And then, 'with a voice like a bull,' he announced: 'My name is William P. Nicholson of Bangor, County Down, Northern Ireland. I was born on 15th April 1880, I was born again on 22nd May 1898, and I was filled with the spirit in November 1898 through the ministry of Dr. J. Stuart Holden of London. And what do I believe? I believe in God the Father Almighty, Maker of heaven and earth, and in Jesus Christ His only Son our Lord. I believe He was conceived by the Holy Ghost. I believe He was born of the Virgin Mary, yes, born of the Virgin Mary. . . .' And so he continued, enunciating each clause of the Apostles' Creed, with briefest comment but without reservation—and when he came to the phrase, 'From whence also He shall come again to judge both the quick and the dead,' and spoke of the Second coming of Christ, a ripple of laughter ran round the room. He reached the last clause: 'I believe in the Life everlasting—yes, the eternity of Hell and the eternity of Heaven. . . . That's me and that's my message.' He then sat down.

The audience seemed stunned; the chairman, somewhat taken aback, rose and announced the closing hymn. As the meeting broke up, wrote Kenneth Hooker of Christ's, 'everybody openly scoffed at what Nicholson had said.' On the platform, a curious incident revealed how highly theological passions were running in 1926. Norwood, a fellow Nonconformist, turned his back on Nicholson, deliberately, so observers concluded, expressing his disapproval; but Temple shook him by the hand and wished him God-speed.

As for the C.I.C.C.U. leaders, they were 'frankly upset

and disappointed.' 'As I walked back across the Market Square,' recalls one of them, 'with Nicholson and Earn-shaw-Smith, the latter said rather touchily, "whatever made you do that? Now you've ruined everything." "Brother Smith," replied Nicholson, "if I had done what you thought, and pleased everybody, it would have been the end of your mission. Now you'll see. *God* will work."'

On the Sunday night, as in 1920, the Missioners were each on their own. The crowds flocked to Great St. Mary's to hear William Temple. Holy Trinity was no fuller than on an ordinary Sunday evening, but such was Nicholson's consciousness of inferiority that he was 'amazed' to see so many. He preached on the text, 'Ye must be born again,' and he preached a full hour. It was startling to hear him in full tilt against the ideas of the age: 'If Jesus only came to this world to be an example of a perfect human life, and a teacher, He has only come to mock poor, helpless, ruined humanity in its helpless, hopeless condition. . . . Christianity is not merely a perfected life presented but it is essentially and supremely a divine life communicated. "Ye must be born again," if you would enter the kingdom of heaven. There is no subject so unpopular in the world today as this, "Ye must be born again."' It was not what he said which astonished so much as his manner, and the man himself. 'It was extraordinary,' said one freshman whom a friend had taken along, 'very vulgar and yet—very attractive at the same time.' Stories and anecdotes flowed from the pulpit. Humour and pathos was unbounded, and a dogmatism which was almost alarming. Many senior members were horrified. 'Alack, a ranting Protestant,' wrote one, 'and this in Cambridge of all places.'

'I was gripped by Nicholson,' wrote a freshman of Caius, Edward Yorke, brought by a school friend to hear the 'Wild Irishman.' 'He was completely unconventional and you wondered what was going to happen next. It was certainly exciting.' As Nicholson came back again and again to his text, 'Ye must be born again,' Yorke found conviction increasing that the man was right. Yet he longed to escape. And then, writes Nicholson,

'I gave the invitation for any who would accept Christ as their personal Saviour to stand up.' 'Is there a man here who has the courage of his convictions?' they heard him ask; 'will you stand up and say "Yes sir, I will." No eyes closed or any of this hokey-pokey business of heads bowed, but just stand up and say "I will."'

Some eight or ten men stood up, and were asked to come forward to the chancel steps. When the service closed they were promptly marched down the aisle by Earnshaw-Smith and taken to the Henry Martyn Hall, where they found assistant missioners awaiting them.

Ted Yorke, for one, did not stand up. He and Clark of St. John's his friend, went back together to Yorke's rooms. For a while they talked trivialities and then Clark remarked abruptly: 'And what about the Lord Jesus Christ?' 'What do you mean?' asked Yorke, though he well knew. 'Are you going to make a decision?' went on Clark, 'you have got to make a decision.' Yorke admitted that he was thoroughly concerned and Clark would brook no delay: 'I will give you ten minutes.' Three minutes later the decision was given. Yorke hesitated when ordered to kneel down and 'Tell the Lord that,' but did so, 'rather sheepishly' and both men prayed. 'It was just on eleven. A sense of overwhelming peace and sense of relief came in,' said Yorke years later, 'and straight away, when left alone, I had my first "quiet time" and then went to bed. My first conscious thought in the morning was of the Lord Jesus' presence.'

The news of Nicholson's first address spread round the University. Numbers increased. Many came from curiosity and amusement. 'There was never a dull or conventional moment,' wrote one man, 'you never knew what he would say next!' Stories of 'Willie Nick' were soon going the rounds. How, when on the text 'The hairs of your head are all numbered,' he pointed at a bald-headed man in the audience and remarked 'Losh man, the Lord wouldna take long over you!' How after some story of an aunt of his who died unregenerate and went to hell, he saw two men leaving the Church and shouted, 'If you leave this

Church unsaved you too will go to hell!' and one of the men shouted back, the remark being lost in the roar of laughter which followed, 'Any message for your aunt?' Nicholson's language was often common and his remarks unguarded: 'It is time that that old bachelor on the Tiber got married,' seemed thoroughly offensive to the ears of dons, whatever their views on the Pope. Small wonder that one of them wrote, 'Listened to Nicholson; sat all through him on purpose and deeply disturbed. Hell and damnation business; a sad caricature of Christianity . . . doubt if my religious tolerance can get as far as this.'

Nicholson's statements were sweeping, yet he knew what he was doing. 'We have come to a place where the Christ of denunciation needs to be preached,' he once wrote. 'Amid the hypocrisies and insincerities which permeate our modern life we too seldom hear in the pulpit the burning indignation, the splendid scorn, and the fiery arraignment which distinguished the old prophets of God when they looked upon social sin and corruption.' It was the year of *Vortex* and *Scotch Mist*; politics and industry were on the verge of the coal stoppage which led to the General Strike. Consciences were easy, such sense of sin as existed was weak and limited: 'we were not worrying about our sins,' was one undergraduate's comment, 'and Nicholson shook us.'

He had no fear of preaching on Hell. 'If this Bible is the Word of God—and it is—and if Jesus Christ is the Son of God—and He is—then there is a hell. You may deny the fact, but that will not destroy it. . . . How are we to escape hell? This is the part of my message that I like. The other part has been very hard to declare to you, but to be true to your soul I had to do it . . . there is mercy with the Lord here and now. Jesus Christ has died, the just, for you the unjust. Surely you will not go to hell with your eyes open and your feet stained with the blood of Christ . . .?'

As men listened some were enraged. But each night more deserted Norwood and even Temple to hear Nicholson. Each night many stood up; some, as Edward Woods believed, 'seemingly rather hypnotised,' but others be-

225

cause they had been reached as they would never have been been reached by moderate men such as Temple or Stuart Holden.

The C.I.C.C.U., for all 'Willie Nick's' violence and rough speech soon felt a new sense of values, a fresh realization of certainties they had been near forgetting. Though some were shocked and offended. most were assured that God's power was at work. They saw men who the week before had been mere nominal Christians or to all intents pagans—one was President of the Drunks' Club—standing at Nicholson's appeal and coming back the next night with friends who would not have come on their own. These friends would bring others on the third night. And the Christian Union knew also that the man who seemed so fierce in denunciation, so intemperate in his words was, out of the pulpit, 'the most lovable and humble of men.'

On Saturday February 6th, the last night but one of the United Mission, none of the Missioners was billed to speak. The C.I.C.C.U. Committee decided that Nicholson ought not to miss a night; he was therefore the only speaker and Holy Trinity was crowded. He preached on the words 'Almost persuaded.' At the close of his forceful address he once more made impassioned appeal. For the first time that week not one man stood up. Whereupon Nicholson leaned back in the pulpit. 'I know what is wrong with this meeting tonight. There are too many hypocrites in the church! Too many blue-eyed, hatchet-faced, lily-livered hypocrites! While we sing the first verse of the next hymn, will the hypocrites please leave the church.' During the singing thirty or forty left the church, many in evident annoyance, among them a college chaplain who wrote the next day to the President, somewhat ingenuously protesting that he had been called a hypocrite.

Still there was no response. As the church emptied the C.I.C.C.U. leaders withdrew to Earnshaw-Smith's rooms in the Market Square, and although uncontrollable mirth sometimes mingled with intercession at odd expressions in Nicholson's petitions, 'the Spirit of prayer was poured upon us.' On the Sunday morning a man who went to fetch Nicholson for breakfast found him on his knees, 'tired and exhausted, after a night of prayer.' In Tupman's rooms in Corpus that morning 'almost continuous' prayer was maintained, 'with men coming and going.'

In the evening the church was full and Nicholson preached on 'My Spirit shall not always strive with man,' the text which, he said, had led him 'to accept Jesus Christ as my personal Saviour.' He spoke of his sailing days, 'several years wandering around, leading a wild life. I came home to Bangor, broken, baffled, beaten. While I was sitting reading the paper by the fireside one Monday morning, the Lord suddenly arrested me: "My Spirit shall not always strive with you." I trembled, and yielded to Christ there and then. It was all so sudden and powerful. I was born again and I knew it. My mother came into the room. I said to her, "Your prayers are answered."' He told how for seven months he 'wandered on, a devoted but a defeated Christian. The Lord brought Stuart Holden to our town to hold a convention. It was then I saw that Christ had purchased me to possess me by His Spirit. I yielded unreservedly and received the Holy Spirit to fill me. What a change. What joy—victory—courage—power.'

At the close of this 'very powerful message,' as it was described at the time, over twenty-five men were found in the Henry Martyn Hall, more than on any previous night. Nicholson himself was impressed by the 'courageous manly way the men decided.'

The next morning after many had been at 7 a.m. to the great Thanksgiving Service of Holy Communion in King's College Chapel, with nearly seven hundred communicants, the Christian Union men met to say good-bye to 'Willie Nick.' 'The send-off they gave me warmed my heart,' he wrote, 'and humbled me. They crowded round the motor that was taking me to London, and sang and shouted. I could hardly see for tears running down my cheeks.'

After that, they paused for breath. 'I rather think,' was the comment of one of the Executive, 'that the University heaved a sigh of relief when he was gone.'

CHAPTER XIX

ON THE DEFENSIVE

THE Mission of William Nicholson loosed a flood of contradictory comment.

Edward Woods, with many senior members regretted that 'missioner and his message extended the gulf between the C.I.C.C.U. and the rest . . . he was not really suited to his job.' The *Cambridge Review*, taking an expression recently imported from America and being used in England as a term of reproach, labelled Nicholson 'fundamentalist.' Of the Christian Union men, for some it was a parting of the ways. 'If that is the sort of direction the C.I.C.C.U. is going,' thought C. K. Sansbury, college representative of Peterhouse, 'then it is not for me.' Incipient dissatisfaction with the tenets or methods of the Union could scarcely survive Nicholson; it was blown away or brought to a head. But others neither dissatisfied beforehand nor unsympathetic afterwards, were disturbed and uneasy when they saw men whom Nicholson had offended rebuff any further approach. 'Of course God used the foolishness of man,' was one comment, 'as we all prayed that He would. But the devil made good use of him too and I wonder who had the best of the bargain?'

The collective reaction of the Union was unstinted gratitude. They expressed their feelings in the words of the 126th Psalm, formally inscribed in the Minute Book over the signatures of the General Committee: 'When the Lord turned again the captivity of Sion, we were like them that dream. Then was our mouth filled with laughter, and our tongue with singing. . . . The Lord hath done great things for us; whereof we are glad. . . .' They recognized that by normal standards Nicholson had been the wrong man. They realized as the weeks wore on into the Easter vacation and the May term that of the fifty or more, a high figure for the times, who had given in their names in profession of new-found faith, some fifteen only had become active members of the Union. Nicholson's personality, and an atmosphere charged with emotion had sown their crop of spurious decisions, and lack of preparation in the Union had cost further loss, for when men had stood in Holy Trinity at Nicholson's appeal, the Union at first had no adequate arrangements to help them. In the Henry Martyn Hall, while assistant missioners and Ridley men, Bibles in hand, had sought to make basic truths plain, C.I.C.C.U. members had been standing about with their hands in their pockets, their Bibles left in their rooms. It was a far cry from the days of Torrey when every convert was someone's responsibility for months to come. Yet the price seemed small beside the gain. 'If he were the only one,' was J. B. Tupman's comment, years afterwards, on the unsparing Christian service of one of Nicholson's converts, 'the Mission would have been worthwhile. He was not the only one. . . .' And the 'tremendous' desire to read the Bible, the 'immediate impression' of the need to tell others of Christ which the Mission imparted to this very convert was typical of the spirit generated.

'Nicholson was quite ruthless with all unreality and hypocrisy,' wrote Tupman, 'his very presence was a call to be the best for God.' Thus his Mission, for all its rough edges and its trail of spiritual castaways was a turning point in the life of the Union. 'We lost our reputation for respectability,' as one man put it, and in an age of confusion, of low standards and indefinite aims, this had become necessary. The characteristics of the Christian Union were brought into clear relief once more. No one could be uncertain of its position. Nor was this all. 'Nicholson's Mission,' in Bishop Gough's verdict, twenty-five years after his presidency, 'produced in the C.I.C.C.U. a generation through which God did certainly work. The effect on the life of members was indelible.'

The rejuvenated Union held a secure but not a highly influential position in the University of the later 'twenties. Sometimes it came into the limelight; in November 1926, it sponsored a visit from Christabel Pankhurst, the erstwhile militant suffragette, who told a crowded Guildhall that 'in my early days I believed that by political action I could set the world right. In the light of what I now know about the Lord Jesus Christ I hold such a view no longer.' Two terms later, in April 1927, the fiftieth anniversary of the founding of the Union was celebrated by Jubilee services, and by a banquet in Caius with speeches from T. R. Glover, Public Orator of the University, T. C. Fitzpatrick, President of Queens' and an array of past members. A pre-war activity was echoed in the production, the same year, of a *C.I.C.C.U. Magazine*, more limited in scope and size than *Cambridge Christian Life* but running for sixteen numbers and five years before the negligence of some hundred and sixty of its subscribers, who forgot their subscriptions, and the growth of the Inter-Varsity Fellowship determined the Union to limit themselves to a Cambridge Supplement in the new *Inter-Varsity Magazine*.

There was no lack of initiative. A C.I.C.C.U. Club was formed, a short-lived experiment, two rooms over a restaurant being rented, a friendly business man providing furniture. A more useful, and a lasting experiment was the adoption in 1927 of a Missionary, regular financial support being undertaken for Dr. J. E. Church of Emmanuel as he sailed to join the Ruanda Mission in Central Africa. 'It is with the humblest sense of gratitude to God,' wrote A. C. Stanley Smith, Director of the Mission, 'that we accept the rich spiritual heritage of the C.I.C.C.U. and welcome Joe Church to a service which your prayers can render victorious.' In the years to come the link with Ruanda was to mean much.

For all this enterprise, the Union found itself in an indifferent University; seldom were there more than forty men at Daily Prayer Meeting. When 'about two hundred' were present in Holy Trinity on the first night of a Mission in 1928 it was considered 'a miraculous answer to prayer.'

The power which the Union had held in Cambridge thirty years earlier seemed passed for ever. Membership, not offered on terms which young men of the late 'twenties found congenial, was little sought after except by those who as freshmen came up seeking it; and the home-life which produced such was on the wane. Yet now and again the manner of life, the prayers and words of a Christian Union man would find their mark, and an undergraduate with little previous thought of personal Christianity would find life running in new channels. Such was Alfred Owen.

A. G. B. Owen, a name which was to become potent in the industrial world, came up to Emmanuel in 1927. Son of an industrialist in the Midlands, a pioneer of motor-cars and aeroplanes, he had already worked in the factory and began to read Engineering. His beliefs, such as they were, he described later as 'mere vague nothingness.' The only other engineering freshman invited him to a college 'squash' where he heard, with mild interest, a talk from the former president Godfrey Buxton. He allowed himself to be persuaded to read his Bible daily and accompanied his friend to the Sunday evening sermons. As the issues became clearer Alfred Owen found himself, as he expressed it, 'counting the cost,' but during the Christmas vacation he was no longer in doubt and the following term he joined the Inter-Collegiate Union.

A year passed. In February 1929 'La Maréchale', the vigorous daughter of General Booth held a series of meetings for town and University, arranged by a local vicar. 'One thing perhaps more than any other which shamed us,' wrote Kenneth Hooker the C.I.C.C.U. President of this woman who had devoted her life to the poor of France and Switzerland, 'was her amazing Love for a human soul, a Love which sent her forth, scorning ease and retirement, to preach to all who would hear, "the unsearchable riches of Christ."' Owen, with many others, went to hear her. At the close of one of the meetings La Maréchale was standing at the door through which, with the crowd, Owen was moving towards the street. 'Suddenly she got hold of me,' was Owen's account, 'looked right into my eyes and said, "Are you a lazy

Christian?" I said I had come to pass an Engineering examination, but she repeated, "Are you a lazy Christian? Are you doing any Christian service? Don't you dare to come and listen to me tomorrow unless you are prepared to work in a Sunday School!"'

The incident was decisive. Not only did Owen arrange for a Sunday School class forthwith, but when, two months later, the employees of the steel works and their wives were entertained, two thousand in all, in celebration of his coming-of-age he did not hesitate to declare in his speech: 'There in only one gift I think more of than those you have given me tonight, and that has been given me by One who died to give me that gift. . . . Just over one year ago I gave my heart and all that I have to Him. Never for one moment have I regretted it. . . .'

At the end of the year his test came. On 30th December 1929 his father died and Alfred Owen left unfinished his Cambridge course to take over his father's position.

He called his men together immediately and told them that the Rubery Owen Company would be run as a Christian business. Corruption would cease; sharp practice would no longer be condoned and nothing that could not be done with clear conscience would be permitted; those who did not wish to work on those terms might leave. His father's right-hand man told him the business would be ruined: 'You cannot bring Christian beliefs into industry.' Another manager, a Christian who, as Owen put it, 'had never shown his light before,' rallied to Owen's side, but doubted the wisdom of his ideals.

Twenty years later A. G. B. Owen could look around on an Owen Organization of twenty-nine companies, the largest privately owned engineering business in the country, 'an industrial giant with all the characteristics of a small firm.' He had determined that welfare should be the foremost concern; and his clinics and nurseries, his convalescent homes and housing estates, his Christian Fellowships and Sunday Schools and the Sons of Rest workshop where, for the first time in Britain, retired employees could continue to earn as and when they wished, testified that his Christianity was not lip-service. He had not lost what he had discovered at Cambridge: 'A profoundly happy man,' commented a journalist, 'A. G. B. Owen never worries. He carries no burdens.'

'After all,' Owen himself could remark, 'if our faith is strong enough, then we must surely know with Paul "that all things work together for good unto them that love God."'

Such achievements of faith, whether in an industrial or other vocation, were latent in the life of any like-minded undergraduate; but as the nineteen-twenties passed into the 'thirties, those in positions of leadership in the Inter-Collegiate Union were burdened again with problems of co-operation and unity.

In the spring of 1928 the Council of Religious Questions once more invited the Union to join a United Mission to the University, for Lent 1929. The Executive, a few weeks before going out of office at the end of their year, accepted, without much study of the issues. During the autumn the details of the mission were prepared. Theodore Woods, now passed from Peterborough to the bishopric of Winchester, was to be the general Church of England missioner and H. H. Farmer the Nonconformist; the C.I.C.C.U. chose Bryan Green, a young Anglican already prominent as an evangelist. 'Loyal co-operation,' wrote the President, 'was demanded from each of the bodies represented.' The Union had no objection to due share in the expenses, though less than a year passed since its own mission of January '28, but the Executive were not happy with the combined preparatory meetings. When the joint letter to all undergraduates was presented for signature and found 'to be of a very nebulous character,' they were thoroughly uneasy. 'The Council of Religious Questions,' so the Executive considered, 'by organizing such a Mission tells the University that every shade of religious opinion has its contribution. The message of the C.I.C.C.U. must therefore be one of these. By joining the Mission the Union consents to there being many messages of equal worth. The C.I.C.C.U., by its tenets, does not believe this. . . .' The conclusion was that if the Union continued in the United Mission, it would be 'sailing under false colours.'

Previous missions had been united; in 1929, as before, the missioners only once would meet on a joint platform and then would be free to carry on as they wished. On the other hand, the Executive knew something of the disappointments of 1920; they had heard how the special circumstances of 1926 had not only nullified the intended unity of that mission but had seemed to underline by contrast the ineffectiveness, from their view-point, of such efforts. Theological differences were if possible sharper than two years earlier; Modernism was at its most extreme. As the Executive said later to the Council, they felt little confidence that 'the C.I.C.C.U.'s stand for the whole Bible as the Word of God, for faith in the efficacy of our Lord's substitutionary sacrifice as the only means of salvation,' would be unhesitatingly preached in the sense they held by other than their own missioner.

On Sunday Novemeber 25th the Executive met to consider their course of action. 'God seems to guide the whole committee in a marvellous way,' recorded the minutes, 'as when we met no single member had come to any definite decision of coming out from the mission, and when we parted everyone was of the opinion that it was the wisest course to take.'

When the General Committee of the Union learned of the decision it was to be asked to endorse there was no such unanimity. The problem brought into the open an undercurrent of controversy. Some had no doubt that the decision was right. They had felt throughout that co-operation was undesirable. It was not so much a matter of dispute over niceties of doctrine nor a refusal to recognize the existence of true Christians outside their own Union but the realization that such bodies as the Student Movement, chief partisan among undergraduates of united missions, were still not propagating much more than a gospel of what the Christian Union called 'moral and social uplift.' Furthermore only a few weeks had passed since the uneasy union between the Oxford S.C.M. and the C.I.C.C.U.'s opposite number had broken down, and the new O.I.C.C.U. had been formed with Cambridge encouragement. Superficial unity seemed indefensible, at Oxford or at Cambridge.

Another wing of the C.I.C.C.U., well represented on the General Committee, welcomed any movement of unity, feeling that what was lost by appearing to subscribe to belief in the equal validity of conflicting gospels was offset not so much by the Christian charity displayed as by the 'great opportunity' presented. 'We believed that the unity would enable us to reach a wider group of students.' They further considered that to renounce commitments at the last moment was wrong, and would bring the Union into contempt. The missioner endorsed this view.

Early in December Bryan Green was asked to Cambridge in order that the General Committee could discuss the position with him. They met in the Henry Martyn Hall after Daily Prayer Meeting; at the last moment Basil Atkinson, who championed those who wished to withdraw, was also asked to attend. An hour's discussion including, in Green's words, 'open and public argument' between himself and Dr. Atkinson won, by a small majority, the case for withdrawal. The Executive then approached the Council of Religious Questions, which called a special meeting to consider their request.

After a lengthy speech from one of the Union's two representatives the chairman, Dr. Alex Wood, came gallantly to the rescue: 'I do not agree with the C.I.C.C.U. on points of doctrine but I respect them for their loyalty to their convictions. If I may be allowed to say so, I was very surprised they had consented to join in the Mission at all. . . . I feel that as they have always acted from principle in the past, they must be left perfectly free to do so again.' In the discussion which followed, one member of the Council, a college dean, exclaimed that it was all nonsense. 'Why should the C.I.C.C.U. withdraw? After all, we all in this room believe in God and that's the great thing!' Another don affirmed that he had known the C.I.C.C.U. some years and 'they have always been giving trouble.' But with the Chairman's support, the proposal was passed that the C.I.C.C.U. should be allowed to withdraw. The Council then adjourned 'in a very happy spirit, there being no bitterness nor resentment.'

Bryan Green, regretting the decision but anxious to help the Executive and Union, came up at their request during the United Mission and held private meetings for members and their friends.

Controversy, however, was by no means finished. In May 1929 it came to a head with a Round Robin sent to the new Executive and signed by thirty-six members, 'who whilst agreeing completely and absolutely with the message of the C.I.C.C.U.' were 'very deeply distressed' by what they considered a dictatorial attitude on the part of its leaders. For a while the Union was in danger of dissolution. But nine months later the new President, Hugh Evan Hopkins of Emmanuel could write, 'the Lord wonderfully brought unity into the C.I.C.C.U. during the year following the incident.' Both at the Keswick Convention and at Old Jordans in Buckinghamshire, where some twenty had met in preparation for the Michaelmas term, many who had signed the Round Robin were present, and the Executive found that 'the matter had fallen into insignificance beside a mutal experience of of Christ and of His will for Cambridge.'

Thus, at heavy cost, the Inter-Collegiate Union had learnt at last that 'there can be no true unity,' as the President for the following year, Norman Anderson of Trinity wrote in 1931, 'with those who are really out for something different.' For young men and women it was essential, if vigorous faith were to survive in after years, that spiritual depth should precede breadth of understanding and sympathy. Whatever was right in a parish, a diocese or on the mission field, the Union now knew that in a University neither wisdom nor value, until conditions should change lay in concurring with attempts to impose, for however good a purpose, a unity which did not exist.

During 1929–30 dispute and controversy was forgotten. Although still small, the C.I.C.C.U. drew to itself men of talent both in academic work and in sport, and was much in the public eye. Few who took part could forget the Open-Air meeting in the Market Place in May week, 1930, which 'gripped the attention of Varsity men in a way we hardly dared to expect'—not least because seven blues were among the speakers. In April a Day of Prayer, 'the real secret to this term,' had given indication of the spiritual determination of the Union, while the claims of mission fields overseas were voiced repeatedly and the proportion of missionary volunteers was high. 'There must have been very few people,' wrote Hugh Evan Hopkins at the end of the year, 'who did not know where they could have found the secret of joy, peace and life, had they wished to do so.'

It was not long, however, before fresh problems arose. Friends and supporters of Frank Buchman had reappeared in Cambridge.

Since his leaving for Oxford in 1921 Buchman had seen his work develop, in extent and in ideas. A tour in South Africa in 1928, of considerable effect on all parties and races, in which he was accompanied by seven Oxford men, had earned his movement the nickname later adopted as official: the Oxford Group. Wherever he went Buchman saw, in his own phrase, 'changed lives.' His methods were startling, seeming to combine the arts of pastor, psychologist and politician. He was certain that both his methods and his message were God-guided—'The Holy Spirit is the leader and director constantly and daily.' 'I can assure you,' he wrote in 1929 to a friend, a C.I.C.C.U. missionary in the East, 'that we still live by the First Epistle of St. John, that we are Bible Christians, as a world-reporter says, that our emphasis is sin, Jesus Christ the Saviour from sin.' His influence was felt both by men whose faith had worn thin and by agnostics and atheists. 'A young fellow who three months ago constantly smoked sixty or seventy cigarettes a day,' he wrote, 'is constantly winning people to our Lord and Saviour Jesus Christ—a mighty work of Grace.' Profound opposition was aroused. 'The Devil's a bit provoked,' was Buchman's view, 'and he is trying to use the saints to throw dust.' 'What I can never understand,' wrote a diplomat, a C.I.C.C.U. man of the 'nineties, 'is the intense and even bitter opposition which the work of the "Groups" encounters from "pi" people. It seems to me that the message is the same as that given at Keswick. . . .' On the other hand one of Buchman's closest friends of Cambridge days could feel that 'the rapid growth, popularity, the suspicion of many orthodox Christians not altogether without reason, and other factors had blunted the edge and diverted the aim.'

For eight years Buchman had been almost unknown in Cambridge. In November 1929 he stayed a week-end with a friend and addressed a few 'squashes,' but no comment was aroused. By the following summer his movement had won the sympathy both of the Dean of Caius and of the Chaplain of Downing, and Buchman had sent a principal American supporter to live and work in Cambridge. Undergraduates began to hear of the Oxford Group, and men whom neither churches, nor college chapels nor the Christian Union had touched were embarking on a militant evangelism.

Members of the C.I.C.C.U. Executive were approached by undergraduate leaders of the Group 'with regard to the possibility of joining with them in work in the colleges,' and on 9th November 1930 the Executive recorded its opinion that 'while they did not wish to dictate in *any way* to individual members of the Union, nor excessively to criticize the methods of the Group Movement, yet the Executive thought it unwise for colleges to join with them. The C.I.C.C.U. had its own work to do in the University and that work must be pursued at all costs.'

In the following eighteen months, widely advertized and active, the Group increasingly filled the Cambridge horizon. All levels and ages were influenced. 'This has proved to be quite the most wonderful term in my experience of thirty years,' wrote B. K. Cunningham, Principal of Westcott House in the summer of '31, 'six of our best men went through a deep spiritual experience in and through the University Group house-party which was held at Selwyn in the week preceding term.' To the ordinary undergraduate, whatever his personal attitude, the Group seemed the natural development of the evangelistic tradition, the unacknowledged heir of the great days of the C.I.C.C.U., and the obvious rallying-point, for all but an obstinate minority, of the enthusiasms and devotion which once had made the C.I.C.C.U. a power throughout the University.

Many members of the Christian Union shared this belief. Attendance at Oxford Group house-parties, together with the increasing support given by leaders in the country and the undoubted effect of Buchmanism on hardened minds and immoral lives appeared convincing. Co-operation in a common cause seemed the only possible response for those who were broad of mind and warm in heart. They suggested that the choice between older ways and the Groups was a choice 'between orthodoxy and life.' Throughout the Union men were shaken and reconsecrated by the emphasis on the Four Absolutes, absolute honesty, purity, unselfishness and love, by the Group's uncompromising attitude to sin and by undiscovered possibilities of the guided life.

Those who were less certain of the Groups were not popular. But Jack Cobb of Fitzwilliam, who took office for 1931–32 was somewhat older than the normal age of presidents and possessed a shrewd understanding of the issues. He saw that the Oxford Group's emphasis on subjective experience as prime authority, almost to the exclusion of doctrine, was giving their converts the weakest of foundations. Cobb, and those who shared his understanding of the position did not decry subjective experience; but they knew that to be lasting it must be securely based on truth and integrated with doctrine. The Groupists were, in effect, preaching repentance unrelated to the redemptive work of the Cross. They taught men to 'tune in' to the Holy Spirit, but spiritual re-birth, in the Biblical sense, was not necessarily a first requirement. Direct guidance in the 'quiet time' was expected, but did not need to submit to the authority of Scripture. Cobb was not surprised at occasional reports, filtering through to Cambridge, of enthusiastic Groupers who, like the Perfectionists of fifty years before, were returning quietly to well-trodden paths or were suffering shipwreck of faith.

At the start of Michaelmas term 1932 the Christian Union was seriously disunited; factions were not openly warring and friendships remained unbroken, but the confusion of methods and aims sapped the Union's strength. One party were eager Groupists; another was pressing the Executive to sanction some of the wilder doctrines of latter-day Holiness teaching; a third had been working on 'Sportsmen's Missions' in the north of England with a missionary bishop on furlough, at that time a strong exponent of methods similar to those of the Groups.

The crisis culminated with the arrangement by the missionary bishop of a campaign in Cambridge, his public addresses to be supported by 'teams' of undergraduates working through the colleges in the Groupist manner, telling of 'changed' lives. 'I knew,' said Cobb, 'that if we as an Executive attemped to forbid, or officially discouraged the attendance of C.I.C.C.U. members at the meetings, perhaps half would have resigned. But to give the campaign official support would have blurred the distinctive witness and would have led also to eventual division.' Cobb took a positive line, and thus was able to lead the C.I.C.C.U. off the defensive. 'Our position must be that of going all-out for winning men to Christ,' he wrote to college representatives, 'with the definite witness for which we stand, so leaving *no time* for all this back-chat business.'

Meanwhile, the Oxford Group had made a formal approach to the President, suggesting that henceforth the Daily Prayer Meeting should become a daily session for 'sharing' sin and experience, and that both the Sunday Bible Reading and the Evangelistic sermon be transformed into Team meetings. 'My reply,' said Cobb, 'was terse.' As it happened, the force of Buchmanism was already spent. The missionary bishop's supporters found themselves less happy with him than when they were on their Sportsmen's Missions. The novelty of Group methods was wearing thin, the weakness of lives 'changed' except through spiritual re-birth was becoming apparent, and too many sweeping moral reformations among undergraduates were followed by radical reactions. Throughout Cambridge men were increasingly dissatisfied with Groupist propaganda, its advertisement of prominent converts, its tendency to dismiss opposition as factious, while Senior members were coming to hear of strange commentaries on Absolute Honesty.

During 1933 the influence of the Oxford Group was on the wane. The Inter-Collegiate Union freely acknowledged a debt to the ideals of the movement but its particular methods and principles they had found wanting. A teaching course on Christian doctrine from a competent theologian, T. C. Hammond, arranged during the May term had the effect of making the issues clear and setting the Union firm on its path. Other undergraduates were losing interest and all but a few senior members were withdrawing such support as they had given. When, several years later, the Group made a further attempt to take Cambridge by storm the response met was shortlived and limited.

CHAPTER XX

IN PEACE AND WAR

THE University of the earlier thirties was comfortable, gay and cushioned against the problems of the age. The increasing sacrifices made by parents were easily forgotten by their sons in the security of an undergraduate life which, for many, could still be undisturbed by concern for the future. Idleness in academic work carried scant stigma. The mounting tensions of international politics were remote.

Christian Union members shared the delights and defects of the world of which they were part. They abounded on the rugger field, at cricket and on the river. The wealthier of them ran explosive motor-cars. They took part in practical jokes, a feature of the age: joining the crowd which sat on cushions across King's Parade on a market day, or the squad of bicyclists who rode, a solid mass, round and round Rose Crescent, Market Hill and Trinity Street at the busiest hour of the day. They invented their own jokes, from the Hoop Race of 1930 to that of the Trinity man of '35 who passed a surveyor's chain through the line of bicycles parked outside a cinema, locked it and withdrew into the darkness to watch results. Like their contemporaries they were easily isolated, content to enjoy their own immediate circle. They tended to ignore responsibilities of church loyalty: 'Most members,' wrote C. G. Scorer, President for 1933–34, 'attended a place of worship in the town, but organized religion was slightly suspect on the grounds of its ineffectiveness. . . . Charles Simeon would have undoubtedly addressed stern words to the Union had he been alive.' Little interest was displayed, save by the missionary minded, in Christianity beyond the immediate horizon. Even the Inter-

Varsity Fellowship meant little, and in reaction to the emphasis in other quarters on social service as the key to the Kingdom the Cambridge University Mission in Bermondsey was ignored except by a handful, though the unemployed still frequently to be met on the streets drew a ready generosity. The extravagances of the time were reflected in the crudity with which the aims of the Union were sometimes expressed. Evangelism too often took the form of rough, insensitive proselytizing, leaving its victims to dismiss, as the emotional expression of the adolescent mind, the spiritual truths so harshly forced on their attention: 'if you loved *me* as much as you loved my soul,' said one man to a C.I.C.C.U. member of his acquaintance, 'you would do better.' The Union's apologia, reacting both to the indifference and to the antagonisms of the day, could also be violent—*Old Paths in Perilous Times*, revised and reissued in 1933, was even more intemperate than twenty years before.

Over and above this share in the weaknesses of their age, Christian Union men had problems of their own. They had scarcely one active sympathizer among senior men of the University. T. R. Glover was aged and to all intents retired; Harold Earnshaw-Smith had left Cambridge in 1927, F. H. Sheldon in '29. Of the dons, Hornsby Wright, bursar of Emmanuel was of the few to give encouragement, although several town parsons, successive Vicars of St. Paul's especially, were thoroughly in sympathy. Of the University staff only Dr. Basil Atkinson was wholeheartedly with them, and he was not a fellow of a college.

The indifference or antagonism of their elders did not, so they felt, 'worry or alarm us in the least—surely God had chosen the "weak things of the world to confound the wise"!' But it did not encourage balance. Further, the theological outlook of the University was still alien. Although the publication in 1931 of Sir Edwyn Hoskyns' *Riddle of the New Testament*, written with F. N. Davey of St. Bene't's Church, had marked the first turning of the Cambridge School from extremes of liberalism, the daily teaching of the divinity faculty still seemed coldly analytical and destructive. 'I found myself,' a Magdalene man

recalled, 'in a severe fight between what I knew to be true
and what I was taught.' When lecturers were heard to
remark, 'Well, gentlemen, there are still some people
who believe in the bodily resurrection of Jesus Christ,' the
reaction was too often to refuse further theological thinking
in any direction. And thus, though it could only be
applied with honesty to a small minority there were
grains of truth beneath the exaggeration of caricature in a
divinity lecturer's impatient criticism of Christian Union
men, voiced a few years earlier: 'they are either highly
suggestible with that strange and almost unearthly look
which is the seal of a childlike faith, or they are hard,
thin-lipped, obviously repressing a mass of unexamined
doubts, men of strong will and narrow bigotry.'

For all shortcomings and weaknesses, the heart of the
Union was sound. In the circumstances of the time its
increase of membership was slow, though in 1934 Basil
Atkinson could claim, perhaps in an over-estimate, that
without it, 'during the five months previous to my writing
this there would have been about thirty men who would
not, humanly speaking, have found the Saviour.' He
could also stress the difficulties which, 'if there were no
C.I.C.C.U.' would have faced those who came up from
school anxious to join such a Union. 'There would be
nothing to unite them, no means of their coming into
touch with each other, and isolation under such circumstances in a University could scarcely fail to mean the
overthrow of spiritual life.' As it was, he concluded,
Cambridge was not only often a 'turning point in their
lives' but a 'training ground of spiritual work and a
school of prayer.'

The Christian Union was continuously active. Each
Sunday evening in summer in the Market Square, some
fifty men would crowd round a piano or harmonium
placed on a table or on a lorry; friends from the town
and other undergraduates would join them, two or three
hundred in all. The preacher for the week-end would act
as leader and eight undergraduates, their names published before hand on college notice-boards and in the town,
would each speak for two or three minutes. 'And what an

THE CAMBRIDGE CAMP AT KESWICK IN THE
NINETEEN-THIRTIES

(*Top*) Visitor's Day: *L. to R.*: Harold Earnshaw-Smith,
E. C. Faithfull and Hugh Gough
(*Below*) The Adjutant, Major Mainwaring-Burton

ordeal it was!' recalled C. G. Scorer. The hour's service was informal. 'Humour was never far away, earnestness predominated.' The brief talks would be interspersed with singing, and the service would end with a straight challenge to decision, from the leader. 'Crowds were near and far and hundreds strolled past. Men from Caius' New Building had their windows wide and sat listening and watching. Sports cars drove by noisily from time to time, as a sort of defiant protest—deliberate but in good spirit. Shouts, cat-calls and whistles were not infrequent. But above the throng would be standing someone telling out in resounding terms, "I *know* Whom I have believed." The faint-hearted Christian achieved new strength when he stood on that table, were his words never so confused. The heedless undergraduate murmured in his heart "Would I had a faith like these men." And from time to time one or another, townsman or gownsman, would come to find new life in Christ.'

In winter Holy Trinity remained, as for many years past, the rendezvous for Sunday evening. The gallery seldom had to be used; not even the transepts were filled. The sermons suffered from the feebleness of national religion: many who at that period would have been giving addresses of depth and power had lost their lives in the war, and although there were notable exceptions many who came to preach had succumbed to the prevalent distaste for theological thought, and failed to balance vivid exhortation with reasoned exposition. This failure showed up also at the Sunday morning Bible Readings. The Henry Martyn Hall would be full, but the speaker, only occasionally given a set subject, generally wandered through some aspect of Christian sanctification, and 'third year men' so one memory runs, 'rather took exception to the monotony of theme and rejoiced when a thoughtful, scholarly exegesis was, on rare occasions, given.'

The primary strength of the Union, however, was neither in its evangelistic services nor in the Bible Readings. Nor even in activity connected with the mission field; each year C.I.C.C.U. men went overseas, in 1934 as many as sixteen, but the general attitude was more of interest than of concern, the Volunteer pledge being reckoned an expression of willingness rather than a declaration of Divine Call. The hub was not even in the Union's corporate prayer, although the Daily Prayer Meeting once again was increasing in meaning and attendance, and the Saturday night meeting, which for some years had drawn only those the most conscious of their responsibilities was growing steadily in importance until obliged, in 1934, to return from its small room up a rickety staircase in a side-street opposite Emmanuel to the Henry Martyn Hall.[1] The strength of the Union depended on the devotional life of its members; on their love to God and their willingness to be used by Him. The true centre of the Union, therefore, was not in public hall or church but in college rooms where men discussed, two or three in frankness of friendship, their problems and opportunities, where one sought to lead another to fresh spiritual experiences or to the first step in the Christian life and where, before the start of the day, each applied himself alone to prayer and the study of Scripture.

There had always been in the Union a nucleus of men who realized that the value of any activities depended on the strength and discipline of personal devotion, on 'a steady, persistent application,' as one man of this time wrote, 'to the task of understanding spiritual truth and interpreting it in holiness of daily living.' Successive presidents had been drawn from this circle. In the mid-'thirties it was slowly widening. And on its further extension hung the future of the Union.

In 1934 the Inter-Collegiate Union numbered some two hundred and twenty members, the Daily Prayer Meeting was attended on an average by thirty-five, and both the feelings of the Union and the attitude of the University were well summed up by Basil Atkinson's words, 'They may laugh at the C.I.C.C.U. but in their hearts they respect it.'

That year proved a turning point. The Executive,

[1] For four terms in 1938–9 this Saturday night meeting was held in the Round Church hall.

convinced that the Union was unprepared, postponed the Triennial Mission from the Lent term until November. The decision shook the C.I.C.C.U., which awoke to its comparative lack of faith. A new spirit of prayer was soon abroad. The Mission, conducted by Colin Kerr in the old Guildhall, then about to be rebuilt, strengthened the Union though provoking no spectacular recovery— 'God seems to be saving individuals rather than masses in these days,' wrote the President, H. T. Hughes of Wesley House, in January 1935.

Each year that followed the Christian Union was recovering lost ground and slowly working towards its former position. Executives were clearer now that at risk of misunderstanding and even resentment, they could not commit the Union without compromise to united approaches to the University, whether sponsored by the Student Movement, the Oxford Group or by the deans and chaplains. On the other hand, 'A really high spirituality must be maintained to give an effective answer to those who accuse us of "dead orthodoxy."' A deeper consciousness was felt of Christian truth and of the essentials of balanced Christian service. 'We need the grace to allow Him to discipline our lives according to His will,' wrote R. J. Knight of Trinity in his presidential letter of January 1937: 'The very nature of the C.I.C.C.U.'s activities being, in a sense, our spare-time work, makes this doubly important. Some of us have erred, no doubt, in spending too much time in C.I.C.C.U. work to the neglect of our reading; some have gone to the other extreme.' With this went increasing impatience of the Union's reputation as a body 'which does not think out its spiritual position.' From time to time it had won a good proportion of Firsts in the tripos lists—the Executive of 1931 was as accomplished in intellect as its immediate predecessor had been in athletics—but not until the later years in the decade did the Union begin to overcome, and then only slowly, its anxiety lest intellectual ability and spiritual power could not be allied. Yet there was no fear of a coldly intellectual approach replacing warmth of spiritual experience. 'The love of God,' wrote a Jesus man in 1937, and his words could have been echoed by many of his friends, 'seems almost too intimate to speak of. Yet without it life would never be the same . . . it is amazingly real and personal.'

It was this personal love of God which was the mainspring, so he hoped, of the Christian Union man's existence. To his casual acquaintance he might seem somewhat apart, subjecting himself to a discipline they supposed irksome and keeping himself aloof from some of their habits and activities; a second or third year man who began to identify himself with the Union might even lose former friends. But as spiritual life deepened he would scarcely notice such petty ostracism. He could not lack companions, and men of varying backgrounds and with interests other than his own, but with the one supreme loyalty, might become his closest friends. He would meet them at the Daily Prayer Meeting, attended on several days each week, and at the Bible Readings. They would work together on Children's Missions at the seaside and go to Keswick together, to the Cambridge Camp which each year gave men fresh vision of the possibilities of the Christian life.

In his college the C.I.C.C.U. man would be increasingly conscious of responsibility towards those who lived on his staircase, or with whom he played games or worked. His desire would be to take them to the sermons at Holy Trinity, to break through indifference and prejudice and to give them the opportunity of understanding the truth and of responding as he had done to the invitation of Christ. He would not therefore break friendship, however hostile to Christianity any of his friends might be. But the primary purpose of Cambridge years, as he knew, was in preparation for the future; and for this he sought the Will of God, while equipping himself intellectually and spiritually for a lifetime of service, whether in the ministry or the mission field or in a profession.

The consciousness of Christ as Saviour and as Friend was the dominant factor in the C.I.C.C.U. man's life; to evangelize was the first aim of the Union. Methods of evangelism, however, were changing with the altered atmosphere of the later 'thirties. The Open-Airs in Market Square were felt out-dated: 'Men may admire us for standing in the market-place to preach the Gospel, but they do not often come within really effective sound of the Gospel and in the past few years we know of very few indeed who have been led to the Lord Jesus Christ as the result of these meetings.' The regular Open-Airs were therefore abandoned in favour of normal evening sermons in Holy Trinity, with Sunday afternoon Garden Parties at Basil Atkinson's house in Grange Road or at St. Paul's Vicarage, and open-air preaching was relegated to neighbouring villages and the further quarters of the town.

Undergraduates were becoming more thoughtful, less biased by a materialism which was beginning to lose ground. As the world outlook darkened the positive approach of the Union, its 'cutting edge' as Max Warren, Vicar of Holy Trinity described it, seemed attractive even to those who would not go the whole way: 'The C.I.C.C.U. stands for something definite,' these men would say to Warren, 'and in a nebulous world like this we want to identify ourselves with such.' The message was still the same and it received a closer hearing and was reaching further afield. 'The one thing that really got hold of me, a Pembroke man could write, 'was the friendliness of the C.I.C.C.U. Their forbearance—and their assurance that the message they had really was the truth of God,' Thus also through the C.I.C.C.U. 'a remote Christianity became a living Christ' for a Trinity freshman, reading Mechanical Science. 'It meant,' he continued 'that I was reorientated to do God's will in God's way, instead of carrying out my ideas of His will in my way.'

The old attitude by which activities often were left to some 'last minute or worked up enthusiasm' was discarded. The mission of 1938 was planned with a thoroughness not known since the Torrey mission of 1911, and its effect followed up carefully. By 1939, though membership was less than two hundred and fifty in a University of over four thousand undergraduates; though the Daily Prayer Meeting was little stronger than five years before, and the Women's Union, already discussing amalgamation, still a scattered handful, yet the general position was more secure than for decades past. And this slow, unspectacular but steady increase might have continued for years to come.

By the outbreak of war the C.I.C.C.U. had continued for over sixty years. Men whose lives had been moulded by the Union were to be found in all parts of the world, serving with missionary societies or working in professions. Some had risen to fame, or had left their mark on areas in which they had been pioneers of the Christian gospel. Others, though unknown beyond their circles were giving themselves to work of which the true value could never be assessed in human terms. Many remembered Cambridge as the birthplace of their faith. Often they looked to the Christian Union to supply their assistants and successors. They relied upon it for support in prayer: 'I am quite definitely of the opinion,' the Union's own missionary, Dr. Church, once commented, 'that as far as human agency is concerned the Ruanda revival owes most to the the prayers of the C.I.C.C.U.'

Past members of the Union had done much also for the Church at home, whether as ordained men in the Church of England or the Free Churches, or as laymen. It was to be expected that countless parishes would have felt the influence of the Inter-Collegiate Union. But scattered over the country were professional and business men whose approach to their work, to those whom they served or who served under them had been moulded by experiences at Cambridge. 'We can describe a business as Christian,' wrote one past president of the C.I.C.C.U., who for many years had controlled a firm in the north-east, 'if its aim and purpose is to glorify Christ. It seeks nothing less than the new birth of all its staff and all whom it serves.' And he, and countless others had proved that such an ambition in professional, business and public life could be fulfilled.

For the next six years, as in 1914-18, this determination to 'do all to the glory of God' was maintained in the changed circumstances of wartime. Meanwhile, at Cambridge, there was no fear that in the Second World

War the C.I.C.C.U. would be extinguished. The University was protected by wiser government policy and never dropped to the level of 1916–17. Freshmen continued to come though reduced in numbers, further space was filled by Army and Air Force cadets, and the corporate life of Cambridge was more than maintained.

The Sunday evening sermons were continued without break, transferring for a few weeks in the Michaelmas term 1939 to the Dorothy café while black-out was installed at Holy Trinity; in 1942 the C.I.C.C.U. service was broadcast, the preacher, appropriately enough, being Harold Earnshaw-Smith. As the war years drew on, membership inevitably declined though towards the end the proportion to the population of the University was higher than before the war. The Daily Prayer Meeting suffered from pressure of Home Guard and Senior Training Corps parades and the tighter requirements of academic work, and attendance in 1943 was reported 'very poor indeed,' while in January 1945 numbers were 'hardly representative' of the size of the Union.

The C.I.C.C.U.'s message stood out more clearly against the background of war, not always with the active assistance of the invited preachers: 'Our difficulty has been partly that there have been some very strong appeals with not very much to go on,' complained one President. 'One or two speakers have hardly mentioned the name of Christ, or the Cross, because their time has been taken up with asking people to "take the step"—some who have come hardly know what "the step" is, I fear.' With no Keswick Convention, no preterminal house-parties or other such aids men were thrown back on to their own study of Scripture. Since, as one of them wrote, 'mature Christians are not made by a series of "thrashes" but rather by a continued and close personal walk with God,' the Union did not unduly suffer.

More than ever the Union depended on the quality of its members. 'It's great being up here,' a Magdalene man wrote during his brief year between school and war service, during which he was killed, 'both the fellowship of other Christians and the undisturbed times of quiet. . . .' 'Last night,' he wrote a few weeks later, 'I had the tremendous privilege of bringing S. to know Him. I am sure that will make you gasp! Jesus took the matter right out of my hands and just put the words into my mouth.' In such ways the Union's work continued, quietly but with lasting effect. 'From my own generation,' wrote one wartime president ten years later, 'I can think of many converts doing first-class work now'; and the names he could list included those of three missionaries, six doctors, two university lecturers, a schoolmaster, two research scientists and two engineers, and three clergymen, 'all brought to Christ through the ordinary course of the C.I.C.C.U.'s activity.'

The summer of 1945 thus found the C.I.C.C.U. active, deepened, reasonably assured, its life unbroken by six years of War, but facing the return of peace and the servicemen without, so far as human eye could see, any certainty for the future.

CHAPTER XXI

ADVANCE

IN 1945 the ex-servicemen returned to Cambridge more slowly than in 1919. Any fears of the C.I.C.C.U. lest past members of the Union would not rejoin were soon proved false. Attendance at Daily Prayer Meeting, the sermons, and at the weekly Bible Reading held on Sunday afternoons beneath the portraits of eighteenth-century noblemen in Trinity Old Combination Room steadily increased.

At the turn of the year the Union, and all other religious bodies and the deans and chaplains were together invited to explore possibilities of unity. A scheme was drawn up, with the name Koinonia, whereby all Christian activities were to present a united front to the University, without, it was hoped, compromising their own distinctive beliefs. Such a movement might transform the religious situation in Cambridge; and the C.I.C.C.U. was needed as Koinonia's evangelistic spearhead.

At first Koinonia received considerable support in the Union, both on the Executive and in the colleges. But during the Lent term 1946 a widespread and spontaneous feeling developed that 'the impetus of such an effort would be slight in view of the loose doctrinal basis and the varied devotional standard of its supporters.' It had appeared to be a bold experiment; on reflection it seemed no different in essence from earlier essays in a unity which must be superficial. By April the Executive, already planning a mission for February 1947, were as certain as their predecessors that in a University 'unity in doctrine is essential as a basis for evangelism.' They therefore withdrew, though agreeing that the C.I.C.C.U. mission should be held at the same time as that sponsored by Koinonia, in the manner of 1920 and 1926.

Koinonia secured the well-known preacher and writer Alec Vidler. The C.I.C.C.U., unable to decide on a suitable missioner reluctantly chose a team of three. Such cumbersome arrangement scarcely bespoke success. The outlook seemed dark. But in April fifteen hundred prayer-letters were sent out.

In July a small Cambridge party led by the President attended the first post-war Keswick Convention. On the last afternoon of the Convention, out of curiosity and because it was raining, the President went to hear an American Presbyterian minister, Donald Grey Barnhouse, whose addresses had already been eagerly discussed by other members of the house-party. While the rain beat on the tent the President sat enthralled as this heavily-built American, with his smiling face and twinkling eye, with vigorous gestures and a voice which no rain could drown expounded the Epistle to the Ephesians. Here was a man who could make the University take notice. He had something to say; and he said it in a way which made men listen. 'The strongest conviction laid hold on me,' wrote the President later, 'that if we can get this man to Cambridge, our problem will be solved.'

An invitation to be missioner in February was issued promptly. A few hours later Dr. Barnhouse replied: he was free for one week only in the next twelve months, and that not in February but November; if the mission could be put forward three months he would come. Without hesitation his offer was accepted and the President returned to his lodgings, to find awaiting him a letter from the Koinonia committee to say that it had proved necessary to advance their mission by a week. Whether the original team of three could have fitted in with such arrangement was highly doubtful. But the difficulty now would not arise. And further, had the President but known it, the date first planned for the mission was to fall in one of the coldest Februaries on record when, with the fuel crisis, Great St. Mary's was to be no place to sit listening to sermons.

.   .   .   .   .

Tales brought back from Keswick of the preaching and personality of Donald Grey Barnhouse, and especially of his skilful and forthright exposition of Scripture gave impetus to the C.I.C.C.U.'s preparations. Whatever the result, if Barnhouse was about the mission could not be insignificant. The Committee, several of its members former staff-officers, planned the mission in close detail, though in 1946 there could be none of the easy-going attitude of 1919 towards academical responsibilities. The publicity reached an effectiveness unknown in any previous year. Despite bread-rationing nearly one hundred 'squashes' were arranged—'to the outsider,' wrote one of them, 'the Mission promised to be great fun. There were unlimited opportunities for having free teas. . . .' By mid-November excitement was rising. Further prayer-letters were sent out all over the world, while in Phila-delphia Barnhouse was calling to prayer his congregation of two thousand and the twenty thousand readers of his expository magazine *Revelation*.[1] The Henry Martyn Hall could witness a spirit of prayer and consecration remini-scent of 1919, and the climax was reached on Saturday November 23rd, when Barnhouse, who had flown into London Airport the previous day, was introduced by the President to a crowded, expectant prayer meeting, and Cambridge heard his voice for the first time.

On the Sunday evening he mounted the pulpit of Great St. Mary's. 'Frankly,' he wrote shortly afterwards, 'I had anticipated a series of meetings at which I would find, at most, two or three hundred students attending. I was amazingly astonished at what I found.' Below him was a sea of faces. Above, to his left and right, the gallery was crowded. Ex-servicemen, freshmen from school, tutors, professors, men and women representing every level of the University, together with townspeople were there, awaiting his opening words. The American voice rang round the Church: 'If we conceive God to be perfect,' he began, each word spoken slowly and with force, as if very life depended on it, 'we must admit His power to hide Himself

[1] He later severed his connection with *Revelation* and founded *Eternity* on similar lines.

from any to whom He does not wish to reveal Himself.'
From this unexpected start he proceeded, his words sometimes fast but incisive, his tone at times pleading, at times
fierce and declamatory, to show 'that men cannot find out
God by themselves but must come in submission to the
revelation of Himself which He has made by the Lord
Jesus Christ as revealed in the Bible.'

He preached for six nights, and he struck the University
forcibly. 'It was impossible to listen and be neutral,'
wrote the President. 'Pagans—and there were plenty of
them—found that decision had to be made; the Holy
Spirit was blocking their path, demanding a verdict for
life or death. Sins were found out, indifference exposed,
and lip-religion proved bankrupt.' But though Barnhouse could convince he could also enrage. His chastise-
ment of contemporary theology angered many, including
some sympathetically inclined towards the mission. His
assertiveness seemed at times to obscure his own message,
merely provoking violent discussion on side-issues; but the
conviction with which he expounded Scripture, his anecdotes, the allusions and references which revealed the
extent of his reading, his wit, his pugnaciousness balanced
by an obvious sincerity and love made each evening an
event. Barnhouse could be scoffed at and the claims of his
message refused, but he could not be ignored. He sent
men scurrying back to take down dusty Bibles from their
shelves and set them arguing into the night. They queued
for private interviews with him—and to any not in earnest
an interview was an ordeal. He precipitated innumerable
talks between those who were Christians and those who
were not.

The whole mission, main addresses, informal meetings,
the missioner's interviews and the work of the assistant
missioners formed a unity. One undergraduate, a scientist
and an agnostic, who after attending a 'squash' had gone
to Great St. Mary's only to be 'amused rather than convinced,' sought an interview with Dr. Barnhouse 'just for a
joke.' They talked for an hour and a half: 'though very
little of what he said convinced me, I realized that however
absurd his belief it was intensely real to him,' and a promise

to attend the remaining sermons was given. 'Every night the challenge passed me by and I never felt the call to do anything personally.' Two days before the mission ended, the scientist reluctantly accepted a further invitation to meet the assistant missioner who had first encouraged him to Great St. Mary's. 'Off we plunged into the same old arguments I had used for years. . . .' But after an hour the assistant missioner 'suddenly changed his tactics. Instead of arguing he told me a few simple stories of how God had worked in his own life—and then, wisely, he sent me away. As he told these stories something had happened. My thoughts as I went out were chaotic. He believed it . . . it worked for him . . . he was sincere, but was it true? . . . Oh, God, was it true? . . . I suppose I was converted even before I reached the bottom of the staircase, but it was in Great St. Mary's that evening before the service began that I really gave myself to God. It was like coming home after a very long time. . . .'

Barnhouse left Cambridge late on the last night of the mission, Friday November 29th, and the next day flew back to America. Behind him were one hundred men and women who had given in their names in token of new-found personal faith; countless others awake to issues hitherto ignored; others angered; and an Inter-Collegiate Union from which hesitancy had been blown away.

The University of the later 'forties was markedly different from that of the 'twenties and 'thirties. National Service made for maturity among undergraduates; the uncertainties of the world situation, the awakening of church and nation to the prevalence of unbelief, and a changing intellectual atmosphere had dismissed much of pre-war indifference to Christianity.

The Inter-Collegiate Christian Union thrived. It was outwardly centred, as it had ever been, on the devotional lives of its members. A time of prayer and Bible study before breakfast was still the key to daily Christian living. Once a week in every college the C.I.C.C.U. Bible Reading would draw members and their friends together. In Trinity thirty or more would crowd into some room on

Great Court. Queens' could count as many. In smaller colleges a dozen or less would sit round, Bibles open, for an exposition from some senior member—Basil Atkinson taking three or four colleges a term—or from a fourth year or Ridley man. In the same room at another time in the week most men met for prayer.

Much depended on the college representative. His work, wrote the President in 1948, 'is twofold: to move, as Christ's ambassador, among the scornful, the indifferent, the religious and the "almost Christians" . . . at the same time to act both as a pastor to lead and a teacher to guide, the members committed to his care.' Even more depended on the six men forming the Executive. They met weekly. Their deliberations were frank, yet never requiring formal vote-taking, and began and ended with a time of prayer which might be extensive, and was always backed by their private prayer meeting at another time. It was for the Executive to arrange the Sunday sermon and the Bible Reading, transferred from Trinity Old Combination Room to the larger St. Andrew's Hall, and now held on Saturdays. Executive and college representatives came together once a term for the General Committee. Here the President could take the tone of the Union, and the Committee catch something of the Executive's vision. Barren politics, into which such committees can degenerate, were excluded by the strong sense of mutual purpose which dominated each member and by the consciousness that it was on the guidance of the Holy Spirit alone that the Union could depend.

The prayer meetings at the Henry Martyn Hall, and the Saturday Bible Readings were each term more crowded. Tyndale House Library, which the Inter-Varsity Fellowship had opened in Selwyn Gardens, gave added encouragement to theological reading. Concern for overseas missions was maintained. Work in Sunday Schools and among the parishes was less widespread than in more leisured ages, but in vacations the seaside missions, arranged by the Children's Special Service Mission, and camps for schoolboys, drew more support than ever. In 1948, women having received full membership of the University, the Women's Inter-Collegiate Union amalgamated with the C.I.C.C.U.

In 1949 Dr. Barnhouse came again. On this second visit the crowds were greater and the division in the University even sharper than before. Disapproval was voiced and prejudice aroused. Yet the mission had marked effect. Doubting and timid Christians were brought into new certainty and throughout Cambridge there were those for whom it was the start of personal faith. Thus a woman research scientist, an atheist and a member of the University Communist party, was taken to the mission. Her views had already been weakened by the consistency with which a college friend had demonstrated, both by her life and her words the truth of Christianity. On the third night she heard Barnhouse invite his hearers to 'pray with me, "As best I know how, I accept Jesus as my Saviour."' She prayed, but felt no different. 'The assurance of the truth of the Christian Gospel' she wrote to Barnhouse a year later, 'came to me during the next fortnight, which was one of the most miserable in my life. It was as though I had been stunned and I recovered slowly to find the Bible a transformed book and a new life in Christ. The misery, needless to say, has not continued. Since surrendering my life completely into the Lord's hands, I find His peace and joy have remained with me constantly. . . .'[1]

It could be an inspiring experience in these next years for a Christian Union member of earlier days to spend a week-end at Cambridge.

Soon after eight on the Saturday evening he would see men and women in academic gowns, though without the mortar-boards of his own day, converging from every part of Cambridge on St. Andrew's Hall. After mingling with the crowd at the entrance he could move straight upstairs where the hall was filling, or stay for a few moments of conversation and for coffee below. A glance during the opening hymn at the three hundred or more around him could not fail to provoke contrast with pre-war Bible

[1] She sailed in 1952 to Japan to work with the China Inland Mission.

Readings in the Henry Martyn Hall. But the deepest impression would be received on the Sunday, not so much at the crowded evangelistic sermon at Holy Trinity in the evening as at the Henry Martyn Hall, between a quarter to and half-past ten in the morning. Having threaded his way through the bicycles which lay outside, mixed with the fairy-cycles of Holy Trinity children's church, he would enter the C.I.C.C.U. prayer meeting. The library doors were open to extend the hall, yet people were standing at the back and sitting on the dais behind the President, one hundred and forty or more, and 'all determined' as one President of the 'fifties wrote, 'to pray at least a one-sentence prayer for somebody or something.' A hymn would be sung, and after a short reading with brief comment by the week-end speaker, the President would rise to announce topics of prayer. A few minutes later the stream of intercessions would begin, prayers short and to the point, from all corners of the hall, with 'Amen' reverberating at the end of each. There was no room to kneel; and there scarcely seemed time for everyone who wished to pray. After a second hymn the President would ask prayer for needs beyond Cambridge; the Oxford Inter-Collegiate Christian Union, stronger with each year since the war, had sent specific requests; a former member of the C.I.C.C.U. asked prayer for his work; a mission was opening in a provincial University; attention was directed to one or other area of the overseas missionary field. And then the flow of intercessions began again. Here was the mainspring of the C.I.C.C.U., and because prayer life was strong, the Union was growing. 'I should say the great feature of the term,' wrote Dr. Basil Atkinson in December 1950, 'has been the spirit of prayer . . . both D.P.M. and the Sunday prayer meeting have been transformed.' 'The Henry Martyn Hall is full every week-day,' the President could report in January 1951, 'and on Sundays the Library is full, too. . . . As a direct result of this there is a weekly congregation in Holy Trinity of six hundred. . . .'

At the end of 1951, having outgrown St. Andrew's Hall the Saturday night Bible Reading moved to the Debating Hall of the Union Society and it was here, on 8th March

A Saturday-Night Bible Reading in the Debating Hall of the Union Society, 1952

1952, that the C.I.C.C.U.'s seventy-fifth anniversary was commemorated. The Bible Reading that night was given by Ralph Taylor, Bishop of Sodor and Man, son of a founder of the C.I.C.C.U. and himself a past president. His words summed up the Union's attitude: 'We have not come here to raise memorials to the leaders of the past. We have come, rather, to look back in order that we may thank God and take courage for the future. . . . We have come that we may take root downward in order to bear fruit upward.' And as he concluded his exposition from the First Epistle of St. John the Bishop spoke of 'Righteousness, love, faith . . . that is what has made the strength of the Union. Not only faith, but real burning love for people, and righteousness of life. As long as these, by the grace of God, mark the members of this Union it will be used.'

The Inter-Collegiate Union had stood the test of seventy-five years. It was true still to its primary aim: 'To present the claims of the Lord Jesus Christ to the University.' In 1877 few had disputed these claims though many might reject them. As the years passed, and generation succeeded generation in the University, the men in the Union had found the prevalent atmosphere increasingly unsympathetic. By 1909 the C.I.C.C.U. as it had been seemed dying. The thirty years which followed the recovery of 1910, though not easy, had proved the unchanging relevance of the Word of God and of the Christian gospel in a world of increasing chaos. The Union had made mistakes; it had not always been certain of its path; often its message had fallen on deaf ears. But the C.I.C.C.U. had refused to seek influence at the price of abandoning essential truths. Since the close of the Second World War men and women were responding each year more readily to a message which had lost nothing of its force. The Union's faithfulness had been vindicated.

This first aim, to present the claims of Christ, led naturally to the fulfilment of the second: 'To unite those who desire to serve Him.' In this Inter-Collegiate Union were men and women from differing denominations and differing backgrounds, 'drawn,' as the undergraduate paper

Varsity commented in 1951, 'from a wide variety of University circles,' and representing diverse stages of development and understanding, yet united. On occasion, unity had been bought at the price of isolation and exclusiveness; at times it had been shallow. But so long as it grew directly from the personal faith expressed in the Union's Basis of Membership, 'faith in Jesus Christ as my Saviour, my Lord and my God,' this unity could not be barren. Nor was it. The third expressed aim of the C.I.C.C.U., 'to extend the work of Home and Foreign Missions,' intrinsic in the very life of the Union, had received new impetus in the summer of 1950 by the creation of Missionary Prayer Groups. The Prayer Group scheme arose from a fresh realization that the spiritual needs of peoples overseas and of those serving amongst them were the responsibility of 'everyone in the Union, not only those who were particularly missionary minded.' Nearly fifty groups, 'each small enough to meet round the table for tea,' were soon coming together regularly for the exchange of information on their chosen field and for prayer; 'the motive behind it being,' as the Missionary Secretary wrote, 'that, as far as God is concerned, prayer is as important a part of any Christian activity as the activity itself.' Thus, in new forms, were maintained the traditions of the Cambridge Seven and of the Student Volunteers.

The influence of the Cambridge movement launched, with little thought of the distant future, by the men of 1877, had been felt far beyond the University. 'If there is a country where the struggle can be successfully maintained for Christendom,' F. J. A. Hort had written to Montagu Butler in 1886, 'it is England. If there is a place where it can be successfully maintained for England it is Cambridge.' In the sixty-six years since Hort wrote, the Inter-Collegiate Christian Union had done much in that struggle, and in the years to come could do more. 'I believe the hope of the evangelization of the world lies in Cambridge,' C. T. Studd had written in 1912; such an expression was sweeping, but it contained truth, and a challenge which the years could not weaken. In Cambridge, and in any university, lies much of the human element in the hope of world evangelization. Wherever it is felt, the spirit which moved Cambridge will promote the further advance of faith. For the Cambridge Inter-Collegiate Christian Union was not the fruit of human energy or of human wisdom. As one leader of the early nineteen-thirties wrote after a visit to Cambridge in the 'fifties, 'The real tradition of the Union is not in any intellectual statement of belief; it lies in a spirit passed from one to another as each generation rises up to receive it, and which is kindled by the Spirit of the living God. To Him alone can the continuing activity and creativity of the Union be attributed.' Thus the Union, looking back in humility, could look forward in confidence if it continued to depend and to depend only, on 'Jesus Christ, the same yesterday, and today and for ever.'

The Michaelmas term 1952, as the Union began the final quarter of its century, could well be taken as an augury for the future. In November the Triennial Mission was conducted in Great St. Mary's by John Stott, Rector of All Souls', Langham Place, a young Cambridge man of high academic record. The church was filled each evening, and on the last night, although chairs were placed in the side aisles and people were sitting in the choir stalls and standing wherever there was space, some of the crowd had to be turned away. But it was not so much the numbers attending which marked the mission as its spirit. The controversial atmosphere of previous years had gone. From the very first night, when in response to the missioner's invitation over one hundred men and women asked for a copy of St. John's Gospel as a sign of 'sincere search for the truth,' there was a quiet determination in all parts of the University to face up to the issues of personal faith. The main addresses were plain unhurried Biblical expositions, almost unadorned with illustrations and without any attempt to force decision; the closest attention was given throughout; such was the desire for the truth that assistant missioners, as one of them commented, 'marvelled at the ease with which men and women accepted the claims of Christ, counted the cost and received Him.' 'This mission,' wrote one undergraduate, 'has taught me most of all that the Bible is the living Word of God.' Once again the relevance of the Biblical message was demonstrated.

For all concerned in the mission the prayer had been 'that they may so present Christ Jesus in the power of the Holy Spirit that men may come to put their trust in God through Him, to accept Him as their Saviour, and to serve Him as their Lord in the fellowship of His Church.' That prayer, which had received such unmistakable answer, summed up the hope of the Union for the years to come.

PRINCIPAL SOURCES

MANUSCRIPTS

(Excluding letters, and excluding memoranda specially contributed by living persons.)

Memoirs of John Barton & His Wife. 2 vols. (Unpublished).

Autobiographical fragments of Barclay Buxton.

Cambridge University Church Missionary Union: Minutes 1879–86. Treasurer's Book 1875–85.

Cambridge Inter-Collegiate Christian Union: Minutes & Records (from 1919).

Cambridge Pastorate Council: Minutes.

Cambridge Prayer Union: List of Members 1848–55 (C.U. Lib. Add. MSS 7039). Minutes 1891–1934 (C.U. Lib. Add. MSS 6791).

Cambridge Women's Inter-Collegiate Christian Union: Minutes 1919–48.

Daily Prayer Meeting Special Requests Book 1873–86.

Memoranda concerning the Early History of the Relations of the C.I.C.C.U. and the I.V.F. with the S.C.M. Compiled by G. T. Manley.

Diaries of H. C. G. Moule, Bishop of Durham.

Reminiscences of Archdeacon W. S. Moule.

Two Etonians in China: By Cecil & Arthur Polhill (-Turner) (unpublished).

Memories of a Varied & Busy Life: by Walter, 9th Lord Polwarth (unpublished).

Student Christian Movement: Minute Books: General Committee. General College Department. Theological College Department.

Student Volunteer Missionary Union: Minute Books.

Diaries of Stanley Smith.

Memorandum (including diary extracts) specially contributed by the late Edward Woods, Bishop of Lichfield.

PRINTED SOURCES

(Place of publication London unless otherwise stated. C = published in Cambridge; (priv.) = privately printed. The probable dates of books Not Dated are given in brackets.)

NEWSPAPERS AND MAGAZINES

Boys' Magazine, Our. (Continued as The:)

Cambridge Christian Life. (1913–15).

Cambridge Chronicle.

Cambridge Daily News.

Cambridge Express.

Cambridge Independent Press & University Herald.

Cambridge Inter - Collegiate Christian Union Review. (and Magazine). (1927–32).

Cambridge Magazine.

Cambridge Review.

China's Millions.

Christian.

Christians' Pathway to Power. (1874–9).

Church Missionary Gleaner.

Church Missionary Intelligence.

Church Missionary Review.

Church Quarterly Review.

Eternity (Philadelphia).

Granta. (C.)

Graphic.

His. (Toronto).

Inter-Varsity Magazine. (continued as Inter-Varsity).

Life of Faith.

Light Blue. (C.)

Pall Mall Gazette.

Record.

Revelation. (Philadelphia).

Scope. Magazine for Industry.

Student Volunteer. (In quotation—no copies available).

Student Movement.

The Times.

Varsity. (C.)

War Cry.

PAMPHLETS

Brief History of the Inter-Varsity Fellowship. (? 1929).

The Cambridge Inter-Collegiate Christian Union. C. 1910.

Cambridge Medical Mission Settlement: An Account. (1914); Some Facts. (? 1917).

Cambridge Missionary Band (1912). Notes. (Sept. 1912 et seq.) (also notes of similar Bands and Prayer Fellowships, printed or stencilled, and privately circulated.)

Griffinhole, C. G. The Story of the S.T.C. C. (priv.) 1915.

Hundred Years Short History of the Cambridge Association of C.M.S. C. 1918.

In Memorian, Rennie MacInnes. 1932.

Life Story of an Eton, Cambridge & All England Cricketer. (C. T. Studd). Belfast. (? 1930).

Livingstone at Cambridge. (Ed. 1907).

Make Jesus King. (Report of Liverpool Conference 1896).

Manley, G. T. Views of Modern Science. Simla 1900.

Miracles of Grace in Bermondsey. (? 1912).

Nicholson, W. P. *Hell: a Sermon.* Bangor (N.D.); *The Unpardonable Sin: a Sermon.* Bangor (N.D.); *Regeneration: a Sermon.* Bangor (N.D.).

Old Paths in Perilous Times. 1913. New ed. 1932.

Raven, C. E. (ed.). *The Mission to Cambridge University.* 1920.

Records of Ridley Reunions. C. (priv.).

Records and Results of Cambridge Prayer Union Gatherings. C. (priv.). 1883.

Scott, W. F. *The Oxford Inter-Collegiate Christian Union.*

Simpson, Sparrow. *The Cambridge Contribution to the Oxford Movement.* 1933.

Student Christian Movement. *Annual Reports.*

Thornton-Duesbury, J.P. *The Oxford Group: its Principles and Growth.* 1947.

Tinling, Christine. *Those Bermondsey Boys.* 1938.

Torrey, R. A. *Why God used D. L. Moody.* New York 1923.

Translated: a memorial of E. G. D. Maxwell by his mother. (1895).

BOOKS

Andrews, C. F. *What I owe to Christ.* 1932.

Babington, Mrs. *Memorials, Journals and Botanical Correspondence of Charles Cardale Babington.* C. 1897.

Ball, W. W. Rouse. *History of First Trinity Boat Club.* C. 1908.

Barabas, Steven. *So Great Salvation: The History and Message of the Keswick Convention,* 1952.

Barton, C. E. *John Barton.* 1910.

Battersby, C. Harford. *Pilkington of Uganda.* 1898.

Benson, A. C. *The House of Quiet.* 1912.

Benson, E. F. *As we were.* 1932.

Biscoe, C. Tyndale-. *Tyndale-Biscoe of Kashmir; An Autobiography.* 1951.

Blackwood. *Stevenson Arthur Blackwood, K.C.B.* by his widow and a friend. 1896.

Blaikie, W. G. *Personal life of David Livingstone.* 1880.

Braisted, R. Wilder. *In this generation.* New York. 1941.

Broomhall, A. J. *Bishop Cassells.* 1926.

Broomhall, B. *A Missionary Band.* 1886. (3rd Ed. 1889 expanded and entitled *The Evangelization of the World.*)

Broomhall, Marshall. *The Jubilee Story of the China Inland Mission.* 1915. (ed.) *John Stuart Holden.* 1935.

Buchman, F. N. D. *Remaking the World.* 1947.

Guy Bullen by his friends. 1938.

Butler, H. Montagu. *Belief in Christ & Other Sermons.* C. 1898.

Butler, J. R. M. *Henry Montagu Butler.* 1925.

Butler, Samuel. *The Way of all Flesh.* 1903.

Bullock, F. N. B. *History of Ridley Hall,* I. 1941.

Burke's *Peerage.*

Buxton, B. G. *The Reward of Faith in the Life of Barclay Buxton.* 1949.

Carus, W. *Memoirs of Charles Simeon.* C. 1847.

Christie, Mrs. Dugald. *Jackson of Moukden.* (? 1921).

Coggan, F. D. (ed.) *Christ and the Colleges.* 1933.

Costain, A. J. *Dr. Arthur Jackson of Manchuria.* 1911.

Coulton, G. C. *Fourscore Years.* C. 1943.

Cranage, D. H. S. *Not only a Dean.* 1952.

Crockford's *Clerical Directory.*

Deane, A. C. *Time Remembered.* 1947.

Dictionary of National Biography.

Elliot, E. B. *Lord Haddo.* (5th ed. 1869).

Eden, G. R. and Macdonald, F. C. (eds.) *Lightfoot of Durham.* C. 1932.

Forman, R. S. (ed.) *Great Christians.* 1933.

Fremantle, W. R. *Memoir of Rev. Spencer Thornton.* 1850.

Gairdner, W. Temple. *Douglas Thornton.* 1909.

Graham, Edward. *The Harrow Life of Henry Montagu Butler.* 1920.

Gray, Arthur. *Cambridge University.* 1926.

Grubb, Norman. *C. T. Studd, Cricketer & Pioneer.* 1933. *Alfred Buxton of Abyssinia and Congo.* 1942.

Guinness, Geraldine. *The Story of the China Inland Mission.* 2 vols. 1899, 1900.

Harford, C. F. (ed.) *The Keswick Convention.* (1907).

Harford, J. B. and Macdonald, F. C. *Handley Carr Glyn Moule, Bishop of Durham.* (1922).

Horton, R. F. *An Autobiography.* 1917.

Inskip, J. H. *A Man's Job.* 1949.

Isaacson, C. S. (ed.) *Roads to Christ.* 1905.

James, M. R. *Eton & King's.* 1926.

Jebb, Eglantyne. *Cambridge: A Brief Study in Social Questions.* C. 1908.

Jones, C. A. and Appleton, R. *The History of the Jesus Lane Sunday School* 1827–77. C. 1877.

Keable, Robert. *Peradventure.* 1922.

The Five Lambeth Conferences (1867–1908). 1920.

Lyttelton, Edward. *Memories & Hopes.* 1925.

MacInnes, Mrs. *Joyfully Ready.* 1886.

Maclean, J. K. *Torrey & Alexander.* 1905.

Masterman, Lucy M. *C. F. G. Masterman.* 1939.

Mather, R. D. *Romance of Black River.*

Matthews, Ronald. *English Messiahs.* 1936.

Milner, Mary. *Life of Isaac Milner.* (abr. ed. 1844).

Montgomery, H. H. *George Alfred Lefroy.* 1910.

Moody, W. R. *Life of Dwight L. Moody.* (1900).

Moorman, John. *B. K. Cunningham.* 1947.

Morgan, G. E. *A Veteran in Revival: R. C. Morgan, His Life & Times.* 1909.

Mott, John R. *Addresses and Papers.* 6 vols. New York. 1946–7. *Five Decades & a Forward View.* New York. 1939.

Moule, H. C. G. *Thoughts on Christian Sanctity.* 1885. *Charles Simeon.* 1892. (ed. 1948).

Mount Temple, Lady. *Memorials of Lord Mount Temple.* (Priv.) 1890.

Nicholson, W. P. *The Evangelist.* (N.D.)

"O.C." (A. H. Lawrence). *Reminiscences of Cambridge Life.* (Priv.) 1889.

What is the Oxford Group? by a Layman with a notebook. 1933.

Pearsall Smith, Logan. *Unforgotten Years.* 1938. *A Religious Rebel.* 1944.

Raven, C. E. *A Wanderer's Way.* 1929.

Robinson, Forbes. *Letters to His Friends.* (1st Public ed. 1938).

Robson, James. *Ion Keith-Falconer.* 1923.

Russell, G. W. E. *The Household of Faith.* 1916. *Lady Victoria Buxton.* 1919.

Rouse, Ruth. *The World's Student Christian Federation.* 1949.

Sankey, Ira. D. *My Life & Sacred Songs.* 1906.

Sidney, E. *Life of the Rev. Rowland Hill.* 1844.

Sinker, R. *Memorials of the Hon. Ion Keith-Falconer.* C. 1888.

Smith, Wilbur M. *Dwight Lyman Moody, an Annotated Bibliography.* Chicago. 1948.

Smyth, Charles. *Simeon & Church Order.* C. 1940.

Somervell, T. Howard. *After Everest.* 1936.

Stead, W. T. *The Revival of 1905.* 1905.

Stephen, Leslie. *Sketches from Cambridge.* 1865 (ed. 1932).

Stock, Eugene. *History of the Church Missionary Society.* 4 vols. 1897–9. *Recollections.* 1910.

Storr, Vernon F. *Freedom and Tradition:* a study of Liberal Evangelicalism. 1940.

Tatlow, Tissington. *The Story of the Student Christian Movement.* 1933.

Taylor, Dr. & Mrs. Howard. *Hudson Taylor and the China Inland Mission.* 1918.

Taylor, Mrs. Howard. *Guinness of Honan.* 1930.

Thomson, G. I. F. *The Oxford Pastorate.* 1946.

Thomson, Sir J. J. *Recollections & Reflections.* 1936.

Thompson, Phyllis. *D. E. Hoste, A Prince with God.* (1948).

Venn, J. A. *Alumni Cantabrigienses.* Pt. II.

Waddington, W. E. and Inskip, J. T. *Charles Vickery Hawkins.* (1896).

Westcott, B. F. *Religious Office of the Universities.* 1873.

Westcott, A. *Brooke Foss Westcott.* 2 vols. 1903.

Wilder, Robert. *The Great Commission.* 1936.

Winstanley, D. A. *Early Victorian Cambridge.* C. 1942. *Later Victorian Cambridge.* C. 1947.

Woods, C.F. *Memoirs & Letters of William Hay Aitken.* 1930.

Woods, E. S. and Macnutt, F. B. *Theodore Bishop of Winchester.* 1933.

ACKNOWLEDGEMENTS

The author wishes to express his thanks to the following for their generous assistance :

The Archbishop of Sydney (The Most Rev. H. W. K. Mowll, D.D.) for a memorandum on the events of 1910–12.

The Bishop of Sodor and Man (The Rt. Rev. J. R. S. Taylor, D.D.) for much information and advice.

The Bishop in North Africa (The Rt. Rev. G. F. B. Morris).

The Dean of Winchester (The Very Rev. E. G. Selwyn, D.D.) for a memorandum on the Church Society of 1906.

The Provost of Nairobi (The Very Rev. H. A. Evan Hopkins.)

B. F. C. Atkinson Esq., Ph.D., Under-Librarian, Cambridge University Library, for a memorandum on part of the early history of the C.P.U., etc., and for other assistance.

O. R. Barclay, Esq., Ph.D., for help in the collection of information and for other assistance.

The Rev. Donald Grey Barnhouse, D.D., of Philadelphia, for information and for other assistance.

Miss Jesse Barton for the MS. autobiography of her father.

The Rev. A. C. B. Bellerby for a memorandum.

The Rev. S. W. Betts, Vicar of Holy Trinity, Cambridge, and the Henry Martyn Hall Trustees for the loan of Church Missionary Union books; the Rev. S. W. Betts and the Pastorate Council for permission to quote from their minute-book.

The Rev. C. W. J. Bowles, Principal of Ridley Hall, Cambridge for the reports of Ridley Reunions and for much other assistance.

The Dowager Lady Buxton for a letter written to the late Sir Victor Buxton, Bt.

Captain B. G. Buxton, M.C., for the MS. autobiography of his father; Captain and Mrs. B. G. Buxton for information.

The Editorial Secretary and staff of the China Inland Mission for the Polhill MS. and for other assistance.

The General Secretary (Canon M. A. C. Warren, D.D.), Librarian and staff of the Church Missionary Society.

The Rev. F. Guy Graham, Vicar of Spaxton, for information on the Agapemonites.

Canon B. S. W. Green for information.

The Rev. C. J. B. Harrison for a memorandum.

The General Secretary and H.Q. staff of the Inter-Varsity Fellowship.

Prebendary C. C. Kerr for information and much other help.

The Rev. G. T. Manley for memoranda, papers and much help.

Headquarters staff, Moral Rearmament (Oxford Group) or literature.

The Rev. A. W. H. Moule for Archdeacon W. H. Moule's MS. autobiography and for other information.

The Rev. Professor C. F. D. Moule, the Rev. A. W. H. Moule, and the Principal of Ridley Hall for the use of some of the Diaries of Bishop Handley Moule.

The Rev. W. Nicholson.

A. G. B. Owen, Esq., O.B.E., for information and other assistance.

Lord Polwarth and the Hon. Mrs. G. Barbour for MS. Memoirs of the 9th Lord Polwarth.

Canon C. E. Raven, D.D., for information.

C. G. Scorer Esq., M.B.E., F.R.C.S., for a memorandum.

Dr. A. C. Stanley Smith for the Diaries of his father.

The Rev. Wilbur M. Smith D.D., of Pasadena, California.

The Rev. S. C. Strong, late Head of Cambridge University Mission, Bermondsey.

The General Secretary and Headquarters staff of the Student Christian Movement.

The Rev. Professor R. V. G. Tasker.

The author is most grateful also to the many others who contributed reminiscences, loaned letters, supplied information or gave other assistance; and he wishes to thank particularly the members of the Inter-Collegiate Union in 1950–52 who assisted him in research at Cambridge.

INDEX

Persons are described as when they appear in the text; designations in brackets refer to later life.

Churches, colleges, etc., without place-name are in Cambridge unless otherwise obvious.